D0915563

MODERN CRIME
AND
SUSPENSE WRITERS

Writers of English: Lives and Works

MODERN CRIME

AND

SUSPENSE WRITERS

Edited and with an Introduction by

Harold Bloom

CHELSEA HOUSE PUBLISHERS
New York   Philadelphia

Jacket illustration: Illustration by J.K. Potter from *The Face That Must Die* by Ramsey Campbell (Scream/Press, 1983) (courtesy of J.K. Potter).

CHELSEA HOUSE PUBLISHERS

Editorial Director Richard Rennert
Executive Managing Editor Karyn Gullen Browne
Picture Editor Adrian G. Allen
Copy Chief Robin James
Creative Director Robert Mitchell
Art Director Joan Ferrigno
Production Manager Sallye Scott

Writers of English: Lives and Works

Senior Editor S. T. Joshi
Series Design Rae Grant

Staff for MODERN CRIME AND SUSPENSE WRITERS

Assistant Editor Mary Sisson
Research Peter Cannon, Stefan Dziemianowicz
Picture Researcher Ellen Dudley

© 1995 by Chelsea House Publishers, a division of Main Line Book Co.

Introduction © 1995 by Harold Bloom

Printed and bound in the United States of America.

First Printing

1 3 5 7 9 8 6 4 2

Library of Congress Cataloging-in-Publication Data

Modern crime and suspense writers / edited and with an introduction by Harold Bloom.
    p.   cm.—(Writers of English)
    Includes bibliographical references.
    Contents: Robert Bloch—Richard Condon—Roald Dahl—Len Deighton—James Ellroy—Thomas Harris—Patricia Highsmith—John le Carré—Elmore Leonard—Robert Ludlum—Robert B. Parker—Mickey Spillane—Andrew Vachss.
    ISBN 0-7910-2222-6.—ISBN 0-7910-2247-1 (pbk.)
    1. Detective and mystery stories, American—History and criticism. 2. Detective and mystery stories, English—History and criticism. 3. Spy stories, English—History and criticism. 4. Novelists, American—20th century—Biography. 5. Novelists, English—20th century—Biography. I. Bloom, Harold. II. Series.
PS374.D4M63 1995
813'.087209—dc20   94-44311
[B]   CIP

Contents

User's Guide   vi

The Life of the Author   vii

Introduction   xi

Robert Bloch   1

Richard Condon   16

Roald Dahl   31

Len Deighton   46

James Ellroy   60

Thomas Harris   74

Patricia Highsmith   87

John le Carré   101

Elmore Leonard   116

Robert Ludlum   130

Robert B. Parker   144

Mickey Spillane   158

Andrew Vachss   173

◈ User's Guide

THIS VOLUME PROVIDES biographical, critical, and bibliographical information on the thirteen most significant modern crime and suspense writers. Each chapter consists of three parts: a biography of the author; a selection of brief critical extracts about the author; and a bibliography of the author's published books.

The biography supplies a detailed outline of the important events in the author's life, including his or her major writings. The critical extracts are taken from a wide array of books and periodicals, from the author's lifetime to the present, and range in content from biographical to critical to historical. The extracts are arranged in chronological order by date of writing or publication, and a full bibliographical citation is provided at the end of each extract. Editorial additions or deletions are indicated within carets.

The author bibliographies list every separate publication—including books, pamphlets, broadsides, collaborations, and works edited or translated by the author—for works published in the author's lifetime; selected important posthumous publications are also listed. Titles are those of the first edition; variant titles are supplied within carets. In selected instances dates of revised editions are given where these are significant. Pseudonymous works are listed, but not the pseudonyms under which these works were published. Periodicals edited by the author are listed only when the author has written most or all of the contents. Titles enclosed in square brackets are of doubtful authenticity. All works by the author, whether in English or in other languages, have been listed; English translations of foreign-language works are not listed unless the author has done the translation.

The Life of the Author
Harold Bloom

NIETZSCHE, WITH EXULTANT ANGUISH, famously proclaimed that God was dead. Whatever the consequences of this for the ethical life, its ultimate literary effect certainly would have surprised the author Nietzsche. His French disciples, Foucault most prominent among them, developed the Nietzschean proclamation into the dogma that all authors, God included, were dead. The death of the author, which is no more than a Parisian trope, another metaphor for fashion's setting of skirt-lengths, is now accepted as literal truth by most of our current apostles of what should be called French Nietzsche, to distinguish it from the merely original Nietzsche. We also have French Freud or Lacan, which has little to do with the actual thought of Sigmund Freud, and even French Joyce, which interprets *Finnegans Wake* as the major work of Jacques Derrida. But all this is as nothing compared to the final triumph of the doctrine of the death of the author: French Shakespeare. That delicious absurdity is given us by the New Historicism, which blends Foucault and California fruit juice to give us the Word that Renaissance "social energies," and not William Shakespeare, composed *Hamlet* and *King Lear*. It seems a proper moment to murmur "enough" and to return to a study of the life of the author.

Sometimes it troubles me that there are so few masterpieces in the vast ocean of literary biography that stretches between James Boswell's great *Life* of Dr. Samuel Johnson and the late Richard Ellmann's wonderful *Oscar Wilde*. Literary biography is a crucial genre, and clearly a difficult one in which to excel. The actual nature of the lives of the poets seems to have little effect upon the quality of their biographies. Everything happened to Lord Byron and nothing at all to Wallace Stevens, and yet their biographers seem equally daunted by them. But even inadequate biographies of strong writers, or of weak ones, are of immense use. I have never read a literary biography from which I have not profited, a statement I cannot make about any other genre whatsoever. And when it comes to figures who are central to us—Dante, Shakespeare, Cervantes, Montaigne, Goethe, Whitman, Tolstoi, Freud, Joyce, Kafka among them—we reach out eagerly for every scrap that the biographers have gleaned. Concerning Dante and Shakespeare we know much too little, yet when we come to Goethe and Freud, where we seem to know more than everything, we still want to know more. The death of the author, despite our current resentniks, clearly was only a momentary fad. Something vital in every authentic lover of literature responds to Emerson's battle-cry sentence: "There is no history, only biography." Beyond that there is a deeper truth, difficult to come at and requiring a lifetime to understand, which is that there is no literature, only autobiography, however mediated, however veiled, however transformed. The events of Shakespeare's life included the composition of *Hamlet,* and that act of writing was itself a crucial act of living, though we do not yet know altogether how to read so doubled an act. When an author takes up a more overtly autobiographical stance, as so many do in their youth, again we still do not know precisely how to accommodate the vexed relation between life and work. T. S. Eliot, meditating upon James Joyce, made a classic statement as to such accommodation:

> We want to know who are the originals of his characters, and what were
> the origins of his episodes, so that we may unravel the web of memory
> and invention and discover how far and in what ways the crude material
> has been transformed.

When a writer is not even covertly autobiographical, the web of memory and invention is still there, but so subtly woven that we may never unravel it. And yet we want deeply never to stop trying, and not merely because we are curious, but because each of us is caught in her own network of memory and invention. We do not always recall our inventions, and long before we age we cease to be certain of the extent to which we have invented our memories. Perhaps one motive for reading is our need to unravel our own webs. If our masters could make, from their lives, what we read, then we can be moved by them to ask: What have we made or lived in relation to what we have read? The answers may be sad, or confused, but the question is likely, implicitly, to go on being asked as long as we read. In Freudian terms, we are asking: What is it that we have repressed? What have we forgotten, unconsciously but purposively: What is it that we flee? Art, literature necessarily included, is regression in the service of the ego, according to a famous Freudian formula. I doubt the Freudian wisdom here, but indubitably it is profoundly suggestive. When we read, something in us keeps asking the equivalent of the Freudian questions: From what or whom is the author in flight, and to what earlier stages in her life is she returning, and why?

Reading, whether as an art or a pastime, has been damaged by the visual media, television in particular, and might be in some danger of extinction in the age of the computer, except that the psychic need for it continues to endure, presumably because it alone can assuage a central loneliness in elitist society. Despite all sophisticated or resentful denials, the reading of imaginative literature remains a quest to overcome the isolation of the individual consciousness. We can read for information, or entertainment, or for love of the language, but in the end we seek, in the author, the person whom we have not found, whether in ourselves or in others. In that quest, there always are elements at once aggressive and defensive, so that reading, even in childhood, is rarely free of hidden anxieties. And yet it remains one of the few activities not contaminated by an entropy of spirit. We read in hope, because we lack companionship, and the author can become the object of the most idealistic elements in our search for the wit and inventiveness we so desperately require. We read biography, not as a supplement to reading the author, but as a second, fresh attempt to understand what always seems to evade us in the work, our drive towards a kind of identity with the author.

This will-to-identity, though recently much deprecated, is a prime basis for the experience of sublimity in reading. *Hamlet* retains its unique position in the Western canon not because most readers and playgoers identify themselves with the prince, who clearly is beyond them, but rather because they find themselves again in the power of the language that represents him with such immediacy and force. Yet we know that neither language nor social energy created Hamlet. Our curiosity about Shakespeare is endless, and never will be appeased. That curiosity itself is a value, and cannot be separated from the value of *Hamlet* the tragedy, or Hamlet the literary character. It provokes us that Shakespeare the man seems so unknowable, at once everyone and no one as Borges shrewdly observes. Critics keep telling us otherwise, yet something valid in us keeps believing that we would know Hamlet better if Shakespeare's life were as fully known as the lives of Goethe and Freud, Byron and Oscar Wilde, or best of all, Dr. Samuel Johnson. Shakespeare never will have his Boswell, and Dante never will have his Richard Ellmann. How much one would give for a detailed and candid *Life of Dante* by Petrarch, or an outspoken memoir of Shakespeare by Ben Jonson! Or, in the age just past, how superb would be rival studies of one another by Hemingway and Scott Fitzgerald! But the list is endless: think of *Oscar Wilde* by Lord Alfred Douglas, or a joint biography of Shelley by Mary Godwin, Emilia Viviani, and Jane Williams. More than our insatiable desire for scandal would be satisfied. The literary rivals and the lovers of the great writers possessed perspectives we will never enjoy, and without those perspectives we dwell in some poverty in regard to the writers with whom we ourselves never can be done.

There is a sense in which imaginative literature *is* perspectivism, so that the reader is likely to be overwhelmed by the work's difficulty unless its multiple perspectives are mastered. Literary biography matters most because it is a storehouse of perspectives, frequently far surpassing any that are grasped by the particular biographer. There are relations between authors' lives and their works of kinds we have yet to discover, because our analytical instruments are not yet advanced enough to perform the necessary labor. Perhaps a novel, poem, or play is not so much a regression in the service of the ego, as it is an amalgam of *all* the Freudian mechanisms of defense, all working together for the apotheosis of the ego. Freud valued art highly, but thought that the aesthetic enterprise was no rival for psychoanalysis, unlike religion and philosophy. Clearly Freud was mistaken; his own anxieties about his indebtedness to Shakespeare helped produce the weirdness of his joining in the lunacy that argued for the Earl of Oxford as the author of Shakespeare's plays. It was Shakespeare, and not "the poets," who was there before Freud arrived at his depth psychology, and it is Shakespeare who is there still, well out ahead of psychoanalysis. We see what Freud would not see, that psychoanalysis is Shakespeare prosified and systematized. Freud is part of literature, not of "science," and the biography of Freud has the same relations to psychoanalysis as the biography of Shakespeare has to *Hamlet* and *King Lear,* if only we knew more of the life of Shakespeare.

Western literature, particularly since Shakespeare, is marked by the representation of internalized change in its characters. A literature of the ever-growing inner self is in itself a large form of biography, even though this is the biography of imaginary beings, from Hamlet to the sometimes nameless protagonists of Kafka and Beckett. Skeptics might want to argue that all literary biography concerns imaginary beings, since authors make themselves up, and every biographer gives us a creation curiously different from the same author as seen by the writer of a rival *Life.* Boswell's Johnson is not quite anyone else's Johnson, though it is now very difficult for us to disentangle the great Doctor from his gifted Scottish friend and follower. The life of the author is not merely a metaphor or a fiction, as is "the Death of the Author," but it always does contain metaphorical or fictive elements. Those elements are a part of the value of literary biography, but not the largest or the crucial part, which is the separation of the mask from the man or woman who hid behind it. James Joyce and Samuel Beckett, master and sometime disciple, were both of them enigmatic personalities, and their biographers have not, as yet, fully expounded the mystery of these contrasting natures. Beckett seems very nearly to have been a secular saint: personally disinterested, heroic in the French Resistance, as humane a person ever to have composed major fictions and dramas. Joyce, self-obsessed even as Beckett was preternaturally selfless, was the Milton of the twentieth century. Beckett was perhaps the least egoistic post-Joycean, post-Proustian, post-Kafkan of writers. Does that illuminate the problematical nature of his work, or does it simply constitute another problem? Whatever the cause, the question matters. The only death of the author that is other than literal, and that matters, is the fate only of weak writers. The strong, who become canonical, never die, which is what the canon truly is about. To be read forever is the Life of the Author.

◈ Introduction

THE COLLAPSE of the Soviet Union and consequent end of the Cold War, a calamity for some writers of international thrillers, scarcely has affected John le Carré. I assume that this is because his authentic agon always has been with his literary father, Graham Greene, and that father's father, Joseph Conrad. Superb as le Carré is at his genre, he has been careful to stay within its limits, avoiding both Greene's lows and highs. Le Carré has no *Brighton Rock*, and he has kept his distance from hopeless comparisons with Conrad's *Under Western Eyes* and *The Secret Agent*. His most ambitious fiction to date, in my judgment, remains *The Little Drummer Girl* (1983), a spy narrative that immerses itself in the Israeli-Arab conflict, while slyly invoking Conrad's *Heart of Darkness* by naming the principal Israeli counterterrorist as Kurtz. In *The Little Drummer Girl*, the name is an irony; Kurtz is a hard professional but a man of strict self-control, and does not succumb to the horror, whether of what he fights or how he has to fight it. One senses that le Carré is far enough away from Kurtz, the Israeli Smiley, so that he experiences considerable ambivalence toward his creation, a protagonist far darker and more enigmatic than the very English Smiley. And yet there is actually very little that is Conradian about le Carré's Kurtz, who is neither High Romantic nor a potential abyss of nihilism.

Graham Greene, in his entertainments, was to Conrad what John Webster was to Shakespeare: like the Jacobean Webster, Greene emulates the master by a simplification into intensity, and thus moral tragedy becomes melodrama, frequently very good melodrama indeed. Le Carré sacrifices Greene's intensity in order to render Smiley's perplexed moral complexity. The result causes a severe loss in dramatic quality in the Smiley novels, particularly in the ambitious *Tinker, Tailor, Soldier, Spy*, le Carré's vision of the Kim Philby case. Yet one feels that George Smiley remains le Carré's most adequate antihero, rather than Kurtz or the suicidal Magnus Pym of *A Perfect Spy*. Compassion, particularly for the outcast, is Smiley's great virtue and makes him le Carré's surrogate. Greene at his best, in *Brighton Rock* and *This Gun for Hire*, is pragmatically little more compassionate than the Webster of *The White Devil* and *The Duchess of Malfi*. Conrad, in *The Secret Agent* and *Under Western Eyes*, approaches something like the Shakespearean disinterestedness that Dr. Samuel Johnson feared as verging upon spiritual nihilism. As readers, we admire le Carré for his compassion, but Pym is far less memorable than Greene's Pinkie and Raven, let alone the nihilistic Decoud of Conrad's *Nostromo*. Le Carré certainly is without peer among living writers in his genre; a call for the dead awakens though some of the ways in which he comes short of (for now) his precursors.

—H. B.

Robert Bloch
1917–1994

ROBERT ALBERT BLOCH was born in Chicago on April 5, 1917, the son of bank cashier Raphael A. Bloch and schoolteacher Stella Loeb. He and his younger sister enjoyed a comfortable middle-class upbringing and were encouraged by their parents to develop interests in reading and the performing arts. Bloch's life was changed irrevocably in 1926 by his viewing of Lon Chaney in *The Phantom of the Opera,* an experience that initiated an early interest in film and a lifelong fascination with the macabre.

Bloch's family moved to Milwaukee in 1927. In that year he discovered the pulp magazine *Weird Tales* and the work of H. P. Lovecraft. A fan letter to Lovecraft in 1933 began a correspondence that would have a major impact on Bloch's future career. Lovecraft encouraged Bloch's efforts as a writer, which hitherto had been devoted to comedy and skits for high school plays. Bloch's first professionally published story, "The Feast in the Abbey," appeared in *Weird Tales* in 1935 and proved the first of a burst of stories that strongly reflected Lovecraft's influence, save for one important difference: many of Bloch's characters were crooks whose grisly fates were a form of sardonic justice.

Following Lovecraft's death in 1937, Bloch branched out into other types of writing. His involvement with the Milwaukee Fictioneers led to his writing science fiction for *Amazing Stories* starting in 1939, and his humorous fantasy helped set the tone for the short-lived fantasy pulp *Unknown.* In the late 1930s the cast of his weird fiction also began to change as he delved more deeply into the twisted motivations of his characters.

Unable to make a living solely from writing fiction, Bloch wrote political campaign material for a Milwaukee gubernatorial candidate between 1939 and 1944. He married Marion Ruth Holcombe in 1940 and, with the birth of their first daughter imminent, took an advertising copywriting position in 1942. He also began writing prolifically for the weird fiction, science fiction, and detective pulps.

In 1943 Bloch wrote "Yours Truly, Jack the Ripper," about the reincarnation of the infamous Victorian psychopath in response to modern society's violent tendencies. The story blended an acute inquiry into the criminal mind with deft social criticism and was recognized as an instant classic. The following year it was adapted for the first of many times for radio and launched Bloch's own scripting of thirty-nine originals and adaptations for the radio program "Stay Tuned for Terror."

Bloch's first novel, *The Scarf* (1947; revised 1966), a first-person portrait of a sexual psychopath, established several themes that came to dominate his crime and suspense writing, among them the miserable lives of his criminals, the banality of their evil, and their society's complicity in either inducing or reinforcing their behavior. Bloch developed these themes over his next four novels and perfected them in his masterpiece *Psycho* (1959), the story of a young man so distraught over his mother's death that a part of his fragmented psyche begins impersonating her. The novel was based in part on the case of Ed Gein, a Wisconsin mass murderer. Interest in it as a film property persuaded Bloch to move his family to California in 1960 and pursue a career in film and television. Alfred Hitchcock's film of the novel became one of the most famous of all time and a source of bitterness for Bloch, who had sold the rights to his story cheaply. Bad feelings were exacerbated when Bloch's novel *Psycho II* (1982) and the script for it were rejected as the source for the film of the same name.

Bloch divorced in 1963 and married Eleanor Alexander the following year. Between 1960 and 1975 he wrote scripts for a wide variety of television shows, including "Alfred Hitchcock Presents," "Night Gallery," "Star Trek," and "Boris Karloff's Thriller." He scripted the remake of *The Cabinet of Dr. Caligari* in 1962 and several films for William Castle. His own stories were adapted for a series of omnibus films throughout the 1960s and 1970s.

All the while he nursed a love-hate relationship with Hollywood, whose business practices he criticized for exploiting the baser instincts of audiences and contributing to the social ills documented in his crime fiction. This became the subject of *The Star Stalker* (1968), his first novel after a hiatus of more than eight years. Bloch returned to writing novels on a regular basis in 1972 with the thriller *Night-World*. His later novels *The Night of the Ripper* (1984) and *Psycho House* (1990) extend his exploration of the criminal's relation to his society, while *American Gothic* (1974), based upon incidents at the Chicago World's Fair of 1893, is an interesting experiment in combining the crime story with the historical novel.

Bloch served as president of the Mystery Writers of America in 1970. Among his many awards are the 1959 Hugo Award for best science fiction story and the World Fantasy Convention's first lifetime achievement award in 1975. His "unauthorized autobiography," *Once Around the Bloch*, appeared in 1993. Robert Bloch died of complications of cancer of the larynx on September 23, 1994.

◈ *Critical Extracts*

UNSIGNED ⟨*The Scarf* is⟩ the case history of a young man who (in the remarkably muted words of the jacket blurbist) is "not quite normal." Daniel Morley, a novelist, because of an early, and very unusual, experience with his English teacher—a lady of amorous impulses—feels impelled to wrap his maroon knitted scarf about the neck of any young woman who especially appeals to him, and then to jot down his emotions in a notebook. In spite of this idiosyncrasy, he prospers until the mortality rate among his fiancées in half a dozen cities attracts attention out in Hollywood, where his maroon scarf is especially admired. Neatly plotted, with one of those endings that are ironic as all getout but not very convincing.

Unsigned, [Review of *The Scarf*], *New Yorker*, 30 August 1947, p. 68

ANTHONY BOUCHER About a year ago I was complaining in this space that Robert Bloch, as a murder writer, is rarely as effective as he can and should be. Now, in his sixth suspense novel, *Psycho*, he is more chillingly effective than any writer might reasonably be expected to be, and I will have my words with *sauce béarnaise* please.

Here Mr. Bloch demonstrates, almost like a male Margaret Millar, that a believable history of mental illness can be more icily terrifying than all the arcane horrors summoned up by a collaboration of Poe and Lovecraft. The narrative surprises and shocks are so cunningly arrayed that it's unwise even to hint at plot and theme beyond mentioning that they seem suggested by a recent real-life monstrosity in the Middle West. It's a short book, powerfully and speedily told; read it in one gulp on a fine spring day when the bright sun *may* restore warmth to your Bloch-frozen bloodstream.

> Anthony Boucher, [Review of *Psycho*], *New York Times Book Review*, 19 April 1959, p. 25

UNSIGNED   Grand Guignol is Robert Bloch's mode in *Psycho* and he manages as splendid a set of creeps as we've enjoyed in some time. His materials look commonplace enough (a motel bypassed by the new highway, its pudgy proprietor, his dominating mama and a girl wondering whether she'd better be on the lam), but Mr. Bloch's employment of them is adroit and bloodcurdling. He doesn't (perhaps by intention) keep his ultimate surprise for the close and, as a pretty crawly sort of fact, this is probably kindness. Of the plot, nothing more should be said here but a hint in a press release seems worth reprinting: "Once a Robert Bloch fan asked what he, Bloch, was like, to which Bloch replied: 'I have the heart of a small boy. I keep it on my desk in a bottle.' "

> Unsigned, [Review of *Psycho*], *New York Herald Tribune Book Review*, 26 April 1959, p. 11

JAMES SANDOE   In *The Dead Beat*, Robert Bloch sketches the later history of a young heel who plays pretty good piano but is trying to parlay himself into means by blackmail. The beating lucky Larry takes is no lesson since it lands him as a guest of Walter and Elinor Harris, concerned, naive and vulnerable. His baby face and Larry's innate shrewdness sustain him through some days of perils for everybody else the more frightening because the others are barely aware of them. Mr. Bloch manipulates his narrative with speed, economy, bite and with appropriately less ruthlessness than he needed last year for the compulsive *Psycho*. But then this is a different book, not by any means a lesser one.

> James Sandoe, [Review of *The Dead Beat*], *New York Herald Tribune Book Review*, 29 May 1960, p. 12

NEWGATE CALLENDAR   Robert Bloch has based his *American Gothic* on an actual criminal who operated during the Chicago exposition of 1893. Bloch in this book really has created an American gothic, complete with castle, hidden passageways and terrified females. The author of *Psycho* knows how to titillate.

Unfortunately, Bloch's book is not as good as some of his previous ones. His ingredients are all too familiar: the evil doctor, the bright girl reporter, the scalpels and dismemberment chamber, and so on. The ending contains no surprises, and the writing is not much above a juvenile level.

> Newgate Callendar, [Review of *American Gothic*], *New York Times Book Review*, 30 June 1974, pp. 32–33

LESTER DEL REY   ⟨Bloch's⟩ loyalty to *Weird Tales* never ceased. In 1943, that magazine printed a story entitled "Yours Truly, Jack the Ripper" ⟨. . .⟩ In it, the London fiend was shown to be still alive and operating in the United States. The story proved to be a milestone in Bloch's career.

Just what makes this story so fascinating is something I cannot analyze. Perhaps it is the quiet, natural development of what could have been melodramatic terror. But the story was adapted several times for radio drama-tization and it quickly began a long series of appearances in anthologies. As a result, Bloch was asked to write a series of such dramatizations of nearly forty of his own stories for the popular radio program "Stay Tuned for Terror." Doing so taught him the art of dramatic writing, which was far removed from his early style that depended almost entirely on narrative development of mood and suspense.

There was a steady evolution going on in his writing, too. Originally, as with most who followed the Lovecraft school of fiction, Bloch had concen-trated on terror from the outside. Men who dared to investigate legends or who were inadvertently drawn into strange events were beset by horrors far beyond their knowledge or control. There was little importance given to what went on in their minds, provided they were duly terrified.

Now, perhaps because his mystery and detective writing required more realism—or perhaps simply because he was growing in skill and scope—Bloch began to look inward, into the strange recesses in the minds of his people. It was in the darkness that lies behind our surface thoughts that he found the real lurking horrors. His stories gained a new dimension.

The terror was more subtle now, but even more real. It crept from the mind, a universal dread that needed no ancient cemeteries or external demons for its effect. The plotting was no less skillful, but a second, deeper level of psychological understanding had replaced or been added to the surface events.

Lester del Rey, "Robert Bloch: The Man Who Wrote *Psycho*," *The Best of Robert Bloch*, ed. Lester del Rey (New York: Ballantine Books, 1977), pp. xiii–xiv

---

ROBERT BLOCH   I can't tell you who first came up with the term "psychological suspense." But I'm forever grateful to him.

Before that phrase was coined, people like myself were referred to—if at all—as "horror-story writers." This designation made me shudder more than my readers. It evoked the vision of a wild-eyed weirdo whose entire wardrobe consisted of two garments—a long black cloak and a short white straitjacket.

But "psychological suspense writer" suggests a more respectable type; a keen-eyed scientific observer whose lucrative analysis of the human condition has enabled him to purchase a whole closetful of tailored clothing.

Actually I don't fit into either category. My eyes are as dull as my conventional outlook and I don't own a single straitjacket, let alone one with a Gucci label.

The real benefit from this change of image accrues to my stories. Over the years what was once dismissed as unworthy of consideration is now frequently given a second glance and a second chance. As a result some of the things I've tried to say have found a new audience. And while my primary purpose is entertainment, it's gratifying to communicate on other levels as well.

To me, writing remains a form of communication. At one time a statement like this seemed self-evident. Now, however, we live in an age of obscurantism, where music and graphic art need lengthy interpretation and the written word must be explained by critics who tell the reader what the writer was "trying to say."

I still believe a writer must do more than *try*—his job is to *succeed* in saying what he means. Obscurantism is for politicians.

In discussing my stories I strive for equal clarity. The material in this collection falls into two genres: supernatural fantasy and the *conte cruel*. But there's a common element—horror, or psychological suspense, if you prefer the term. And that's about all the explanation that seems necessary.

Chronologically the stories represent a sampling of my output over the past three decades. During that time there have been many changes in the world of reality—but the world of unreality, of imagination and aberration, remained constant.

Despite extensive and expensive investigation, the field of parapsychology has not been greatly illuminated. Dispute still wages and rages over the validity of supernatural manifestations, and we know not one whit more about death than we do about life.

Equally elaborate attention has been paid to the examination of criminal behavior and mental disorder, without resulting in any consensus of scientific opinion. The mind has not yielded up a tithe of its secrets.

And so—since we fear that which we do not know and cannot explain—my subject-matter remains pertinent, or impertinent.

> Robert Bloch, "Author's Afterword," *Such Stuff as Screams Are Made Of* (New York: Del Rey/Ballantine, 1979), pp. 284–85

BRIAN STABLEFORD   Bloch reached a kind of crossroads in his career in 1942, when his work diversified in two different directions. For *Unknown* in 1942, he wrote "A Good Knight's Work," a slapstick comedy influenced by Damon Runyon which brought a parody of Arthurian legend into contemporary America. For *Weird Tales* in the same year, he wrote "Nursemaid to Nightmares," another comedy, this time in the vein of Thorne Smith, while in *Fantastic Adventures*, he began the long-running series of burlesques featuring the amiable Lefty Feep with "Time Wounds All Heels." Although he wrote sequels to both of the first-named works (these are the stories collected in *Dragons and Nightmares*), neither *Unknown* nor *Weird Tales* continued to provide a market for such lighthearted fantasies as these, and Bloch deemphasized this aspect of his production. 〈. . .〉

The other direction taken by his work during the late 1940's was signalized by one of his most famous stories: "Yours Truly, Jack the Ripper" (1943). In this story, an Englishman approaches a Chicago psychiatrist with the claim that Jack the Ripper is alive and well and continuing his career in that American city. It turns out that he is right, but fate subjects him to a particularly ironic betrayal. It was in this story that Bloch demonstrated for the first time the ability which lies at the heart of his artistry: the ability to strike a perfect balance between the obvious and the covert. His mastery of the surprise ending depends on his ability to contrive denouements which fit perfectly that which has gone before but which the reader never quite guesses in advance. The risk run by authors of this type of story is that in planting the clues that make the ending fit they will telegraph their surprise and defuse it; no one is better than Bloch at walking on the very edge of this pitfall while not falling into it.

> Brian Stableford, "The Short Fiction of Robert Bloch," *Survey of Modern Fantasy Literature*, ed. Frank M. Magill (Englewood Cliffs, NJ: Salem Press, 1983), Vol. 3, pp. 1453–54

TOM EASTON   Bloch first came to public attention with "Yours Truly, Jack the Ripper" in 1943. Now, 41 years later, he returns ⟨in *The Night of the Ripper*⟩ to his origins as a writer with a full-scale docudrama, and it's gripping, gory stuff. It's not for the bodice-ripper fans, either, for Jack didn't pay much attention to bodices. He liked juicier stuff, and Bloch shows it all to us, with details straight from the public record and ambience that feels grittily true to the period. Only the story is fiction. ⟨. . .⟩

The story has its relevance for today, for the Ripper was one of the first private mass murderers and, as the detective says, "America is young yet. . . . Wait and see." At the same time, we see the world in a more innocent age, when blood-obsessed psychopaths needed no ideological justification for their acts. To my mind, the Ripper, while evil, is less evil than any terrorist.

Read the book. And laugh at yourself when you hesitate to go out at night.

> Tom Easton, [Review of *The Night of the Ripper*], *Analog* 105, No. 4 (April 1985): 183–84

LES DANIELS   Bloch's novel ⟨*Psycho*⟩ is an indisputable tour de force, the distillation of twenty-five years of experience and experimentation: it provided not only the plot for the movie, but many of the clever little touches most critics assume are Hitchcock's own. For instance, those who praise the director for the suspenseful scene in which a car carrying incriminating evidence sinks with agonizing slowness into a swamp should realize that the incident is also in the book, and in fact was prefigured fourteen years earlier in the story "Enoch." ⟨. . .⟩

Bloch got his inspiration from the factual case of a Wisconsin killer named Ed Gein, but the story and its treatment are largely original. What is most memorable is the cleverness of the trick (since Bates believes his mother is responsible, the reader does as well), but the story is so well told that it is gripping even when no surprise is expected. *Psycho* is a landmark, if only because after its appearance horror stories were more likely to deal with madmen than monsters. Yet more than a touch of the supernatural is implied; despite all the glib psychological explanations, the fact remains that Norman Bates has been, in one way or another, possessed by the spirit of his dead mother.

Les Daniels, "Robert Bloch," *Supernatural Fiction Writers*, ed. E. F. Bleiler (New York: Charles Scribner's Sons, 1985), Vol. 2, pp. 904–5

RANDALL LARSON   *Night-World* is not entirely a psychological thriller, since the character of the killer is almost constantly off-stage. If anything, *Night-World* is more the study of the *victim*, Karen Raymond, and her responses to events that transpire around her. Yet the malevolent character of the psychotic killer is revealed, little by little, even in his absence.

An introductory chapter starts the novel off with an ominous foreboding, as the unidentified killer muses over his plans for destruction, and Bloch affords us our first glimpse at the madman's psyche. His initial thought is one of mayhem: "the sun is dying in the west and it's blood stained the sky." His thought patterns seem disjointed and rambling, yet there is one thread that constantly links them: death.

Eventually, we realize that the killer shares much in common with Bloch's other psychopaths. Like Dan Morley in *The Scarf*, he does not view his victims as real people. "The world is my idea," he remarks to himself. Other people are only actors in a play that *he's* designed—a morality play, a Passion Play, a Grand Guignol extermination of all performers save himself. The killer fails to notice the irony in that he, too, is an actor, playing out various roles: the dutiful patient for Dr. Griswold in the asylum, the man in the closet for Dorothy Anderson, and so on. *Night-World's* killer is the quintessential Bloch villain. Like all those who have gone before him—Dan Morley and Steve Collins and Larry Fox and Charles Campbell and all the rest—when he ceases to consider others as being real, as mere objects to suit his megalomaniacal fancy, that's when he becomes truly dangerous. He can justify anything.

Another theme in *Night-World* is that of lunatics taking over their asylum, an idea Bloch dealt with before in short stories such as "Mannikins of Horror" and "A Home Away from Home." It's not only a frightening thought (and one Bloch is quick to credit Poe's "The System of Dr. Tarr and Prof. Fether" for initial inspiration), but one that dovetails into Bloch's own preoccupation with the schizophrenic personality. The lunatics are taking over because we can't recognize them for what they are. It's no longer Peter Lorre or Boris Karloff grinning in mayhem, no longer the obvious skulking villain. It's the boy next door; it's Good Neighbor Sam or John Q. Psychopath or the Fuller Brush Man. *Look carefully*, Bloch nudges. *He may not be who he seems. Watch out or they'll get you.*

Randall Larson, *Robert Bloch* (Mercer Island, WA: Starmont House, 1986), pp. 97–98

STEFAN DZIEMIANOWICZ   The centerpiece ⟨of *Unholy Trinity*⟩ is *The Scarf*, to which a chapter cut from the original has been restored. That chapter does not "open up" the book in any new way, as restored texts of Faulkner, Joyce, and Lovecraft seem to be doing these days, but it does show the difference between what the publishers (whom Bloch says cut it out because it was "too farfetched") may have perceived Bloch's writing was all about and a singular idea Bloch introduced here and would explore further in much of his post-pulp work.

The narrator of *The Scarf* is a character seen in different guises in all three novels: a loner, psyche slightly off-kilter, who adapts to his environment by murdering those who get in his way. In the purged chapter, which occurs halfway through the book, Daniel Morley fantasizes in a notebook entry what it would be like to climb up on top of a tall building at a busy intersection and randomly pick off passersby with a rifle (anticipating the Charles Whitman killings by almost twenty years).

At this point in the story Morley has strangled two, possibly three, women he has known intimately, and he has justified it to himself on the grounds that they would have held him back in life. The anonymous and wanton murders in his fantasy, though, reveal something deeper and more insidious than his seeming misogyny: a detachment from and total lack of empathy for other human beings. It's evident in his feelings of superiority over his victims, seen symbolically in his god-like perch on the building and in his literal description of victims as "dots" and "bugs" (indeed, in *The Couch*, the murderer indulges the thought that his ability to dispense death makes him god-like). Morley is a full-blown misanthropist, a point shrilly under-scored at the end of the fantasy when he decides that if the authorities storm his hideout he'll jump, in the hope of taking some bystanders with him when he hits the pavement.

Perhaps Bloch's editors, reading this chapter, assumed it would distract readers from the psychological "center" of the book: the opening sexual encounter that presumably unbalances Morley and imbues his scarf with its fetishistic power. What Bloch seemed to be getting at, though, is that there was already a gaping wound in Morley's psyche long before that incident that no amount of psychotherapy could cauterize shut (in fact it is later revealed that he was the seducer and not the seducee, as he claims). His difficulty with women isn't the problem—it's just a *symptom* of something more malign. Thus the uneasy feeling the reader has at the end of the story, when this proto–Norman Bates speaks as though he is cured and ready for a new start in life. No one in his right mind, reading the last sentence of *The Scarf,* could believe in a psychosis-free future for Daniel Morley.

Stefan Dziemianowicz, [Review of *Unholy Trinity* and *Night-World*], *Crypt of Cthulhu* 6, No. 5 (Roodmas 1987): 57–58

DAVID PUNTER   I would like here to mention another of Bloch's novels, *American Gothic* (1974). The central character is again a murderer of women, G. Gordon Gregg; and again here Bloch is taking the frame of an actual criminal history and searching in it for clues about the kind of psychic structure which might lie behind these crimes.

Gregg's story is replete with Gothic trappings: it is set in a modern castle full of secret passageways, slaughterhouses, hidden doors, and comes to an appropriately melodramatic conclusion. Among other things, Gregg is a pharmacist and a master-hypnotist, a clear descendant of villainous alche-mists in the tradition of Frankenstein. But in the end it appears that Bloch is as puzzled about his motivations as we are, and offers two interlocking but disparate accounts.

Below the surface, we are allowed to surmise that this is another pathologi-cal account, and that Gregg enjoys his grisly work. But this, of course, is not the way he sees it. He again regards his victims as simply objects; what he wants from them, or so he believes, is simply their money. But he wants this not in any empty spirit of acquisition: 'it wasn't swindling', he explains to Crystal, who is intended to be another of his victims; 'it was a business matter. Building a place like this, carrying out my plans. You've got to find working capital, that's the primary rule of economics.' ⟨. . .⟩

We may go in several directions from this point. On the one hand, we may trace the psychic effects of capitalism, the implanted need for success and profit, the apparent need to treat other people as objects in the process of engaging successfully in business. On the other hand, we may think about the psychological need for domination and possession which the castle represents. The concentration on detail connects with the need for secrecy; it is only through an intense absorption in detail that one can escape from the all-seeing eye of mother, and simultaneously prove one's command of the outer world.

But this need to command is itself merely the psychic residue of unaccommodated problems with omnipotence; if anybody were allowed to penetrate the bedroom, all of the child's secrets would be revealed, all that lies behind the accurate and neat accounts, the ledgers of profit and loss. And the term 'loss' perhaps reminds us of what is most important for Bates and Gregg: that there should be no loss to the self, no further erosion or leakage of that which is to be so preciously guarded because it is so fragile, the sense of a maturity precariously achieved and maintained only through an increasingly detailed elaboration of an overarching fiction.

> David Punter, "Robert Bloch's *Psycho*: Some Pathological Contexts," *American Horror Fiction: From Brockden Brown to Stephen King*, ed. Brian Docherty (New York: St. Martin's Press, 1990), pp. 102–3

S. T. JOSHI   *The Scarf* is the first-person account of Dan Morley, who tells of a traumatic experience he had as a youth. A handsome boy, he has attracted the attention of one of his teachers, a lonely woman in her late thirties named Miss Frazer. One day she invites him to her home and proceeds to tie him up with a maroon scarf, seal up the house, and turn on the gas so that the two of them can die together as lovers. He manages to escape, but Miss Frazer dies in the process. As a result, he confesses that "For years I hated women, books, everything."

It is at this point that the paradoxes begin. Although he hates women, he attracts them and is attracted to them; although he hates books, he becomes a writer of them. He undergoes a pattern of latching on to a woman, writing stories about her, then killing her with the scarf. Words and reality have become inextricably confused in his mind, and it is as if he kills his women only so as to provide a fitting climax to a story: "I killed Rena because she was just a story character to me. She wasn't real. She didn't exist at all." In a fascinating and highly prophetic disquisition, Morley ponders on words and their ubiquity: "A jumble of words on a slip and a mumble of words on a lip and you're married. Or divorced. Or buried, for that matter. You can't buy, sell, or contract without a magic formula. It's all words now." Is there a reality beyond the facade of words? Yes, but only one: "Murder isn't a word. Murder is a deed." Morley kills not only to vent his hatred of women but, in a twisted way, to confirm his own existence.

The quasi-weirdness of this novel comes from several directions. Morley begins writing a "Black Notebook," a notebook filled with his innermost thoughts, in which he records not only his murders but the terrifying night-mares he suffers; they are among the more effective dream-sequences in modern weird literature. Moreover, it is precisely because there is no doubt of Morley's guilt, and accordingly no mystery or suspense element aside from the matter of whether he will ever be caught, to distract us from the perception of his increasingly aberrant mental state. The latter part of the novel does indeed take on a suspense element as certain characters finally begin to suspect Morley of the murders and set about to entrap him; and the conclusion—rewritten in the 1966 version—is more than a little con-trived. Here we find that Miss Frazer did not in fact die, and she maintains that it was Morley who was in love with *her* and sought to tie her up and commit joint suicide. I believe we are to interpret this, however, as a lie fabricated by Miss Frazer in order finally to gain Morley for herself—and Morley now seems resigned to such a fate ("Miss Frazer and I are going to be married . . ."). I am not especially happy with this conclusion, but perhaps Bloch felt that this ending allowed him to give Morley a more satisfactory comeuppance than merely death or incarceration. Nevertheless, *The Scarf* is a powerful work of psychological horror; because of its singleminded focus upon a disturbed mentality, it can take a place with the best weird fiction of its kind.

S. T. Joshi, "Weird Tales?," *Armchair Detective* 26, No. 1 (Winter 1993): 43–44

◈ Bibliography

Sea-Kissed. 1945.

The Opener of the Way. 1945.

The Scarf. 1947, 1966.

The Kidnapper. 1954.

Spiderweb. 1954.

The Will to Kill. 1954.

Shooting Star. 1958.

Terror in the Night and Other Stories. 1958.

Psycho. 1959.

The Dead Beat. 1960.

Pleasant Dreams—Nightmares. 1960.

Firebug. 1961.

Blood Runs Cold. 1961.

The Couch. 1962.

Terror. 1962.

Yours Truly, Jack the Ripper: Tales of Horror ⟨The House of the Hatchet and Other Tales of Horror⟩. 1962.

Atoms and Evil. 1962.

The Eighth Stage of Fandom: Selections from 25 Years of Fan Writing. Ed. Earl Kemp. 1962.

Horror-7. 1963.

Bogey Men. 1963.

Tales in a Jugular Vein. 1965.

The Skull of the Marquis de Sade and Other Stories. 1965.

Chamber of Horrors. 1966.

The Living Demons. 1967.

The Star Stalker. 1968.

Ladies' Day; This Crowded Earth. 1968.

Dragons and Nightmares: Four Short Novels. 1968.

The Todd Dossier. 1969.

Bloch and Bradbury (with Ray Bradbury). 1969.

Fear Today—Gone Tomorrow. 1971.

It's All in Your Mind. 1971.

Sneak Preview. 1971.

Night-World. 1972.

American Gothic. 1974.

Cold Chills. 1977.

The Laughter of a Ghoul: What Every Young Ghoul Should Know. 1977.

The Best of Robert Bloch. Ed. Lester del Rey. 1977.

The King of Terrors: Tales of Madness and Death. 1977.

The Best of Fredric Brown (editor). 1977.

Reunion with Tomorrow. 1978.

Strange Eons. 1978.

There Is a Serpent in Eden. 1979.

Out of the Mouths of Graves. 1979.

Such Stuff as Screams Are Made Of. 1979.

The First World Fantasy Convention: Three Authors Remember (with T. E. D. Klein and Fritz Leiber). 1980.

Mysteries of the Worm. Ed. Lin Carter. 1981, 1993.

Psycho II. 1982.

Twilight Zone: The Movie. 1983.

The Night of the Ripper. 1984.

Out of My Head. 1986.

Unholy Trinity: Three Novels of Suspense ⟨The Scarf, The Dead Beat, The Couch⟩. 1986.

Selected Stories. 1987, 1990 (as *Complete Stories*). 3 vols.

Midnight Pleasures. 1987.

Lost in Time and Space with Lefty Feep. Ed. John Stanley. 1987.

Fear and Trembling. 1989.

Screams ⟨The Will to Kill, Firebug, The Star Stalker⟩. 1989.

Lori. 1989.

The Robert Bloch Companion: Collected Interviews 1969–1986. Ed. Randall D. Larson. 1989.

Psycho House. 1990.

The Jekyll Legacy (with Andre Norton). 1990.

Psycho-Paths (editor). 1991.

Three Complete Novels ⟨Psycho, Psycho II, Psycho House⟩. 1993.

Once Around the Bloch: An Unauthorized Autobiography. 1993.

Richard Condon
b. 1915

RICHARD THOMAS CONDON was born in New York City on March 18, 1915, the son of Richard Aloysius and Martha Irene (Pickering) Condon. When he was eighteen he sailed around the world as a waiter on a cruise ship. Back in New York he worked as an advertising copywriter, which led in 1936 to a job as a publicist for Walt Disney Productions. In 1941 he moved to Twentieth Century–Fox, and then—after briefly attempting his own publicity firm, Richard Condon, Inc. (1945–48)—he worked for Paramount (1948–53) and United Artists (1953–57).

During his years as a publicist Condon wrote abundantly in his spare time. He had one play, *Men of Distinction*, staged on Broadway in 1953 and was also coproducer with José Ferrer of two other Broadway shows, *Twentieth Century* and *Stalag 17*, in 1951–52. In 1957, however, Condon developed duodenal ulcers as a result of his publicity work, and he decided to become a full-time novelist, even though he had previously written very little fiction. His first novel, *The Oldest Confession* (1958), was cordially received, but it was eclipsed by what many critics believe is still his best work, *The Manchurian Candidate* (1959). This novel of political intrigue is a prototype for many of Condon's later novels and underscores his own political beliefs; as he has commented in an interview, "Every book I've ever written has been about abuse of power. I feel very strongly about that. I'd like people to know how deeply their politicians are wronging them." *The Manchurian Candidate* was made into a successful film, as several other of Condon's novels have been.

For the next twenty years Condon continued to write while traveling widely with his wife, Evelyn Hunt (whom he married in 1938), and their two daughters; the family lived at various times in France, Switzerland, Spain, and Ireland. Among his later novels are *An Infinity of Mirrors* (1964), *Mile High* (1969), *The Vertical Smile* (1971), and *Winter Kills* (1974), a thinly disguised account of the assassination of John F. Kennedy.

Many of Condon's novels of the 1960s and 1970s were poorly received, and some critics believed that he had written himself out; but his career gained new life with *Prizzi's Honor* (1982), a vibrant and witty story of organized crime. It was lavishly filmed by John Huston and starred Jack Nicholson and Anjelica Huston; Condon wrote several drafts of the screenplay but then developed an aneurysm of the abdominal aorta, and the screenplay was revised by Janet Roach. Condon has written several more sequels to this novel, including *Prizzi's Family* (1986), *Prizzi's Glory* (1988), and *Prizzi's Money* (1994). Other recent novels are *Emperor of America* (1990) and *The Final Addiction* (1991), transparent satires on Ronald Reagan and George Bush.

Condon has also written a historical novel, *The Abandoned Woman* (1977), and has collaborated with his daughter Wendy on a cookbook, *The Mexican Stove* (1973). Since 1980 he has lived in Dallas, Texas.

Critical Extracts

WHITNEY BALLIETT   Richard Condon's first two novels—*The Oldest Confession*, published last year, and *The Manchurian Candidate*, just issued by McGraw-Hill—are brilliant, highly individualistic, and hopelessly unfashionable demonstrations of how to write stylishly, tell fascinating stories, assemble plots that suggest the peerless mazes of Wilkie Collins, be very funny, make acute social observations, and ram home digestible morals. They demonstrate, in short, a good many of the things that were expected of the novel before the creative-writing courses got its practitioners brooding in their mirrors. ⟨. . .⟩

Mr. Condon's story ⟨*The Manchurian Candidate*⟩, which is balanced on an infallible use of suspense and surprise, is ingenious. It involves a Communist effort, painstakingly carried out between 1936 and 1960, to have the pawn of an American sympathizer elected President of the United States. The principal figures are Raymond Shaw, his mother, and his stepfather, Senator (formerly Governor) Iselin, who represent extraordinarily hideous caricatures of, respectively, an American egghead, a domineering American mother, and an American demagogue with more than a passing resemblance to Senator McCarthy. ⟨. . .⟩ Mr. Condon oils this nonsense with such self-caricaturing horrors as a foolproof type of brainwashing, developed by a Chinese Communist and dependent on long-range posthypnotic suggestion; no fewer than nine startlingly cold-blooded murders; two suicides; some orgies; and an amazingly complex species of incest, executed between a daughter and her father and between the daughter and her son. But these bulging irregularities are always contained by Mr. Condon's Roman-candle prose, which effortlessly shoots off words like "zymurgist," "monotreme," "langrel," and "luetic," indelible descriptions like "His face began to fill with a claret flush that clashed unpleasantly with the Nile-green wallpaper directly beside him," and lunatic images such as "The sergeant's rage-daubed face would shine like a ripped-out heart flung into stones in moonlight." Very likely, many of *The Manchurian Candidate*'s liberal readers will clap their hands over its savage parade of bourgeois decadence and the wicked political deception it outlines, while an equal number of conservatives will disbelievingly humph and bridle at such soiled, un-American images. Both groups, of course, will have missed its heartening and robust intent, and for a simple reason. The book is about them.

Whitney Balliett, "Made in the U.S.A.," *New Yorker*, 30 May 1959, pp. 105–7

JAMES KELLY   A measure of the wildly wonderful quality of *Some Angry Angel* is that there's really nothing with which to compare it. A gargantuan, gothic, quixotic stew served up with crazy eloquence. A polemic against modern foolishness, with a compassion that is all the more effective because it is indignant. For starters, imagine the friendly echoes of Robert Nathan, Nathanael West, Joyce Cary (in the Gulley Jimson mood), Robin Hood, George Orwell, and "This Is Your Life" . . . yes, with a Dylan Thomas swing to the roistering, image-haunted prose which threatens every minute to burst into genuine iambic. Every reader is offered his chance and choice from a bottomless grab bag which has been filled by larceny and opens at a touch. In this sensual, informed tale of an abominable newspaperman-turned-gossip columnist, whose tracks lead all the way to the top of the mountain before they stop, Richard Condon has more than lived up to the clues and promises of his two previous novels, *The Oldest Confession* and *The Manchurian Candidate*. In fact, Mr. Condon could become a Cult as quickly as you can say Kafka or Kerouac.

James Kelly, "Modern Gothic with Guilt Edges," *Saturday Review*, 2 April 1960, p. 21

MORDECAI RICHLER   *An Infinity of Mirrors* ⟨. . .⟩ has what film
people call a strong story line as well as plenty of hotsy scenes. In fact the
basic plot, like too many TV salesmen's faces, could move any product. It
fits a western as well as a thriller. In this case, it just happens to be intercut
with the holocaust. The story, briefly, is about Bernheim's daughter Paule,
rich and lovely, who marries a German staff officer, Veelee, tall, blond, and
handsome. Paule and Veelee go off to live in pre-war Berlin where a sexually
depraved S.S. officer, who secretly adores Jewesses, attempts to rape her,
and then turns up again in war-time Paris where Paule has fled with her
son. In Paris, the S.S. officer has the son (half-Jewish) picked up on the
night of an S.S. *razzia*. The boy dies. Paule and Veelee avenge themselves
by beating up the S.S. officer and having him put on a train bound for
Dachau. Only then does Paule "come to realize" that now she is a monster
too.

Such a summary, however, does not do justice to the big scenes and
audacities en route. Hitler himself, for instance, is brought into the story
twice. Once to congratulate Veelee on his soldiermanship, but most memora-
bly at a ball in Berlin where he "wore evening dress, extremely well-tailored"
and made straight for Paule to kiss her hand. "My dear lady, may I have
the pleasure of bidding you good evening." Hitler, it seems, is also crazy for
Jewesses, but Paule makes up for allowing the kiss by kicking "that awful
Goebbels woman" in the ankle. Goering and of course Eichmann also enter
into the action, for the story is only barely underway when the separation
between real newsreel content and fictional characters is dropped—tan-
gles—and results in a suspension of disbelief.

All the same, it's only fair to add that *An Infinity of Mirrors* is very
readable, fast-moving, and rich in romantic detail of the high life. In fact
what Mr. Condon has succeeded in doing is to make the rise of Hitler seem
glamorous and sexy. There is even a comic sub-plot about secret agents in
the best British film tradition. My chief complaint, then, is not that Mr.
Condon has written a bad novel, it is that he has written an immoral one.

> Mordecai Richler, "A Captivating but Distorting Image," *New York Herald Tribune
> Book Week*, 13 September 1964, p. 19

KURT VONNEGUT, JR.   The sixth novel ⟨*Any God Will Do*⟩ by
Richard Condon, an American, of course, seems very middle-European to

me. I hear echoes of Friedrich Dürrenmatt, Max Frisch, *und so weiter*—and the theme, I take it, is the loss of identity by modern man. I might as well add the name of Thomas Mann, since a lot of the action takes place in a Swiss sanitarium, and since this is such a serious book (or have I been had again?). It is serious despite a plot rigged along the lines of low comedy. What could be more middle-European than that? ⟨. . .⟩

The best parts of the book are its celebrations of food. Francis Vollmer becomes such a great cook even French chefs praise him. My guess is that Condon is almost that good himself, since he is able to write, for instance: "During this monologue, Francis had stripped the boiled chicken, covered its flesh with a layer of farce à quenelles à la panade and sprinkled truffles on top. He kneaded it into a firm lengthwise roll, having packed it with filets of tongue, chopped truffles and another layer of quenelles." Yummy.

The poorest parts of the book are its characters. The leading man ⟨. . .⟩ is hollow and is supposed to be hollow, and the supporting players who put junk into him or take it out are cartoons. Consider the monologue that goes on while Vollmer is fixing the chicken, delivered by a Frenchman who is discussing mistresses: "Sensibility, good health and a good disposition—these things combined with utter selfishness. That is what makes a great mistress." This may be true, but it is not fresh. Such Gallic outrageousness goes on for pages, and would bore anyone but Maurice Chevalier.

The book is an honorable failure—a failure because it is boring, despite many game and clever efforts on the author's part to bring it to life. It is honorable because it has tried to say some big things without a trace of meretriciousness. Condon has not solved a technical problem which may well be insoluble: how to write interestingly about a man who is truly empty. Kafka and other literary successes have wisely written about people who weren't truly empty, but only felt as though they were. That is probably as far as fiction can go, and still find readers.

Too bad.

> Kurt Vonnegut, Jr., "The Fall of a Climber," *New York Times Book Review,* 25
> September 1966, pp. 5, 42

JULIAN SMITH   Not long ago, a Yale psychologist conducted a series of experiments demonstrating how easily well-intentioned, responsible, honest, ordinary men can be turned into machines for torturing other men ⟨. . .⟩ When I discussed this experiment with my colleagues in the humanities here, they almost unanimously exclaimed not at the psychologist's findings, but at the fact that he made the study in the first place. Their reaction has a lot to do, I think, with the difference between the literary reputations of writers such as Faulkner and Ambrose Bierce. Both examine the grotesque in human nature, but Faulkner sugar-coats the pill and assures us that man will endure. Condon, like Bierce, makes the unpopular assertion that man will endure only in ignorance, cruelty, and perversity. Even when a director as tough as John Frankenheimer made a film of *The Manchurian Candidate*, he meliorated the novel's cynicism by changing the ending: whereas in the novel Major Marco orders Raymond Shaw to kill his parents and then himself, the film version has Raymond break free of his conditioning (Man Can Escape the Trap! says the film) and, to what is now Marco's absolute horror, kill his parents and himself. That is, if in film vernacular Marco is a good guy, he cannot order a victim of hypnosis and brainwashing to commit political murder, matricide, and suicide.

Half of Condon's value is that he does not affirm the goodness of man. The other half is his independence from currently "stylish" subject matter—while Updike, Malamud, Bellow, and their followers generally treat ordinary men and commonplace, dull, and "realistic" events, Condon writes of power politics, assassination, the world's largest ranch, its most famous movie stars and columnists, madmen, honest thieves—but rarely anyone we might know. For this reason, he is among the very few good writers who live on their craft without the help of foundations and universities. Translated into nineteen languages, he remains neglected by our literary opinion-makers, one of whom sniffed verbally in a letter to this writer: "He lives in another world from ours." Well, thank God he does live in that "other world," for "our" supposedly sane world is increasingly in danger from that other world. Dantes all, we need Virgils such as Condon to guide us through the new Inferno.

Julian Smith, "The Infernal Comedy of Richard Condon," *Twentieth Century Literature* 14, No. 4 (January 1969): 228–29

CHARLES NICOL   Richard Condon's best known novel is *The Manchurian Candidate*, which *Time*, with its hopelessly perverse sense of the clever and the possible, labeled as black humor; its author was compared with Joseph Heller. That analysis and that comparison were, of course, the only black humor connected with that book.

The Manchurian Candidate was an ambitious thriller and converted nicely into film. You all remember Laurence Harvey, brainwashed, preparing to assassinate a presidential candidate. Condon has more recently moved toward the "straight" novel, but the characters who march behind him still seem to be suffering from advanced Pavlovian conditioning. Perhaps Condon is like Vonnegut's typical scientist: people aren't his specialty. He is a plotter and a plodder, and we may say kindly that he is indeed a craftsman, an artificer; his novel is an impressive *ballet mécanique*. Like a clockwork mouse, its life is solely in its style. No matted hairs cling.

Not that this style is particularly admirable, merely curious. Condon's sentences are sturdy rather than flashy, and rarely very lively. But his paragraphs are strange constructions, for Condon starts with a statement about his story, offering a reasonable bit of plot or character, and then forces that small item until it fits into place on top of his paragraph like a handle on a lunch bucket. The lunch bucket however, large, black, rusty, and unfortunately empty, is Condon's main concern: listing irrelevant, trivial facts, his characteristic paragraph grinds until it produces a footnote.

> Charles Nicol, "Plotter and Plodder," *Atlantic Monthly* 224, No. 3 (September 1969): 115

MILES DONALD   No one could possibly guess from the crude and silly cover of *Arigato* that it is in a limited sense (and I am trying to be precise, not patronising) a masterpiece. The cover shows: the hero who is a retired naval officer kitted out in his uniform looking like a reject from Madame Tussauds; two cardboard girls, one of whom, naked and leering, improbably combines skinny ribs and buttocks fit for the most anally fixated; and daubed in the middle of it all a roulette wheel so that the casual reader might quite reasonably assume the whole was a weary and low-grade follow-up of Bond. It is nothing of the kind. Although Mr Condon is a thriller writer (remember *The Manchurian Candidate?*) and although *Arigato* is nominally a thriller its delight comes from the skill with which its author alternately keeps his tongue in his cheek and sticks it out at his audience; it is in fact a novel of impudent wit. ⟨. . .⟩

⟨. . .⟩ The success of the first two-thirds of the book depends upon our recognition that all this is the most splendid nonsense. We enjoy events and characters without being in the least bit committed to or moved by them. Gradually, and certainly Mr Condon does it very skilfully, things start to matter. The issues which were merely jokes before become serious; crime involves death and dishonour—the world is no longer the Captain's own little snobbish oyster. Shifts of this kind aren't easy to effect, and although I am not completely sure that Mr Condon has managed it there isn't any doubt that his novel as a whole is as enormously entertaining as it is enterprising.

Miles Donald, "Impudent Wit," *New Statesman*, 17 November 1972, pp. 731–32

REED WHITTEMORE   One has to piece together the Condon life—its details being inseparable from data about bathtubs in Indianapolis and zoning laws in Portugal—but the confusing evidence suggests that he got into writing late (except for an early monograph for *Esquire* on Mickey Finns) via a curious Hollywood route. He had been "chief braggart" for a number of films, then decided one day to leave press agency, scribble up some scripts and thereby "be fitted for gold toenails"; but when he sat down to his Olivetti he slopped inadvertently into the past tense and so turned novelist.

Maybe some of the extravagance of such tales as *The Manchurian Candidate* and *The Vertical Smile* derives from his Hollywood braggart period, but more likely it goes further back; as he says somewhere in this crazy new book ⟨*And Then We Moved to Rossenarra*⟩ he was perfectly modest until he was six. Anyway you would think that in dealing with dear old reality rather than fiction he would slow down. He is not noveling in the new book—and he is nearer 60 than six—but it makes no difference; he is still a glorious verbal braggart. ⟨. . .⟩

⟨. . .⟩ Right after the assassination of President Kennedy, the movie of *The Manchurian Candidate* was "frozen" because it was about a presidential assassination, hence politically infectious, and a journalist called Condon to ask him if, because he had written the novel, he felt responsible for Kennedy's death. Condon replied that he "had contributed to form the attitudes of the assassin by being an American, not particularly by writing that novel," and that the novel was largely an attempt "to suggest that for

some time all of us in the United States had been brainwashed to violence"
but that now the brainwashing tempo was speeding up. ⟨. . .⟩ It is true
enough that a lesson against brainwashing, which *The Manchurian Candidate*
is, can still become part of conditioning *to* violence, especially in the movies
where the vividness of the violence so easily drowns out the message that
This Is Bad. Condon has been one of our smashingly best violence writers
and has therefore presumably contributed more—despite his modest
denial—than the average citizen's quota to the national violence pool. But
as he points out, we are all—we Americans—in need of redemption, which
may or may not be achieved by emigration (*The Manchurian Candidate* was
written before emigration, right in NYC), but can hardly be delayed by it.

Reed Whittemore, "Trouble in the Whoopee Pit," *New Republic*, 2 June 1973, pp.
26–27

LEO BRAUDY   ⟨In *Winter Kills*⟩ Condon's hero, Nick Thirkield, is
the half-brother of Tim Kegan, the rich, young, charismatic, handsome,
womanizing, liberal Irish President who had only begun to deliver on his
promise of America when he was assassinated by a lone fanatic in Philadelphia's Hunt Plaza in 1960. Now, almost 15 years later, a man who claims
to be the second gun has made a deathbed confession and Nick is on the
trail to find the power behind the gun, whoever it is: the right-wing Texas
oil billionaire; the head of the Tubesters union; the film studio chief upset
that his greatest star (and one of Tim's hundreds of mistresses) has committed
suicide; the prostitute turned Mafia capo; or some other shadowy figure from
the maze of stories, rumors, half-truths, and myths that pass for reality in
America.

But *Winter Kills* is not a commercial ripoff of recent events in the style
of Harold Robbins and Irving Wallace (themselves the butt-end of natural-
ism), nor is it another Condon novel like the last few, filled with the
forgettable frenzy of a mechanical satirist. *Winter Kills* is instead a triumph
of satire and knowledge, with a delicacy of style and a command of tone
that puts Condon once again into the first rank of American novelists.
Condon's hero is the lineal descendant of the ineffectual avengers who
stalked the movie world of the 1950s. But while they were trying to hold
on to a warped dream of individuality, Nick Thirkield is merely trying to
find a fact. And Condon goes with him, less interested in facts than in

nonfacts and superfacts, not historical truth but the Macy's parade of history, the overblown images from which we have each manufactured our own paranoid vision of the true connections of American society. ⟨. . .⟩

   Winter Kills, then, is "some kind of bummer through American mythology," in which almost all of Condon's characters, from highest to lowest, are driven by the American dream of being someone, making a difference, having power and control. *Winter Kills* isn't the world; it's the way we think about the world, the distortions and how they are created, "the application of the techniques of fiction playing like searchlights on a frenzied façade of truth." Condon has created a paranoid novel that does not leave us trapped inside its world, but functions instead as a liberation, exposing through the gentler orders of fiction the way we have been programmed to believe anything in print. By mingling historical reality with his own fabulous invention, Condon savagely satirizes a world in which fiction and reality are mingled to manipulate, exploit, and kill.

   Leo Braudy, "*Winter Kills* by Richard Condon" (1976), *Native Informant: Essays on Film, Fiction, and Popular Culture* (New York: Oxford University Press, 1991), pp. 268–70

ALAN BOLD   To suspend disbelief long enough to accept the events described in Richard Condon's latest novel ⟨*Prizzi's Honor*⟩ it is necessary to believe, first, that an abstract concept like honour can dehumanize the individuals who subscribe to it; and, second, that language can be reduced to a euphemistic rubble which these men of honour can deploy in place of conversation. Honour, in Condon's book, is a Sicilian defence of the family. For Charley Partanna, enforcer of the New York–based Prizzi family, this is an ethical obligation: "the family were what he had been since Sicily started breeding people. They were his food. They had been with him forever. There were hundreds of thousands of them, most of them ghosts, some of them bodies."

   Charley Partanna's first loyalty, then, is to Prizzi's honour. To protect it—and the millions of dollars invested in it—he is willing to break legs and influence people or massacre them and dispose of their bodies. Charley and his Mafia colleagues do not speak like other American citizens. They have their own colourful jargon and it enables them to operate on an Us versus Them basis. They think like a persecuted minority and members of the family know that "the environment" means the Prizzi organization, that to "zotz" means to eliminate, that a "hitter" is a hired killer and that "a little problem" involves a lot of bloodshed. Charley doesn't talk a lot but when he does he uses the jargon. When he thinks, which is often, he has his own way with words. ⟨. . .⟩

Condon's hyperbolic prose turns every event into an issue so that the novel is strung out tight on its own tension. Charley's understanding of the nature of Irene's work is traumatic, so Condon piles on the metaphorical effects: "The furniture of Charley's mind suddenly began to come loose, the pieces crashing into each other like unfastened objects aboard a ship at sea ploughing through a hurricane." If that sounds a trifle clumsy then it has to be said, in Condon's praise, that he consistently gives an impression of Charley as a blunt instrument or as an obstacle in a subhuman race. The reader is persuaded that if such men actually exist then Charley is an accurate representative of the species.

> Alan Bold, "How to Zotz the Hitter," *Times Literary Supplement*, 11 June 1982, p. 642

JOE SANDERS   Condon's subject in most of his novels is political-social life in contemporary America. In novel after novel, he shows as much fascination with the world we live in as Dante did with Hell. In Condon's novels, politics determines the shape of society, but politics is not a voluntary, cooperative activity, entered into for some common end; it is a device by which a few clever people manipulate many others to gain their selfish ends. In some cases, it seems, they go on manipulating after any practically satisfying ends have been gained, out of unthinking inertia or the sheer joy of control. Each novel focuses on a device of control, a tool that a character in the novel has managed to systematize until it can be utilized with scientific precision: brainwashing in *The Manchurian Candidate* (and *The Whisper of the Axe*), media manipulation to encourage frustrated impotence in *Winter Kills*, and bribery in *Mile High*. In this way, by their extrapolation in the soft sciences, these novels resemble science fiction.

Furthermore, if science fiction may be defined as a branch of literature that not only involves some significant extrapolation but that believes humanity will be able to understand or control the conditions of life, Condon's novels again very obviously border on science fiction. By depicting characters who are easily recognizable analogs of historical figures and by a carefully woven tapestry of invention and verifiable facts, Condon appears to be revealing the secret truth about the forces that control us. The first three novels under consideration show the problems people face while gaining and acting on an understanding of their situation. Ben Marco, hero of *The Manchurian Candidate*, must fight his way through the thoroughly perfected brainwashing he has undergone before he can act. Meanwhile, a Senator Joe McCarthy–analog lets himself be controlled by his ambitious wife who wants to make him president. And at the same time, Raymond Shaw, the Manchurian puppet of the novel's title, also brainwashed by the Communist Chinese, operates as the perfect, unknowing assassin controlled by a master secret agent planning to take over the American government. In *Winter Kills*, the hero must resolve mutually exclusive combinations of fact and interpretation to find out who killed his brother, a Kennedy-analog president, and he also must find out who is killing all the people who could help him answer that question. He is more hindered than helped by the information-gathering services owned by his Pa, which provide so much data that the hero is overwhelmed. Finally, the content of *Mile High* shows how American politics and idealism are manipulated and corrupted over the years by Edward West, while all the time he is becoming more murderously insane. Eventually, West's younger son must penetrate the illusions that his father has spun, in order to save his wife from West's plan to murder her.

In general, the extrapolation in these novels proceeds in a rather odd direction. Rather than working forward into the future, Condon works backward into the past. The main action is set in the present, or at the most perhaps a day or so in the future. Otherwise, although what he shows has clear implications for the future, Condon deals primarily with reinterpretations of the causes of present conditions. In each novel, his characters constantly are brought up short by the recognition that the past they have believed in is a lie, that the "truth" they are living by now is illusion, and that they must learn to see events from another angle. This reemphasizes the issue of "control," for the characters must become aware that they have been deliberately manipulated before they can act freely, gaining some control of their own lives.

Joe Sanders, "The Fantastic Non-fantastic: Richard Condon's Waking Nightmares," *Extrapolation* 25, No. 2 (Summer 1984): 129–30

KEITH JEFFERY   In a solid corpus of entertaining political novels,
Condon has provided a vivid analysis of power in modern America. In these
fables, art imitates life to an extraordinary degree. In *Winter Kills*, a hugely
libidinous and popular President is assassinated; in *The Star-Spangled Crunch*,
a foul-mouthed wheeler-dealer chief executive is brought down by a scandal
involving the burglary of the opposition party's campaign headquarters. In
The Final Addiction, the President, a rather dim man, has "extremely dainty
morals, except perhaps where money and Nicaraguans and his appointees
are concerned". Goodie Noon, who succeeds this man, has vowed never
again to eat broccoli.

Someone remarks in the book that Washington "is not a city. It is a
place on another planet." This is apt since Condon's characters all possess
an alien quality. It is as if they were androids, constructed to look perfect,
but individually flawed; they have been programmed wrongly, so that while
they appear to possess real human emotions and motivations, they are
actually completely amoral and utterly without any human feeling. Condon
provides an amplified and Americanized interpretation of the epigraph which
Simon Raven chose for his *Alms for Oblivion* series of novels, which, roughly
expressed, asserted that, whatever goodness and kindness there is in the
world, the shits always end up on top. In Condon's stories, it is merely a
case of whether the nice shits or the really nasty ones triumph in the end.
The only decent people in his novels are those who are too dim to be
otherwise.

> Keith Jeffery, "Moving among Powerful People," *Times Literary Supplement*, 19 July
> 1991, p. 21

JOE QUEENAN   *Prizzi's Money* is the latest riotously funny install-
ment in a series of novels that includes *Prizzi's Glory*, *Prizzi's Family* and
Prizzi's Honor, the last of which was the basis for a fine movie starring Jack
Nicholson as the likable hit man Charley Partanna. As was the case in
Prizzi's Honor, the infamous don, his vile sons and their assorted *vindicatori*,
intimidatori and even what Mr. Condon refers to as "assistant *intimidatori*"
and "apprentice *intimidatori*" now find themselves confronted by a force of
nature that they are culturally unequipped to deal with: a perfidious woman
10 times more cunning and determined than they are. As the long-suffering
don gloomily laments: "Sixteen months ago this Asbury woman was a simple

housewife, now she runs 137 companies and wants to take over the biggest conglomerate in America. It's that . . . woman's movement that puts these crazy ideas into their heads." ⟨. . .⟩

Of course, what really makes the novel work is Mr. Condon's acid prose. "If taxis wore clothes they would resemble Charley," he writes. Of Julia, he says, "She had a passionate Sicilian nose and—God!—what a mouth—an army could feed on that mouth and be able to march for 10 days."

> Joe Queenan, "Swept Away by the Hit Man's Daughter," *New York Times Book Review*, 6 February 1994, p. 9

◈ *Bibliography*

The Oldest Confession. 1958.

The Manchurian Candidate. 1959.

Some Angry Angel: A Mid-Century Faerie Tale. 1960.

A Talent for Loving; or, The Great Cowboy Race. 1961.

An Infinity of Mirrors. 1964.

Any God Will Do. 1966.

The Ecstasy Business. 1967.

Mile High. 1969.

The Vertical Smile. 1971.

Arigato. 1972.

And Then We Moved to Rossenarra; or, The Art of Emigrating. 1973.

The Mexican Stove: What to Put on It and in It (with Wendy Bennett). 1973,
    1988 (as *¡Ole Mole! Great Recipes in the Classic Mexican Tradition*).

Winter Kills. 1974.

The Star Spangled Crunch. 1974.

Money Is Love. 1975.

The Whisper of the Axe. 1976.

The Abandoned Woman. 1977.

Bandicott. 1978.

Death of a Politician. 1978.

The Entwining. 1980.

Prizzi's Honor. 1982.

A Trembling upon Rome. 1983.

Prizzi's Family. 1986.

Prizzi's Glory. 1988.
Emperor of America. 1990.
The Final Addiction. 1991.
The Venerable Bead. 1992.
Prizzi's Money. 1994.

Roald Dahl
1916–1990

ROALD DAHL was born in Llandaff, South Wales, on September 13, 1916, the son of a Norwegian shipbroker who died when he was four. Dahl always considered Norway home, but his mother honored her late husband's wish to have their son educated at English schools. He attended Llandaff Cathedral School, St. Peters Boarding School, and Repton, where he showed little promise as a future writer. At Llandaff an incident at a neighboring sweet-shop, recounted in his memoir, *Boy: Tales of Childhood* (1984), helped inspire his most popular children's book, *Charlie and the Chocolate Factory* (1964; rev. 1973).

After school, given the option to attend either Oxford or Cambridge, Dahl elected instead to work abroad. He was hired by the Shell Oil Company, which sent him to Tanganyika (now Tanzania). At the start of World War II he joined the Royal Air Force in Nairobi, Kenya. A crash landing in Libya due to the misdirections of a commanding officer left him badly injured, but he recovered in time to rejoin his squadron in Greece, where he fought in the air battle above Athens. Invalided in 1942, he was transferred to Washington, D.C., as an assistant air attaché. There he wrote up for C. S. Forester, who was interviewing him, an account of his crash landing, which Forester then submitted without changes to the *Saturday Evening Post*. With the success of this story, "A Piece of Cake" (published under the misleading title "Shot Down in Libya"), Dahl wrote a number of other wartime flying stories, later collected in *Over to You* (1946). He also published a children's book, *The Gremlins* (1943), and a novel-length fantasy, *Some Time Never: A Fable for Supermen* (1948).

Starting in the 1940s, however, Dahl began to make his reputation as an author of macabre short stories for adults. These clever and finely crafted stories appeared in such magazines as the *New Yorker* and *Playboy*, and were issued in three major collections: *Someone Like You* (1953), *Kiss Kiss* (1959), and *Switch Bitch* (1974). He would win three Edgar Allan Poe Awards from the Mystery Writers of America. One volume of stories, *Roald Dahl's Tales of the Unexpected* (1979), would be the basis for a television series.

In 1953 Dahl married Patricia Neal, an American actress, with whom he had five children. Making up bedtime stories for his children led to his career as a prolific author of children's books, starting with *James and the Giant Peach* (1961). Some critics were disturbed by these books' sadistic streak, but they were favorites with children, in part because, according to Dahl, children have a more vulgar sense of humor than adults. Apart from a short novel, *My Uncle Oswald* (1979), he wrote very little for adults in his final years, claiming to have run out of story plots.

After his wife suffered a stroke in 1965, Dahl turned to screenplay writing to make money, including a script for the James Bond novel, *You Only Live Twice*, and *Willie Wonka and the Chocolate Factory*, an adaptation of *Charlie and the Chocolate Factory*. Dahl and Neal divorced in 1983; that year he married Felicity Ann Crossland. He died on November 23, 1990, in Oxford, England.

Critical Extracts

WILLIAM PEDEN   By their very nature artificial rather than realistic, most of these stories ⟨in *Someone Like You*⟩ rely heavily upon a carefully worked-up climax for their effect. So skilful is Mr. Dahl that he makes some of his predecessors in this field appear amateurish. Like Dickens (whom I suspect Mr. Dahl has read and at one time enjoyed), he exploits to the full the principle of contrast. These bizarre stories are heightened by the matter-of-fact and realistic method with which the author approaches his surprising endings. And, like the good entertainer he is, Mr. Dahl never works a good effect to death.

> William Peden, "Collection of Curiosos," *Saturday Review*, 26 December 1953, p. 15

UNSIGNED   Eleven is the number of further stories from the inimitable Mr. Dahl, whose craft has a gruesome, almost Dali-ish eye, and twelve would be too much, because Mr. Dahl's macabre realism stretches the intellectual nerve almost beyond bearing. What is unique is the cunning used to persuade the reader that characters and plots are really ordinary, and this is accomplished through a deadly urbanity of detail selected from the superficially familiar. Such matters are possible is the final conclusion, although afterthought persuades the imagination to rest from its Dahlish fever in more rational thoughts. Where Mr. Dahl differs from the common run of spine-chillers is in the verisimilitude of his caricature of human weakness, showing this to the edge of extravagance, revealing a social satirist and moralist at work behind the entertaining fantast. In this many of these stories ⟨in *Kiss Kiss*⟩ recall Mr. Angus Wilson's earlier work, although Mr. Wilson's scope is basically a wider social one, whereas Mr. Dahl does not look far beyond the individual's frailty. Animal lovers, vegetarians and cranks are Mr. Dahl's natural victims, and the dangerous territory of the over-devoted and the over-dedicated is inexorably explored.

Unsigned, "Sweet and Sour," *Times Literary Supplement,* 28 October 1960, p. 697

JAMES P. DEGNAN   Although ⟨John⟩ O'Hara and Roald Dahl can hardly be compared—the former being an ambitious, a "serious" writer, the latter unambitious, an "entertaining" writer—there is much about constructing short stories that O'Hara could learn from Dahl; for Dahl's stories, even at their worst, seldom suffer from the defects of construction so charactertistic of O'Hara's. Perhaps it is because of Dahl's lack of ambition, his indifference to imposing a "vision" on his stories, his lack of obsessions—sexual and otherwise—that he can focus always on narrative action. Whatever the cause, the stories in his new collection ⟨*Selected Stories of Roald Dahl*⟩ make clear that, unlike O'Hara, he knows the difference between merely interesting episodes and characters (of which there are many in these stories) and a finished work. Rather far-fetched but eminently readable and, despite their lack of pretension, a great deal more profound in their insight into human nature than much fiction passing as profundity today (e.g. most of the Grove Press Black Humor nonsense) are the widely anthologized Dahl classics: "Taste" (about a wine snob), and "Lamb to the Slaughter" (about a particularly ingenious murder). And there are many new stories in this collection that demonstrate Dahl's ability to combine craft and insight. One such, "The Rat-Catcher," the story of a rat exterminator with, to say the least, bizarre methods of extermination, provides a fascinating and horribly real picture of depravity. Told by a less-gifted narrator—by, for example, a typical Black Humorist—the story would emerge as little more than Gothic farce; but, told by this highly skilful writer, it comes across as low-keyed, serious, and totally compelling.

James P. Degnan, "Sex ex Machina and Other Problems," *Kenyon Review* 31, No. 2 (1969): 274

MARGOT HENTOFF   Roald Dahl writes good obsessional books that I (not sharing his obsessions) find a little repellent—which does not make them any the less good. *Charlie and the Chocolate Factory* takes place in the canals of a huge subterranean chocolate factory through which runs a river of chocolate. The owner of the factory allows some rather bizarre but fascinating things to happen to bad children who visit. He also experiments on tiny black pygmies he has brought, as workers, from Africa. (These pygmies sing and dance while they work because they are so happy not to be starving in Africa.) Finally, having no heirs, he gives away his factory to a good but starving boy.

In Dahl's new book, *Fantastic Mr. Fox*, Mr. Fox and his family, living snugly in a hill, are being starved by an unwholesome trio of farmers (one of whom eats nothing but goose livers mashed "into a disgusting paste" and then stuffed into doughnuts). The farmers are prepared to dig into the hill until they find and destroy Mr. Fox, who has been coming out to steal their fowl. Mr. Fox happily escapes with only his tail cut off. (In children's stories, such mutilations happen *only* to animals—which fools no one but adults.)

Mr. Dahl has apparently been touched by the feathery fingers of Consciousness III, for Mr. Fox and the other neighboring animals resolve their problem of survival by creating a communal underground world which includes a network of tunnels leading to the storehouses of the three farmers. Mr. Fox instructs Badger:

> My dear old furry frump, do you know anyone in the *whole* world who wouldn't swipe a few chickens if their children were starving to death? . . . If *they* want to be horrible, let them. We down here are peace-loving creatures.

And the animals all decided to live together and never had to come above ground again. A story more satisfying than most.

> Margot Hentoff, "Little Private Lives," *New York Review of Books*, 17 December 1970, p. 11

ELEANOR CAMERON   We come now to Charlie, that starved child Roald Dahl dreamed up to go and live forever in pure bliss in Mr. Willy Wonka's chocolate factory. The more I think about Charlie and the character of Willy Wonka and his factory, the more I am reminded of ⟨Marshall⟩ McLuhan's coolness, the basic nature of his observations, and the kinds of things that excite him. Certainly there are several interesting parallels between the point of view of *Charlie and the Chocolate Factory* and McLuhan's "theatrical view of experience as a production or stunt," as well as his enthusiastic conviction that every ill of mankind can easily be solved by subservience to the senses.

Both McLuhan's theories and the story about Charlie are enormously popular. *Charlie and the Chocolate Factory* (together with *Charlotte's Web*) is probably the book most read aloud by those teachers who have no idea, apparently, what other books they might read to children. *Charlie*, again along with *Charlotte's Web*, is always at the top of the best sellers among children's books, put there by fond aunts and grandmothers and parents buying it as the perfect gift, knowing no better. And I do think this a most curious coupling: on the one hand, one of the most tasteless books ever written for children; and on the other, one of the best. We are reminded of Ford Madox Ford's observation that only two classes of books are universal in their appeal: the very best and the very worst.

Now, there are those who consider *Charlie* to be a satire and believe that Willy Wonka and the children are satiric portraits as in a cautionary tale. I am perfectly willing to admit that possibly Dahl wrote it as such: a book on two levels, one for adults and one for children. However, he chose to publish *Charlie* as a children's book, knowing quite well that children would react to one level only (if there *are* two), the level of pure story. Being literarily unsophisticated, children can react only to this level; and as I am talking about children's books, it is this level I am about to explore.

Why does *Charlie* continually remind me of what is most specious in McLuhan's world of the production and the stunt? The book is like candy (the chief excitement and lure of *Charlie*) in that it is delectable and soothing while we are undergoing the brief sensory pleasure it affords but leaves us poorly nourished with our taste dulled for better fare. ⟨. . .⟩

What I object to in *Charlie* is its phony presentation of poverty and its phony humor, which is based on punishment with overtones of sadism; its hypocrisy which is epitomized in its moral—stuck like a marshmallow in a lump of fudge—that TV is horrible and hateful and time-wasting and that children should read good books instead, when in fact the book itself is like nothing so much as one of the more specious television shows. It reminds me of Cecil B. De Mille's Biblical spectaculars, with plenty of blood and orgies and tortures to titillate the masses, while a prophet, for the sake of the religious section of the audience, stands on the edge of the crowd crying, "In the name of the Lord, thou shalt sin no more!"

If I ask myself whether children are harmed by reading *Charlie* or having it read to them, I can only say I don't know. Its influence would be subtle underneath the catering. Those adults who are either amused by the book or are positively devoted to it on the children's level probably call it a modern fairy tale. Possibly its tastelessness, including the ugliness of the illustrations, is indeed (whether the author meant it so or not) a comment upon our age and the quality of much of our entertainment. What bothers me about it, aside from its tone, is the using of the Oompa-Loompas, and the final indifference to the wishes of the grandparents. Many adults see all this as humorous and delightful, and I am aware that most children, when they're young, aren't particularly aware of sadism as such, or see it differently from the way an adult sees it and so call *Charlie* "a funny book."

> Eleanor Cameron, "McLuhan, Youth, and Literature," *Horn Book* 48, No. 5 (October 1972): 438–40

RHODA KOENIG   We know that God has a sense of humor, said de Maupassant, from the manner he has chosen for us to reproduce ourselves. This view of copulation as undignified and absurd is the theme of Roald Dahl's novel ⟨*My Uncle Oswald*⟩, a short, snappy burlesque of sex novels and sex. ⟨. . .⟩

Dahl's style is a sort of comic-strip version of Frank Harris. Oswald and Yasmin speak in modern, staccato rhythms, yet much of their vocabulary echoes Victorian porn—facetious names for the penis, "wench" used as a noun and verb. "Oh," cries a French wench on whom Oswald has used his mighty engine, "I feel like my boiler has exploded!" Sometimes—as in a rather brutal representation of sex as medieval combat—Dahl's imagery is a bit sickening; but that, I suppose, is part of his merry contempt for polite entertainment. He has written a very impudent, jolly farce; I just hope other readers are able to suspend disbelief at the rather far-fetched idea of a geniuses' sperm bank.

Rhoda Koenig, [Review of *My Uncle Oswald*], *New Republic*, 19 April 1980, pp. 37–38

ROALD DAHL and LISA TUTTLE   T⟨wilight⟩ Z⟨one⟩: You're very famous as a children's writer these days, but I want to talk to you about your short stories.

DAHL: Ah, good. We will. They were the result of, I suppose, twenty-five years of solid work, doing nothing else, and not many people have devoted themselves to that. Twenty-five years of solid work, absolutely nothing but these short stories.

TZ: I know the story of how you wrote the stories that were collected in *Over to You* . . .

DAHL: Good! Thank God I don't have to say all that again.

TZ: But once you'd written them, you went on to write more short stories. Why? Why not a novel?

DAHL: I think I had a very strong feeling that it was my *métier*, you know. And if you find that you can do something, you don't rush off and try to do something else. I think I was probably right. I'm not a novelist, and, on the whole, the pure short-story writer is not a novelist. People like Katherine Mansfield. I don't think she ever wrote a novel. You see, the short-story writer has got to get everything so tight, so close, and so concise. It's the opposite of a novel. The novelist can spread himself or herself. They can take a page or two to describe the fucking landscape, can't they? You can't do that in a short story. It's as different as . . . I don't know . . . the only thing you can say about it is that they're both writing. But they're entirely different. Quite a number of fine novelists have done fine short stories . . . Who? Ah, Hemingway. I don't think Hemingway's short stories are as great as people say, but he's a wonderful novelist, early novelist anyway. Everyone has a go at them—Somerset Maugham, Graham Greene, everyone—but they're all primarily novelists, aren't they?

TZ: And short-story writers who try to write novels?

DAHL: Usually it's a cock-up. I mean, Maupassant never wrote a novel, did he? I don't think he did. The modern great short-story writers, to me, are John Collier—we were all of a bunch in *The New Yorker* in the late '40s, you know—John Cheever, J. D. Salinger. He did one novel, *Catcher in the Rye*. Super. But just the one. He was really a supreme short-story writer, but he only had eleven good ones, then he ran out. ⟨. . .⟩

TZ: Why did you take the direction that you did? The short stories in *Kiss, Kiss* and *Someone Like You* tend to be on the macabre, disturbing side. What drew you to that sort of horrific story?

DAHL: I can't answer that question. Nobody can answer that. It's like, on a much higher level, let's say old Beethoven was sitting here, and you were interviewing him, and you said, "Mr. Beethoven, how did you come to think of the Fifth Symphony?" Or, "Why did you suddenly write the later quartets? What got into you?" How the hell would he know? ⟨. . .⟩

TZ: Then why did you begin to write for children?

DAHL: Ah, that's a whole different thing. After having done my twenty-five years of short stories, the three volumes, I think I probably ran out of plots, and that's the hardest thing in the world. If you write the sort of short stories I write, which are *real* short stories, with a beginning, a middle, and an end, instead of the modern trend, which is mood pieces. I'm judging right now a short-story competition, a very serious big one, and there's not one single short story I've read so far with a plot. They're all mood pieces. You know: I went down to the kitchen and my wife was there and she had a saucepan and we had a little row and threw the carrots out the window and the dog came in and—they're concentrating on their writing, and not on the content. Well, the average reader doesn't care about the writing. They want something which will keep them reading, wondering what's going to happen next. None of these stories says what's going to happen next. And then to finish it satisfactorily, so the reader says ha ha, I wouldn't have guessed that, how fantastic, how fascinating, ooh, golly! That's jolly hard.

I found about thirty-five plots, and then I probably ran out of them. I don't know many now. I don't know *any*, I don't think. I couldn't sit down and write a short story now—it's very hard. And these people who are writing them now, they don't have any plots, they don't bloody well have them. Maupassant had them. Salinger had them. That's why they were so sparing. Salinger found eleven.

Roald Dahl and Lisa Tuttle, "TZ Interview: Roald Dahl," *Twilight Zone* 2, No. 11 (January–February 1983): 71–72

BEN P. INDICK   Dahl, like ⟨John⟩ Collier, enjoys exploiting the relations of man and woman, husband and wife. ⟨. . .⟩ In "Neck", Sir Basil, a wealthy landowner, whose estate is filled with beautiful sculpture, has, as well, a beautiful, if unfaithful wife. Walking with the narrator, he observes his wife with another man, gamboling near a Henry Moore sculpture carved of wood. The woman playfully puts her head through the inevitable hole in the Moore and the two exchange kisses while the husband and the embarrassed guest watch. Then they note she is having trouble extricating her head. They saunter up, as by accident. Head tightly wedged, the wife shouts at her husband to release her. "Most obvious," says her lover, "we're going to have to break up this lump of wood." The narrator notices a smudge of red on his moustache, "like the single extra touch of colour that ruins a perfect painting." Equally detached, Sir Basil debates. "You mean break the Henry Moore? . . . What a terrible pity. My beautiful Henry Moore." In response, the wife begins "abusing her husband in a most unpleasant manner." Just then the gamekeeper comes up, and Sir Basil sends him for "a saw or something." He returns with a saw—and an axe. He hands the two implements to his master, the axe held out perhaps a fraction of an inch further. Dahl orchestrates the moment in perfect, precise, suggestively horrible words: "It was so slight a movement it was barely noticeable—a tiny pushing forward of the hand, slow and secret, a little offer, a little coaxing offer that was accompanied perhaps by an infinitesimal lifting of the eyebrows." In a "dreamy sort of way" Sir Basil takes the axe, and "the instant he felt the handle in his grasp, he seemed to realize what was required of him and he sprang to life."

The narrator now is stunned, thinks with shut eyes of the horror when a child runs into the street before a car and one can only await the noise. The last laugh, however, is shared by the husband—and the author. ⟨. . .⟩

⟨*Charlie and the Chocolate Factory*⟩ is a cautionary tale in the manner of *Pinocchio*, its good hero differentiated from a group of naughty children, a girl who is very spoiled, another who chews gum incessantly, a gluttonous boy and another who is addicted to television. Each, including the humble Charlie, gains admission to Willie Wonka's incredible chocolate factory, with its mouth-watering delights, and, as in the Italian classic, the lessons taught to each ingrate are plain, if literally candy-coated, in uproarious incident. The book was a great success, its young readers readily accepting the dreadful fates of its characters as their due. A sequel resulted, *Charlie and the Great Glass Elevator*, eight years later. Except for the naughty children, the characters are the same; however, the factory is quickly forgotten for a sciencefictional atmosphere, with space stations, extraterrestrials, spacemen, etc. Lacking the pungent didacticism of the first book, dependent upon a succession of adventures and puns, it misses the Dahl strength, tension. Nevertheless, an adult who recalls the joy of reading novel-length stories to his children may find in its frenetic pace and sound-oriented nature an inviting read-aloud. ⟨. . .⟩

The "sardonic" implies a certain distance between the observor and the observed. It is a comfort, of course, to observe the comeuppance of others who are so obviously sinners, in the safety of our own easy chairs; their fate possibly affirms our own sanctity. The magic of Roald Dahl, however, is that he does not quite allow us total freedom: to some degree, we are ourselves involved in that world—anxiously watching the wine-taster, dying for a mouthful of gushing chocolate, making passionate and mysterious love in the darkness of the desert night, impotent against bookmakers as crooked as ourselves, raising the axe before that lovely head so neatly exposed, as it were, on an executioner's block—and when, at last, we laugh, it is because we, unlike his protagonists, have escaped.

Ben P. Indick, "Sardonic Fantasistes: Roald Dahl," *Nyctalops* No. 18 (April 1983): 62–64

ALAN WARREN   Dahl's fourth collection ⟨*Switch Bitch*⟩ was published in 1974. It is significantly different from the others in that it comprises only four stories, and all four deal with more overtly sexual material than previously. "For twenty-five years I was able to write stories that were untarnished by sexual undertones of any kind," Dahl noted. "But now, in my late middle age, they're riddled with sex and copulation. What, I wonder, is the reason for this?"

One reason is surely the relaxation of laws pertaining to the publication of such material. "Perhaps," J. D. O'Hara wrote in *The New Republic*, "like so many writers, he feels that the public demands coarseness now." Whatever the reason, it has added yet another dimension to Dahl's writing. Not coincidentally, all four stories in this tetralogy first saw publication in *Playboy*.

"The Visitor," which leads off the collection, is Dahl's masterpiece in the short story form. When originally published it was greeted with thunderous applause. The editors of *Playboy* awarded it their annual prize as the best major work of fiction, and many readers wrote in saying it was the finest work of fiction the magazine had ever published. It is a tour-de-force by a master at the absolute top of his form.

It opens with an apparently arbitrary and unnecessary framing device in which the narrator receives a large box containing elaborately bound books, 28 in all, "identically and superbly bound in rich green morocco," all containing the hardwritten memoirs of the narrator's uncle, Oswald Hendryks Cornelius, wealthy *bon vivant*, connoisseur, collector of spiders, scorpions, and walking sticks, and "without much doubt, the greatest fornicator of all time."

The narrator, unsure of which of Oswald's reminiscences to publish, settles on one—he dubs it "The Sinai Desert episode"—and reproduces it verbatim from Oswald's diary, informing us that it is the very final entry, and adjuring us to keep that in mind. ⟨. . .⟩

A synopsis such as the foregoing can only do injustice to a story like "The Visitor." The richness of the story, its verbal texture, and its compelling narrative drive make it almost unique among twentieth century short story writing. One reason it succeeds so well is Uncle Oswald himself. He is so fastidious, so obsessed with germs and diseases, that his narration possesses a unique, slightly surreal, paranoid quality:

> For breakfast I ordered a poached egg on a piece of toast. When the dish arrived—and I tell you, it makes my stomach curdle just to write about it—there was a *gleaming, curly, jet-black human hair*, three inches long, lying diagonally across the yolk of my poached egg. It was too much. I leapt up from the table and rushed out of the dining room. *"Addio!"* I cried, flinging some money at the cashier as I went by, *"addio valle di pianti!"* And with that I shook the filthy dust of the hotel from my feet.

Surprisingly, "The Visitor" is not as well known as it deserves to be, probably because, like so much of Dahl's work, it does not fit into a convenient fictional niche. It has elements of the fairy tale and the horror story, but it does not fit either of these categories. The genre it belongs to, more than any other, is that of the ribald anecdote, as other Oswald adventures will make clearer.

Alan Warren, *Roald Dahl* (Mercer Island, WA: Starmont House, 1988), pp. 49–52

MARK I. WEST   In almost all of Dahl's fiction authoritarian figures, social institutions, and societal norms are ridiculed or at least undermined. Many of his children's books satirize authoritarian adults, and some, such as *Matilda,* include stinging attacks on schools and other institutions. Most of his children's books also poke fun at the propriety of the adult world. In these books adult notions of what is proper and in good taste come across as being hypocritical and dehumanizing. Like his children's books, Dahl's stories for adults criticize social norms, but they do so in a somewhat different way. These stories generally show how meaningless life can be when conforming to societal norms is the primary motivating force in people's lives. For the most part the characters in these stories appear to be respectable members of society, but they are basically unethical and uncaring people. So long as they are able to rely on societal norms to govern their behavior they seem civilized enough, but as soon as these norms break down they quickly become savages.

There is one major exception to Dahl's pessimistic view of social structures, and that is his attitude toward the family. As is made clear in *Boy* and *Going Solo,* the happiest moments of Dahl's youth were those spent with his family. During his years at boarding school he saw his family as a sort of oasis in an otherwise hostile world. Even when he was working in Africa or flying in the RAF, he tried to stay in close contact with his family. Every week, for example, he wrote a letter to his mother.

Dahl's sense of the importance of families is reflected in his fiction. In most of his adult stories families are conspicuously absent. There are many couples in his stories, but most of them do not have children. This absence of families is in keeping with the meaninglessness of these characters' lives. Perhaps if they had children they would not be so self-centered and obsessed with their social status. Families, however, do figure in several of Dahl's children's books. In the case of *Matilda* the family is not much more than a collection of individuals who live in the same house, but the families in some of his other children's books are much more like the family Dahl knew as a child. The family of foxes in *Fantastic Mr. Fox,* the father and son in *Danny, the Champion of the World,* and the grandmother and grandson in *The Witches* all have loving and close relationships. The members of these families are often at odds with the rest of the world, but they always support each other. Thus, even though Dahl's fiction presents a pessimistic view of modern civilization, it holds out hope that individuals can find happiness and meaning within the bosoms of their own families.

Dahl's fiction clearly reflects his values and beliefs, but he seldom discussed this aspect of his writing. When interviewers questioned him about his vision of human nature or the meaning of his stories, he generally gave evasive answers. If pressed he argued that the job of analyzing his stories rested with critics and scholars; his job, he maintained, was simply to entertain his readers. During one of his last interviews, however, he admitted that entertainment was not his only goal as a children's author:

> When I'm writing for adults, I'm just trying to entertain them. But a good children's book does much more than entertain. It teaches children the use of words, they joy of playing with language. Above all, it helps children learn not to be frightened of books. Once they can get through a book and enjoy it, they realize that books are something that they can cope with. If they are going to amount to anything in life, they need to be able to handle books. If my books can help children become readers, then I feel I have accomplished something important.

As one of the most popular children's authors in the Western world and certainly the best-selling one from England, Dahl helped turn countless children into avid readers. This accomplishment gave him greater satisfaction than the critical acclaim he earned or the awards he won. The immense popularity of his children's books also guarantees that Dahl's work, despite its controversial nature, will leave a lasting mark on the history of children's literature.

Mark I. West, *Roald Dahl* (New York: Twayne, 1992), pp. 128–30

◼ *Bibliography*

The Gremlins. 1943.
Over to You: 10 Stories of Flyers and Flying. 1946.

Some Time Never: A Fable for Supermen. 1948.

Someone Like You. 1953.

Kiss Kiss. 1959.

James and the Giant Peach: A Children's Story. 1961.

Charlie and the Chocolate Factory. 1964, 1973.

The Magic Finger. 1966.

Selected Stories. 1968.

Twenty-nine Kisses from Roald Dahl. 1969.

Fantastic Mr. Fox. 1970.

*Charlie and the Great Glass Elevator: The Further Adventures of Charlie Bucket
    and Willy Wonka, Chocolate-Maker Extraordinary.* 1972.

Switch Bitch. 1974.

Danny, the Champion of the World. 1975.

The Wonderful World of Henry Sugar and Six More. 1977.

The Enormous Crocodile. 1978.

The Best of Roald Dahl. 1978.

Roald Dahl's Tales of the Unexpected. 1979.

Taste and Other Tales. 1979.

My Uncle Oswald. 1979.

The Twits. 1980.

More Tales of the Unexpected. 1980.

George's Marvelous Medicine. 1981.

Roald Dahl's Revolting Rhymes. 1982.

The BFG. 1982.

Roald Dahl's Dirty Beasts. 1983.

The Witches. 1983.

Roald Dahl's Book of Ghost Stories (editor). 1983.

Boy: Tales of Childhood. 1984.

The Giraffe and the Pelly and Me. 1985.

Going Solo. 1986.

The Roald Dahl Omnibus. 1986.

The Complete Adventures of Charlie and Mr Willy Wonka. 1987.

Ah, Sweet Mystery of Life. 1989.

Matilda. 1988.

Rhyme Stew. 1989.

Esio Trot. 1990.

The Minpins. 1991.

Collected Short Stories. 1991.

Roald Dahl's Guide to Railway Safety. 1991.
Memories with Food: At Gipsy House (with Liccy Dahl). 1991.
The Vicar of Nibbleswicke. 1992.
My Year. 1993.

Len Deighton
b. 1929

LEONARD CYRIL DEIGHTON was born on February 18, 1929, in Marylebone, London. He attended St. Martin's School of Art in London and graduated from the Royal College of Art. He married Shirley Thompson, an illustrator, in 1960.

After a succession of miscellaneous jobs, including assistant pastry cook at the Royal Festival Hall (1951) and steward for BOAC (1956–57), Deighton published the first of a series of successful espionage novels, *The Ipcress File* (1962). With his elliptical, parodic style and nameless working-class hero, Deighton established a place for himself, especially after *Funeral in Berlin* (1964), in the front rank of the spy genre, along with Graham Greene, Ian Fleming, and John le Carré. In later novels he has become less oblique and more expansive, trying for more subtlety and deeper characterization. He has written two trilogies, the first bearing the generic title *Game, Set and Match* (*Berlin Game*, 1983; *Mexico Set*, 1984; *London Match*, 1985) and the other entitled *Hook, Line & Sinker* (*Spy Hook*, 1988; *Spy Line*, 1989; *Spy Sinker*, 1990). Nonseries novels include *SS-GB: Nazi-Occupied Britain 1941* (1978) and *Winter: A Berlin Family 1899–1945* (1987).

Along with a number of cookbooks, Deighton has also published such well-researched works of military history as *Fighter: The True Story of the Battle of Britain* (1977), *Blitzkrieg: From the Rise of Hitler to the Fall of Dunkirk* (1979), and, most recently, *Blood, Tears and Folly: An Objective Look at World War II* (1993). He has written television scripts and has had a weekly comic strip on cooking in the *Observer* since 1962. *The Ipcress File* and *Funeral in Berlin* have both been made into films, in which his nameless British spy was given the name Harry Palmer.

Deighton's most recent novels are *Violent Ward* (1993) and *Faith* (1994). He continues to live and write in London.

◈ *Critical Extracts*

G. W. STONIER   Now a thriller, *The Ipcress File*. I like this:

> 'You may as well go in,' said a tall, bespectacled city gent behind
> us opening the door with a key. We went in, partly because it was
> convenient for us, partly because there were two more city gents
> behind us, and partly because they were all holding small 9m.m.
> Mod. 34 Beretta automatic pistols.

I like the very secret-service hero, who is liable to go round with a squashy
parcel of butter and garlic sausage in his pocket. His first-person adventures
across Charlotte Street, Whitehall, a Pacific atoll, and a brainwashing hideout bristle with a self-discovering, atmospheric talent. The publisher wish-
fully drags in Ian Fleming's name; but on the face of it Mr Deighton is a
good deal more expert and twice the writer. There has been no brighter
arrival on the shady scene since Graham Greene started entertaining. A
first book, and the first of a planned series.

G. W. Stonier, "Beast People," *New Statesman*, 7 December 1962, p. 84

RICHARD SCHICKEL   Len Deighton clearly has many masters.
He shares the late Raymond Chandler's taste for over-complicated plotting
and occasionally over-strained metaphors. He shares the late Ian Fleming's
interest in technological gadgeteering, his easy—though possibly fraudu-
lent—knowledgeability about the more exotic locales, materialisms and
techniques of violence available to the modern spy and his predilection for
grotesque villains. He shares John le Carré's attitude of distrust toward those
arrested-in-adolescence bureaucrats who "run" spies and the conviction that
out there in the gray, ambiguous cold all the cats, theirs and ours, look
alike, are alike morally (or perhaps amorally) speaking and are, indeed,
completely interchangeable.

If this suggests that Mr. Deighton is a multi-voiced impersonator of well-
tested mannerisms instead of a highly gifted innovator, I don't want to be
too pejorative about it. He has the merits of the consolidator, and a talent
for sheer entertainment that compares very favorably to most of his current
competitors. His new story ⟨*The Billion Dollar Brain*⟩ about his nameless (as

usual) hero's penetration of a private, Right-wing, American-based intelligence network, the aim of which is to turn the cold war hot, reads faster and livelier than most of the stuff you pick up in the drugstores these days. He gets off a lot of sharp, tough, most un-English wisecracks and for all the tortuousness of his route through the labyrinthine plot, one cannot help but admire the gimmicks that pop up, like surprise targets in a shooting gallery, along the way. ⟨. . .⟩

It is Mr. Deighton's annoying habit to adorn his work with footnotes and appendices to explain the current jargon of espionage and to set forth the latest true information about Russian military districts and the like. This is supposed to generate what the blurb writer calls "the strong feeling that it is all really happening." But information is no substitute for sound novelistic observation and, if anything, the scholarly apparatus underscores the writer's failures of purely literary craft.

Richard Schickel, "Not So Secret Formula," *Washington Post Book Week*, 1 May 1966, p. 10

GENE LYONS   *Spy Story*, like the author's previous novels in the series, *Funeral in Berlin* and *The Ipcress File*, is a superior entertainment. Since Deighton seeks a literate audience, it is essential that his narrator-protagonist be of relatively limited physical competence (as compared to James Bond, for example) and that he display a carefully measured amount of ironic reluctance about the proceedings he is involved in, together with a degree of fastidiousness with regard to murder. For all the deftness of his wit and his technological expertise, he must remain a British hobbyist at heart and display only the vestigial personal memory needed to flesh him out, so that he may neither learn significantly from previous adventures, nor (God forbid) intellectualize overmuch. One happily tolerates a stylistic assertiveness, particularly in the politics of the book, that one would find tendentious or bothersome if required to accept it as very much more than a given upon which to hang a plot. ⟨. . .⟩

Altogether, Deighton's self-conscious irony about the form he is using works to his advantage, and even imparts greater impact to a grisly conclusion on the arctic icepack for which the reader has not been overprepared by the sententious metaphors that occasionally mar the work of other form novelists like Ross Macdonald.

Gene Lyons, [Review of *Spy Story* and *Declarations of War*], *New York Times Book Review*, 13 April 1975, pp. 5, 10

ROBIN W. WINKS   By 1969 Len Deighton had written his four best spy thrillers, beginning in 1963 with *Ipcress File*, and going on quickly to *Horse under Water* and *Funeral in Berlin*. ⟨. . .⟩ By 1969 the Deighton touch was clear, both the plots and the style almost instantly recognizable, and Nicolas Freeling, creator of the Dutch detective Van der Valk, led his hero to contemplate Deighton along with Maigret and Raymond Chandler as modes of thought possibly productive to the resolution of the crime in *Tsing-Boom*. In fine, Deighton had carved out his own niche by then.

What was this special niche? Roughly Deighton had decided to apply to the reader, and therefore to his style, the principle so honored in spy fiction (if not necessarily in real life), that of "need to know." His plots seem more complex than they are, as most mundane lives no doubt do, because very little is stated explicitly, sequences appear to begin in mid-passage, and only through observation of the action does one come to understand either the motives of the villains, or the thought processes of the heroes. Adam Hall would be the closest imitator in style, and those who compared Deighton to Ian Fleming seemed to have missed the obvious point that Fleming wrote in the standard way recommended to Alice, while Deighton had patented a style in which every third paragraph appeared to have been left out.

It worked stunningly well, not only as pure thriller, but as a not too subtle way of sharing Harry Palmer's confusion with the reader. In a sense, Deighton's interest was increasingly in the question of what an agent might be led to believe was true rather than in any fictional truth to be revealed to the reader. And it worked brilliantly in *Horse under Water*, even well in an otherwise extravagant and unconvincing book, *An Expensive Place to Die*. Appearances increasingly became everything. ⟨. . .⟩

Deighton worked this style to its height in his last spy thriller, entitled simply *Spy Story*, the title itself warning one that a spade is a spade, words count, visions discredit. *Spy Story* was inexpressibly boring but it also showed that he had a serious idea about style and that he wanted to grow as a writer. For the problem of the writer to formula remains: once the audience is hooked, how does one lead them to other things? ⟨. . .⟩

So now Len Deighton has thumbed his nose at us and ⟨in *Yesterday's Spy*⟩ written his best book since *Funeral in Berlin*, all in the same gesture, which is surely a kind of grace. For he has written a book which reviewers may well hail as Deighton returning to the style and mannerisms of his earlier successes. Having tried to grow and experiment, without critical success, and having thus shown far more courage than an Alistair MacLean (who in his next to last, *Breakheart Pass*, couldn't even bother to check the most simple of facts, building the Union Pacific Railroad 19 years too soon to please his plot), Deighton has written a book that is self-parody so cunningly constructed as to please at almost any level. Even Deighton's metaphors read like those that used to be reprinted in *Reader's Digest* (and may still be for all I know; I've changed my dentist). This is "the mixture as before" with a difference.

Robin W. Winks, [Review of *Yesterday's Spy*], *New Republic*, 13 December 1975, p. 32

JULIAN SYMONS   ⟨. . .⟩ *SS-GB* is a triumphant success. It is Mr. Deighton's best book, one that blends his expertise in the spy field with his interest in military and political history to produce an absorbingly exciting spy story that is also a fascinating exercise in might-have-been speculation.

The year is 1941, and the Germans control Britain. The British armed forces surrendered in February, after a successful invasion. Churchill was summarily tried and executed, the King is in the Tower of London, the Queen and Princess in New Zealand. Germany and Russia are still allies, Joseph P. Kennedy is American Ambassador to Britain. It is a scenario that gives immense opportunities for the sensational approach. Instead, everything is played down, so that it becomes at once plausible and frightening. We learn about Churchill's death in an aside, the King's whereabouts is mentioned casually in conversation. On the surface, Nazi-occupied Britain hasn't changed much. The German presence is carefully muted: "The Soldatenkino sign outside the Curzon cinema was small and discreet, and only if you tried to enter the Mirabelle restaurant did a top-hatted doorman whisper that it was now used exclusively by Staff Officers." The signs that

say "Jewish Undertaking" are discreet, although they keep out all but the
boldest customers. And Detective Superintendent Douglas Archer ("Archer
of the Yard" in the press) is still able to regard himself as a policeman
steering clear of politics, even though his wife was killed in a bombing raid
and the Police Commissioner has been replaced by Gruppenführer Fritz
Kellerman. ⟨. . .⟩

All this is how it might very well have been, but mercifully was not, as
any adult who lived through those years in Britain will know; and the
picture of Nazi-occupied Britain is so good that at times we are bound to
feel the criminal problems facing Douglas Archer as an intrusion. But that
would be a mistaken view. Len Deighton is in the entertainment business,
and any social and political conjectures prompted by the book are strictly
subsidiary to the telling of an exciting story. In the process of entertaining
us, however, he shows that a masterly thriller can be written that makes
few sacrifices of seriousness in tone.

Julian Symons, "Deutschland über England," *New York Times Book Review*, 25 February 1979, pp. 1, 37

JOHN GARDNER   The success of "series" novels, like the Bond
books, automatically brings a backswing. It came first from Len Deighton,
with his working-class, ex-NCO, nameless narrator (later to be named Harry
Palmer in the films of his books; and played with cool insubordination by
Michael Caine).

At first sight, Deighton's early books seem to be the complete antithesis
of the Bond novels. They are certainly brilliant in their conception of
character, and eye to detail. But, on deeper examination (I speak as an
ardent and jealous admirer of Deighton), they contain a form of inverted
snobbery which one likes to think is the author's intention.

In the four major early novels, *The Ipcress File*, *Horse under Water*, *Funeral
in Berlin*, and *Billion-Dollar Brain*, we find the narrator as an habitué of
Mario & Franco's Terrazza (one of the really "in" restaurants of "swinging
sixties" London); a gourmet at home (Deighton is also a cook of some
standing); and very knowledgeable about food and wine, just as he is with
regard to locations, weapons, and military matters. He is a music lover (the
works of Charles Ives receive special attention in one book), and knows
his onions in that field also.

But the early Deighton spy novels are a delight; not on account of their plotting, but solely because of character and the standard of writing. Julian Symons writes of him as ". . . a kind of poetry of the spy novel", which, in those early books, is exactly what he is. (Deighton's *An Expensive Place to Die*, not his best book by far, incidentally contains my own favourite opening line in all espionage fiction: "The birds flew around for nothing but the hell of it. It was that sort of day: a trailer for the coming summer.")

Rightly, and to his lasting credit, among others, Len Deighton began to diversify after *Billion-Dollar Brain*, producing, among others, his *tour de force*, which has nothing to do with espionage—*Bomber*, a work that can be read again and again and is, undoubtedly, *the* classic novel of the air war against Germany during World War II.

His abiding interest is, obviously, military history, and, of late, Deighton has taken to producing works on that subject, *Fighter*, *Blitzkrieg*, *The Battle of Britain*, of a very high standard. Happily, though, he has not entirely left the espionage field, and his last book at the time of writing, *XPD*, contains some of his best prose and observation.

> John Gardner, "The Espionage Novel," *Whodunit?*, ed. H. R. F. Keating (New York: Van Nostrand Reinhold, 1982), pp. 75–76

H. R.   Aficionados of Deighton's work might reasonably expect to be offered here ⟨in *Goodbye, Mickey Mouse*⟩: the lives and loves of men at war, revelations of cowardice or treachery, quaint British stuff, brave boys proving their mettle, the West Point martinet hated-by-his-men, death in battle, dense clumps of useful information—and, above all, a sturdy plot guided with such a swift and skillful hand that readers will gratefully overlook clunky characterization or wooden dialogue en route to the denouement.

Many of these delights are delivered. But the sad truth is that Deighton has unwisely opted for character this time, leaving the plot to lumber along without any coherent narrative thread. The denouement is too late and perfunctory to be convincing. ⟨. . .⟩ Devoid of emotional authenticity, the book is oddly anemic—except on the subject of fighter planes. Deighton's obsession with planes makes the combat sequences lurid and exciting. If only the rest of the book were too.

> H. R., [Review of *Goodbye, Mickey Mouse*], *Harper's* No. 1560 (November 1982): 76

JANE STEWART SPITZER   I had a feeling of *déjà vu* reading
Len Deighton's latest spy novel, *Berlin Game*. The plot—uncovering the
identity of a Soviet double agent in the British intelligence service—is so
similar to that of John le Carré's *Tinker, Tailor, Soldier, Spy* that *Berlin Game*
seemed slightly flat and disappointing by comparison. And, perhaps because
of having *Tinker, Tailor . . .* on my mind, or perhaps because of Deighton's
clues, I wasn't really surprised by the ending. ⟨. . .⟩

Given the limits of the genre, it is inevitable that there will be familiar
echoes in plots and characters. It is unreasonable of me to expect otherwise.
But I can hope, because although it rarely occurs, this genre can produce
a novel that is fresh and unique, such as John le Carré's *The Little Drummer
Girl*. But if a spy novel is intelligent and well-written, and if it has an
exciting and suspenseful plot, interesting and believable characters, and
information about foreign places, politics, and people, it succeeds, and the
echoes should not matter.

Although a little weak on plot suspense, *Berlin Game* does contain all
of these elements. Deighton's characters seem to be like real people, having
likable and unlikable qualities. He draws a fascinating portrait of divided
Berlin—its history, its ambiance, and its people. *Berlin Game* is a very good
spy novel—interesting, entertaining, and at times, exciting. I enjoyed the
book. But I would have enjoyed it more without that feeling of *déjà vu*.

Jane Stewart Spitzer, "Clear Echoes of 'Tinker, Tailor, Soldier, Spy,' " *Christian Science Monitor*, 3 February 1984, pp. B6, 8

ANDY EAST   Len Deighton's popularity is somewhat surprising,
considering his acumen for intricate technological detail. But his place in
the history of the Cold War spy thriller speaks for itself. *The Ipcress File*
(1962—U.K.; 1963—U.S.) was an instant sales and critical success. ⟨. . .⟩

Reading Len Deighton can be linked to examining the facets of a Tiffany
diamond. The beauty is obvious from the initial encounter, but, to comprehend its depth, each side must be evaluated separately. In other words, to
fully comprehend the substance of a Deighton novel, additional readings
may be required.

Where le Carré concentrated on the desolation of The Circus, Deighton
accented the cynicism of an agent who might conceivably approach a
perilous mission differently than Bond. In its section devoted to Michael

Caine's superb portrayal of Harry Palmer (in *The Ipcress File* [1965], *Funeral in Berlin* [1966], and *Billion Dollar Brain* [1967]), the celluloid counterpart of Deighton's elusive hero, *Whodunit?* (edited by H. R. F. Keating) offered this interpretation of the author's selection of an obscure protagonist: "In the books, cunningly, it is never stated that he is each time the same individual. . . . In this way, he can be stretched over an inordinate length of contemporary history."

In his five series of spy thrillers of the Cold War era, *The Ipcress File* (1962—Britain; 1963—U.S.), *Horse under Water* (1963—Britain; 1968—U.S.), *Funeral in Berlin* (1964—Britain; 1965—U.S.), *The Billion Dollar Brain* (1966), and *An Expensive Place to Die* (1967), Deighton adopted a dossier format which emphasized the political or technological aspects of global intelligence. It is this single characteristic of Deighton's work that motivated later advocates to be more perceptive of the mechanics of the spy trade. *The Ipcress File*, *Funeral in Berlin*, and *The Billion Dollar Brain* featured top-secret appendixes, each authentically simulated, which contributed to the plot. Deighton's second thriller, *Horse under Water*, which involved a currency cache for renegade Nazis hidden on a sunken German tanker off the Portuguese coast, contained a code translation document, a high-level Cabinet letter (dated 1941), and an "Eyes Only" file register. These latter elements were introduced before the first chapter, which indicates the importance Deighton assigned to these devices throughout his books.

Funeral in Berlin has endured as Deighton's most celebrated novel. Deighton's spy is ordered to execute the defection of a valued Russian scientist, and, within the plot, Deighton constructs perhaps the definitive commentary on the East-West tensions of the Cold War, next to le Carré's *The Spy Who Came In from the Cold*. It is in this pulsating thriller that Deighton's hero first encounters Colonel Stok, a high-ranking K.G.B. strategist, and their interaction symbolizes the rising fever of U.S.–Soviet hegemony following the Berlin Wall crisis. Deighton's integration of elementary chess rules as chapter headings in *Funeral in Berlin* prove to be a master stroke on the author's part—in addition to complementing the East-West allegory throughout the book.

The Billion Dollar Brain is regarded as Deighton's most technologically oriented thriller. Assigned to penetrate a fanatically right-wing organization, Facts for Freedom, Deighton's spy uncovers a megalomaniacal blueprint by its head, Colonel Midwinter, to devise a computerized war strategy against the Warsaw Pact powers. His first objective is to launch an invasion of the Soviet republic of Latvia.

The futility of le Carré is poignantly reflected in *An Expensive Place to Die*. The major Western intelligence networks engage in a paranoid battle of wits over the political value of an American nuclear genius and a Chinese Communist scientist. The battleground for these intrigues is Paris, and, in a bitter narrative style more indigenous to détente than the Cold War, Deighton portrays the City of Lovers with a prophetic sense of desolation. Unquestionably, *An Expensive Place to Die* is Deighton's understated classic of Cold War espionage.

Andy East, "The Spy in the Dark: A History of Espionage Fiction," *Armchair Detective* 19, No. 1 (Winter 1986): 37–38

EDWARD LENSE   Len Deighton and John le Carré virtually re-invented the secret-agent novel in the early 1960s, each in his own way, by grafting the conventions of earlier thrillers onto the conventions of murder mysteries. Le Carré's Smiley embodies the ratiocinative detective of British tradition, while Deighton's nameless hero steps out of Raymond Chandler and into the offices of W.O.O.C.(P.). ⟨. . .⟩

Deighton's hero is a man with a vivid personality, which gives his narrative voice its Chandleresque tough-guy tone, but his personality is secondary in these novels to his role as a spy. He is so perfectly a spy, hidden from everyone else, that he is left without a name. He has many names, but all of them are false; his real name is unknown to the reader, just as his real self is unknowable to the other characters in the stories. This device suggests that, in the world of these novels, all names are disguises and all persons are essentially unknowable. Because he takes this to be an essential fact of human relationships, the hero is completely isolated but can accept his isolation as a necessity, even as his greatest asset. For one thing, all other people may be as isolated as he but not so clearly aware of their condition. The eagerness with which other characters define themselves in terms of class or ideology suggests that they need to construct identities to hide their solitude from each other and themselves. The nameless hero's ability to live with his isolation rather than deny it makes him an authentic person whether anyone knows his name or not.

In any case, for Deighton, even more than for the American "hard-boiled" mystery writers who served as his models, human relationships are irreducibly mysterious because they are based on motives so irrational that they can never be completely understood and are therefore not predictable. Harvey Newbegin, for example, is a former CIA agent who, in *The Billion Dollar Brain*, defects to the Soviet Union and tries to take along biological secrets; he does this on the grounds that his family was originally Russian and therefore he is going home to his true country. Even the nameless hero is nonplussed by this behavior but recovers his poise in time to murder Harvey in Leningrad. Since he must depend on many people in his job, any of them presumably capable of equal lunacy, the hero isolates himself as much as possible, not only on grounds of philosophy but simple prudence. He understands that it is impossible ever to know another person fully and is too wise or cautious ever to base his trust on imperfect understanding of another person. Harvey, not being so wise or cautious, ends up under a bus.

Edward Lense, "They've Taken Away Your Name: Identity and Illusion in Len Deighton's Early Novels," *Clues* 12, No. 2 (Fall–Winter 1991): 67–69

D. T. MAX   During the Cold War things were simpler. Len Deighton's master spy Bernard Samson marked the halfway point between Ian Fleming's James Bond and John le Carré's cerebral George Smiley. With Deighton maybe you couldn't quite figure out the plot but at least the secret agents had guns. But with the razing of the Berlin Wall in 1989 (*annus horribilis* for espionage writers), everything changed. Now John le Carré writes about drugs-for-arms deals in Curaçao and Len Deighton ⟨in *Violent Ward*⟩ has taken literary refuge in, of all places, Los Angeles.

Deighton, who has had a long and distinguished career moving spies in and out of enemy lines, tries out a new and more humble protagonist here: Mickey Murphy, a criminal lawyer working out of a rundown office near South Central L.A. Murphy's law firm functions according to Murphy's Law. Murphy has two Asian partners, one of whom has a sideline in obtaining for living clients fake death certificates. He gets hit by an RV; his colleague has a heart attack. Murphy's ex-wife Betty, who in the book's first scene stands on his window ledge threatening suicide, winds up a successful Hollywood agent. ⟨. . .⟩

Murphy himself is a mass of inconsistencies. He's supposed to be a Southern Californian born and bred but sounds more like Lord Peter Wimsey than Sam Spade. He "posts" his mail, calls football players "footballers," and, giving the once-over to Pindero's house, asks: "Why did a guy leave so hurriedly that he didn't even grab his soap and razor?"

The backdrop for *Violent Ward* are the riots following the Rodney King verdict, about which Deighton seems to want to make an editorial point: "Like most of the city's inhabitants, I spent many of those early hours of the riots comparing the TV coverage with wary glances out the window, until eventually I could hardly distinguish between those two distorting sheets of glass. . . . Is it television, is it reality or is it neither?"

Or is it Marshall MacLuhan?

D. T. Max, "Nerve of Steel," *Los Angeles Times Book Review*, 29 August 1993, p. 13

KEITH JEFFERY   ⟨*Blood, Tears and Folly*⟩ is an ambitious book, which seeks to tell the story of the Second World War up to the involvement of the United States of America at the end of 1941, at which point it became a fully global conflict and the defeat of the Axis powers was ensured. It is written by a self-styled "amateur historian", who was reassured earlier in his career by the opinion of A. J. P. Taylor—incontestible enough—that "an amateur historian is an historian nevertheless".

Len Deighton begins explicitly in a revisionist mode, referring on the first page to the "delusions from the past" which afflict the "collective British mind" (as well, he notes, as those of other nations). He declares his intention "to deal with some of the misconceptions that cloud both our preferred vision of the war, and our present-day view of a world that always seems to misunderstand us. . . ." ⟨. . .⟩

The strengths of *Blood, Tears and Folly* lie in the sustained narratives of action—Dunkirk, "Operation Barbarossa", Pearl Harbor, and so on—and in the technical details. As might be expected from the author of *Fighter* ("The true story of the Battle of Britain"), which with *Blitzkrieg* ("From the rise of Hitler to the fall of Dunkirk") has been reissued in paperback to accompany *Blood, Tears and Folly*, the coverage of the air war is meticulous and comprehensive. At times, however, the sense of personal involvement in the war which so powerfully illuminated Deighton's novel, *Bomber*, is lost in a welter of facts about Japanese fighter development or the relative merits of radial and liquid-cooled aero engines. ⟨. . .⟩

This volume contains the kind of iconoclastic revisionism which such historians as A. J. P. Taylor, Corelli Barnett and, more recently, Clive Ponting (in *1940: Myth and Reality*) have already provided us with. While some of Deighton's interpretations may be suspect, we may rely on the technical detail; here is historical "truth" (always a slippery customer) of a type which will not date as the sometimes arid debates of professional historians can. This history, too, may be the sort of thing that most *aficionados* of war history prefer to read. As such, it will contribute to the survival of the Second World War in mythology as much as it will to the "real" history of the conflict.

> Keith Jeffery, "The World's Only Hope," *Times Literary Supplement*, 3 December 1993, p. 23

◒ *Bibliography*

The Ipcress File. 1962.

Horse under Water. 1963.

Funeral in Berlin. 1964.

Drunks-man-ship: Town's Album of Fine Wines and High Spirits (editor). 1964.

Action Cook Book: Len Deighton's Guide to Eating. 1965.

Où Est le Garlic; or, Len Deighton's French Cook Book. 1965, 1979 (as *Basic French Cooking*).

The Billion Dollar Brain. 1966.

An Expensive Place to Die. 1967.

London Dossier (with others). 1967.

The Assassination of President Kennedy (editor; with Michael Rand and Howard Loxton). 1967.

Only When I Larf. 1968.

Len Deighton's Continental Dossier: A Collection of Cultural, Culinary, Historical, Spooky, Grim and Preposterous Fact. Ed. Victor and Margaret Pettitt. 1968.

Bomber: Events Relating to the Last Flight of an R.A.F. over Germany on the Night of June 31, 1943. 1970.

Declarations of War. 1971.

Close-Up. 1972.

Spy Story. 1974.

Yesterday's Spy. 1975.

Twinkle, Twinkle, Little Spy ⟨*Catch a Falling Spy*⟩. 1976.

Fighter: The True Story of the Battle of Britain. 1977.

SS-GB: Nazi-Occupied Britain 1941. 1978.

Airshipwreck (with Arnold Schwartzman). 1978.

Blitzkrieg: From the Rise of Hitler to the Fall of Dunkirk. 1979.

Tactical Genius in Battle by Simon Goodenough (editor). 1979.

Battle of Britain. 1980.

XPD. 1981.

Goodbye, Mickey Mouse. 1982.

Berlin Game. 1983.

Mexico Set. 1984.

London Match. 1985.

Game, Set and Match ⟨*Berlin Game, Mexico Set, London Match*⟩. 1986.

Winter: A Berlin Family 1899–1945. 1987.

Spy Hook. 1988.

Spy Line. 1989.

ABC of French Food. 1989.

Spy Sinker. 1990.

MAMista. 1991.

Hook, Line & Sinker ⟨*Spy Hook, Spy Line, Spy Sinker*⟩. 1991.

The Last Marxist. 1991.

City of Gold. 1992.

Blood, Tears and Folly: An Objective Look at World War II. 1993.

Violent Ward. 1993.

Faith. 1994.

James Ellroy
b. 1948

JAMES ELLROY was born in Los Angeles on March 4, 1948, to Geneva Hillaker, a registered nurse, and her husband, an accountant for the Hollywood studios. An only child, Ellroy learned to read from his father when he was three and in the years ahead turned to it as a refuge from family tragedies. Ellroy was four when his parents divorced and ten when his mother was strangled to death by a bar pickup.

Following his mother's unsolved murder, Ellroy began reading true crime documentaries and detective fiction voraciously, in books often stolen from Hollywood bookstores. His acquaintance with the works of Rex Stout and Mickey Spillane inspired dreams of becoming a writer. However, he was expelled from high school for fighting and truancy in 1965, and his father arranged for him to join the army. When his father died while he was in basic training, Ellroy faked a nervous breakdown to secure his discharge from the military.

Between 1965 and 1977 Ellroy spent most of his time living on the streets of Los Angeles, stealing, drinking, taking drugs—and reading. He first encountered the work of Raymond Chandler, Ross Macdonald, and Joseph Wambaugh in the early 1970s and found that the tragic dimension of their fiction resonated with his direct experience of being driven by circumstance to a life of petty crime. He was arrested approximately fifty times for a variety of misdemeanors, ranging from public drunkenness to disturbing the peace, and served a total of six months in jail sentences.

A life-threatening bout of double pneumonia related to his self-destructive habits encouraged Ellroy to join Alcoholics Anonymous in 1977 and rehabilitate himself. He took work as a caddy at a Hollywood golf course and began writing his first novel, *Brown's Requiem*, in 1979. Published in 1981, it wove together a number of elements that have since become trademarks of Ellroy's writing: unsympathetic protagonists caught in morally ambiguous situations, urban settings and characters grotesquely shaped by crime, and sex as a motive for evil *and* good. His second novel, *Clandestine* (1982), a period *noir* thriller set in the 1950s, was based loosely on his mother's murder and earned an Edgar Award nomination from the Mystery Writers of America.

With his third novel, *Blood on the Moon* (1984), Ellroy introduced Lloyd Hopkins, a sexually aggressive detective whose character is juxtaposed to that of a homicidal maniac he pursues. Ellroy began writing full-time after its publication and turned out three more Lloyd Hopkins adventures over the next two years. The publication in 1987 of *The Black Dahlia*, a fictionalized rendering of a notorious unsolved 1947 crime, inaugurated Ellroy's L.A. Quartet, a gritty and graphic look at the underbelly of Los Angeles as representative of American culture for the last half-century. The other three novels, *The Big Nowhere* (1988), *L.A. Confidential* (1990), and *White Jazz* (1992), have earned Ellroy the reputation as the leading exponent of the modern hard-boiled school of writing.

Ellroy moved east in 1984 and married Mary Doherty in 1988. He lives in Connecticut, where he continues to pursue his ambition to become the world's greatest living writer of crime fiction.

◈ *Critical Extracts*

DONNA GRAY   Written in the first-person, *Clandestine* has an almost autobiographical feel to it, especially in the familiarity with which the author leads us through the dark and seamy underside of Los Angeles, from Silverlake to Watts. The story is centered around the strangulation murders of two LA women, and ⟨Frederick Upton⟩ Underhill, cockily looking to make a name for himself as well as earn the title of Detective, sets out on his own, unauthorized, to find the killer. The path his search leads him on is both gripping and complex, with the intervention of several finely-detailed characters along the way, including an old Irish cop whose brogue is as thick as molasses, as well as a mulatto homosexual who runs a gay bar in Venice. There's even some old-fashioned romance thrown in for good measure, in the form of a crippled lady from the DA's office, whose father is a movie producer called Big Sid.

Ellroy certainly seems to know his stuff. Read it. You'll like it.

Donna Gray, [Review of *Clandestine*], *West Coast Review of Books* 9, No. 1 (January 1983): 43

DUANE TUCKER   *JE:* I'm interested in people who tread outside the bounds of conventional morality; displaced romantics ill at ease in the 1980s; people who have rejected a goodly amount of life's amenities in order to dance to the music in their own heads. The price of that music is very, very high, and no one has ever gotten away without paying. Both cops and killers fall into that category, to varying degrees, walking the sharpest of edges between their own music and the conventional music of the world that surrounds them. Think of the potential conflicts. A modern-day policeman, equipped with technology and a pitch-black skepticism, a man who would have been a good medieval warrior, meets a psychopathic killer who maneuvers in the real world yet is fueled by an indecipherable, symbolic language—in other words, pure insanity. I've given you an admittedly extreme example, and a brief synopsis of *Blood on the Moon.* Within that framework, though, think of the opportunities to explore psyches and moral codes under incredible duress. Think of how precious physical sacrifice and human love stand out when juxtaposed against the severely contained universe I just described.

DT: One which you yourself describe as extreme, though.

JE: Extreme only because its facts are made explicit. Beyond that, highly prosaic, even vulgar. Eschewing the tabloids completely, pick up a copy of any newspaper. You'll find elliptically worded accounts of psychopathic slaughter in most of them.

DT: A frightening thought. Is there a salient motivating factor in this "universe" of yours?

JE: Yes, sex. I've gone back and read through my four novels recently and was astonished how close to the surface it has been from the beginning. In this specific "universe" you just mentioned, the dividing point is obvious: in the hellish unreality of the psychopath, sex is a weapon; in the displaced romantic cop's quasi-reality, it is the love of unattainable women, unattainable only because the cop would have to submit to vulnerability to earn their love, which of course he would never do. Again, one example, and an extreme one. Pauline Kael once wrote, "Sex is the great leveler, taste the great divider." As these themes become more dominant in my work, I'm going to have to learn to offset them in subtle variations, and, in general, infuse this so-called "universe" of yours with a greater degree of recognizably human behavior. Literature is tricky, Daddy-O. Just when you think you've got something down pat, you realize you have to shift gears or go stale. Tricky.

DT: Shifting gears slightly, do you have an overall goal or ultimate goal as a writer?

JE: James M. Cain said that his goal was to "graze tragedy." My goal is to hit tragedy on the snout with a sixteen-pound sledge hammer.

> Duane Tucker, "An Interview with James Ellroy," *Armchair Detective* 17, No. 2 (Spring 1984): 153

HARRIET WAUGH   The only thriller I have read in the last two months that finishes as strongly as the story engages is James Ellroy's *Brown's Requiem*. Set among the fairways of Los Angeles golf courses, Mr Ellroy tells a violent story through the eyes of a mixed-up alcoholic ex-cop private eye, called Fritz Brown. He is hired by a psychopath golf caddy who is fixated on his sister to investigate her relationship with a Jewish business man who is sponsoring her music training. Fritz Brown falls in love with the sister and turns his attention on the brother. Out of the derelict scum that hang out around the golf courses comes the smell of corruption, violence, death and money. Fritz Brown's unattractive righteous violence piles up the corpses. The reader needs to concentrate hard to follow the many twists in the fast moving action, and for once the solution does not seem quite arbitrary.

> Harriet Waugh, "Thrillers," *Spectator*, 21 July 1984, p. 29

NEWGATE CALLENDAR   *Blood on the Moon* ⟨is⟩ an ambitious book that does not come off. It is the story of two men. One is a brilliant detective sergeant in the Los Angeles Police Department. He is a loner who is able to make quantum jumps that leave his less gifted colleagues far behind. The other is a mysterious psychopath who murders attractive young women and then takes out after the officer when he starts getting close.

The murderer is supposed to be as brilliant in his way as the policeman, and the book tries to be a study in polarities. But there is very little to suggest that the killer is brilliant; the only thing really established about him is that he is shrewd and cunning. And for a supposedly smart policeman, the sergeant does some dumb things. He theorizes that there is something in common about murders that have occurred on June 10 in the past. So he goes to the library and spends the day with microfilms of old newspapers, looking up the date in previous years. He comes up with nothing. Naturally. Someone should tell him that most newspapers and all morning newspapers carry the news of June 10 on June 11.

In addition, the writing, though it does show talent, tends to be a bit hysterical and self-conscious. Also hyperventilated—the characters always seem to be shouting or screaming. Mr. Ellroy tries too hard, ending up with mannerism rather than a natural style. One peculiarity of his writing is his use of blood and colors as symbols. There is more blood and blood symbolism than there is in "Pierrot Lunaire." Thus "His peripheral vision throbbed with red." And there is sun symbolism: "Lloyd began to see pure white light in the space, growing in and around and out of Kathleen." At the end, "Floral-scented terror merged with metal filing cabinets, wanted posters, and a map of the city, producing pure white light." This is like a *pas de deux* in which each star does a series of solo turns before they come together in a final dance of death. But the author's manipulative hand is too much in evidence.

Newgate Callendar, [Review of *Blood on the Moon*], *New York Times Book Review*, 22 July 1984, p. 32

JOHN R. DORAN   For all those fans of hardboiled police procedural novels, Ellroy ⟨in *Suicide Hill*⟩ delivers his goods with all the subtlety and grace of an ice pick in the eye. It's obvious that the series featuring the exploits of Police Sgt. Lloyd Hopkins has appeal since this is the third offering by Ellroy on the wacky cop with a psycho mentality and an IQ of 170. If you can stand the asinine clichés, the overblown street talk, the pages full of insipid dialogue and unattractive, tough guys, you'll probably *love* this book.

Those in search of a more finely crafted mystery will likely want to bypass this piece. It's simply impossible to relate to any of the people in this novel. At least for this reader. There is no ballast of reality on which to grab hold. But maybe that quirkiness would make the book pay off for some readers.

Hopkins is a certified loony case and everybody knows it, including his supervisors in the police department. He's been off the force because of his craziness but in another case of bureaucratic pretzel logic Hopkins is invited to return to the department to take on another case. His suspension, by the way, is for breaking the very laws he's been sworn to uphold. This is a very dirty Dirty Harry. His assignment this time is to aid the feds in their investigation of a series of bank robberies. Lloyd has his personal problems, too. He's separated from his wife and three daughters and wants them back. Very few readers will disagree with the family's reluctance to return. Lloyd, also, by the way, has a panicky conviction that the head of Internal Affairs has just dedicated the rest of his life to persecuting him.

The unsavoriness of the lead character, the street talking hard noses all make this an unsavory novel. Perfect for those who love sensationalized grubby fiction.

> John R. Doran, [Review of *Suicide Hill*], *West Coast Review of Books* 12, No. 3 (September–October 1986): 27

CHARLES DE LINT   ⟨*Suicide Hill*⟩ begins with ⟨Duane⟩ Rice's release from prison and his obsessive attempts to track down his girlfriend Vandy. Needing money, Rice borrows a diabolically clever plan overheard while in prison and, after enlisting the aid of the Garcia brothers, sets out on a bank-robbing spree. The bank jobs get increasingly violent, ending in the deaths of two policemen and an immense manhunt.

Sgt. Hopkins is in disgrace—with Captain Gaffney after his head no matter what it takes—but he is called back in to handle the case simply because he is the best that the department has and there are three cop killers out on the streets. Only Hopkins really is not much better than the men he is hunting. He is willing to do anything to get the job done, and that is what makes the novel so fascinating.

The lines between protagonist and antagonists blur. Ellroy is strong on characterization, painting highly believable portraits of disturbed individuals with the same skill of a William Goldman (*Control, Heat*) or a Thomas Harris (*Red Dragon, Black Sunday*). The reader is thrust straight into the heads of the characters and left there for the duration of the ride.

A multiple viewpoint technique is used to its fullest potential for both characterization and tension. The writing is hard and gritty and certainly not for those who prefer their mysteries cozy and safe. And, while the concept of the "hot-dogging" cops—fabricating evidence, beating up suspects, breaking and entering, indiscriminately firing their guns—is unrealistic in terms of how real police departments operate, it still makes for a rollercoaster of a read.

Charles de Lint, [Review of *Suicide Hill*], *Armchair Detective* 20, No. 2 (Spring 1987): 206–7

NICK KIMBERLEY   The central character of James Ellroy's *Silent Terror* is ⟨. . .⟩ Martin Plunkett, a convicted multiple killer who refuses to apologise for his sins, instead setting out to show that he's even worse than the public suspects. The book takes the form of a confession which he's preparing for publication, in which he reveals that the handful of murders for which he's been convicted are just the icing on the cake—he asks for dozens more to be taken into account.

Ellroy is working with our obsession with mass murderers; at one point, his hero confronts Manson in prison and suggests that, when it comes to gore, Charlie doesn't really cut the mustard. Ellroy maintains that faintly comic edge throughout ⟨. . .⟩ He engineers his mother's suicide, then drinks her blood; brings himself to an orgasm while disembowelling a dog; and sets off on a nationwide tour of sexually tinged murder. This is a sort of *Bildungsroman* in which the hero finds his identity through murder. The elements of pastiche are well-controlled: we get a primal scene; a homosexual encounter with a cop who's a twin figure, using his authority to conceal his own series of murders; and a wonderful climax in which Plunkett makes his stand against 'the bankruptcy known as HAPPY FAMILY LIFE'—dismembering corpses in all directions, he tosses one set of limbs 'into a dusty chair covered with tennis balls', another 'in the sink along with the dishes'.

⟨. . .⟩ Plunkett survives partly by an ability to assume a variety of forms appropriate to each vile act. While Ellroy has cast his novel in the form of a psychological investigation—'a chilling journey into the mind of a serial killer' says the cover—it becomes apparent that Plunkett ⟨. . .⟩ has no real psychology, but is animated evil. Although overlong, *Silent Terror* is a witty mix of horror novel, thriller and black comedy.

Nick Kimberley, "Slippery as Sin," *New Statesman*, 19 June 1987, p. 31

JACK SMITH   On the morning of Jan. 15, 1947, the body of a nude young woman, severed at the waist, was found in a vacant lot on Norton Avenue.

This macabre discovery touched off a police investigation and a newspaper extravaganza that have not been equaled since. The unfortunate victim turned out to be Elizabeth Short, 22, a Hollywood tramp from Medford, Mass. Her killer has never been caught. ⟨. . .⟩

James Ellroy's novel ⟨The Black Dahlia⟩ is not the first entertainment derived from this event, but it may be the most imaginative and bizarre.

The narrator is Bucky Bleichert, a cop and ex-prizefighter; his partner and friend is Lee Blanchard, also a cop and ex-prizefighter. Both seem to be in love with Kay Lake, ex-girlfriend of an imprisoned robber-pimp whom Blanchard busted. Bleichert won't touch her because she is living with Blanchard, although they don't have sex.

This strange menage à trois is made all the more peculiar by the pathological influence of the dead Black Dahlia. Blanchard is obsessed with finding her killer, because he feels guilty for the mutilation murder of a younger sister; Bleichert has an erotic fixation on the Black Dahlia, so that she intrudes on his sex life—when he's making love to another woman, he sees her face. ⟨. . .⟩

The book is turgid with passion, violence and frustration; the dialogue is suitably obscene for a cop book, and the prose is riddled with such graphic synonyms as "eyeballed" for looked at.

Jack Smith, "Making a Legend More Macabre," Los Angeles Times Book Review, 13 September 1987, p. 16

NEWGATE CALLENDAR   If The Black Dahlia by James Ellroy were a play, it would be reviewed as overwritten, overdirected, overproduced and overwrought. ⟨. . .⟩

If Mr. Ellroy had only stuck to the straight story line, the book would not have been bad. He can be an entertaining writer. But, as in some of his previous novels, he gets submerged in a quicksand of psychobabble. His two central characters are hard to take and even harder to believe. For experienced cops they are mentally unstable. They let their emotions get the better of them. They cry. They do completely irrational things. After a while the book becomes so turgid and unrealistic that it is a real effort to finish it.

Newgate Callendar, [Review of The Black Dahlia], New York Times Book Review, 8 November 1987, p. 28

NICK KIMBERLEY   It's more or less a rule of crime fiction that, when the supernatural intrudes, the point is lost. James Ellroy's *Because the Night* is a Los Angeles cop story, with Detective Sergeant Lloyd Hopkins tackling two cases which slowly intertwine. The necessary paranoia and violence saturate the book, but from the emblematic opening paragraphs a divide is established between *this* side of life and the *other*, where crimes of murder happen.

What we end up with is a quasi-supernatural view where the mayhem takes place in a world not subject to the rules we live by. Thus, anything can happen. Psychology here becomes an occult science, revealing all, explaining nothing. As is so often the case, homosexuality is the archetypal site of all repressions, so fearful that Hopkins can barely pronounce the word. Ellroy is certainly teasing us here with his refusal to be reasonable, but he can still only function in a world where violence comes from somewhere "beyond the beyond"—one of his characters' favourite sayings.

Nick Kimberley, "No Hiding Place," *New Statesman*, 22 January 1988, p. 33

JOHN GROSS   James Ellroy's previous book, *The Black Dahlia*, was a fictional reworking of a celebrated California crime. In *The Big Nowhere* he offers another mixture of Los Angeles as it was—in 1950—and Los Angeles as it might have been. The terrain is lovingly mapped, the mood of the period is adroitly conjured up, and some choice real-life characters put in an appearance: Howard Hughes, Johnny Stompanato, the ganglord Mickey Cohen.

Two major themes weave their way through the story. A Hollywood union is being investigated in the name of anti-Communism (though the investigation·is in effect a self-serving racket); an unknown murderer is at large, killing homosexuals in a peculiarly gruesome fashion. ⟨. . .⟩

*The Big Nowhere*is a big, sprawling book, which lays on the atmosphere rich and thick. Sometimes, indeed, Mr. Ellroy supplies background detail to the point of being garrulous; but his characters are drawn with a firm brush, he has an excellent line in flinty, sardonic dialogue, and you terribly want to know how the whole thing is going to work out in the end.

John Gross, "A Nondescript Victim, and Los Angeles Shames," *New York Times*, 9 September 1988, p. C24

RAYMOND SOKOLOV   For something in that classic vein written by a man alive and in full noir-lit vigor, the strong of heart will want to read James Ellroy's *The Big Nowhere*. Buffs will already know about Mr. Ellroy from *The Black Dahlia* and six other novels. He is in the grand tradition, maybe even too wholeheartedly for his own good. The violence in this hefty new book is so savage it almost makes you giggle. The main crime cannot be described in a family newspaper. Most people would find it hard to recount in private to friends. Suffice it to say that the murder discovered by Los Angeles sheriff's deputy Danny Upshaw involves not only death, but the most lurid imaginable violation of the human body (don't even try to guess) as well as the desecration of an animal (the wolverine, a savage beast best known as the emblematic creature of the University of Michigan; will this book be burned in Ann Arbor?). ⟨. . .⟩

Period flavor—oh, call it historical depth, why not?—is Mr. Ellroy's goal. He's done his research and, without writing a real *roman à clef,* he makes you feel as if you really are in the Hollywood of 1950. This is effective in several ways, for the flavor of the time itself, for the extra plausibility it gives to some pretty implausible crimes against the person, and for the implicit tribute it pays to the high period of noir literature and film. But for all his respect for the past and his great talent for re-creating it, Mr. Ellroy adds his own personal and up-to-date twists to the genre. *The Big Nowhere* is completely unhobbled by any of the taboos or notions of good taste that Chandler and Hammett had to observe, and yet it is written with a curious delicacy of craft and an instinct for keeping the reader intrigued, amused and even a bit scared.

Raymond Sokolov, "What's New in Noir," *Wall Street Journal,* 29 September 1988, p. 28

KEVIN MOORE   Ellroy ⟨. . .⟩ has made a well-publicized bow to the steamy *noir* atmospherics of the period, acknowledging the subtle influence of Dashiell Hammett and Raymond Chandler. *L.A. Confidential* opens with a bang, literally, as 13 people get gunned down after a hijacked drug deal. And that's only the prologue. ⟨. . .⟩

The action and characters cascade along at a surreal pace Cornell Woolrich would have applauded. And James M. Cain never orchestrated violence any better than Ellroy does. *L.A. Confidential* undoubtedly will heat up the summer, especially for those who have never considered the garbage disposal as an interrogation tool.

Still, the characters, especially the women, seem to become reflexes rather than personalities toward the end (the book is 50 or so pages too long). By then, though, Ellroy has constructed his world so completely that the plot plays itself out with all the impact—and excess—of a shotgun blast. *L.A. Confidential* will make the contemporary reader feel he has been dumped into a wrestling ring against a tag team of Joseph Wambaugh and Mickey Spillane.

> Kevin Moore, "Summertime Crime-Travel: James Ellroy and Stuart Kaminsky Visit the Steamy California of the Past," *Chicago Tribune Books*, 10 June 1990, p. 1

MARPESSA DAWN OUTLAW   Strictly on the QT, I know what Sandra Bernhard meant when she confessed in a recent interview that she'd always wanted to be the victim in a Weegee photograph. It's got nothing to do with a death wish; it's about immortality. Weegee's grisly inner-city vision of the '40s and '50s is compelling because he not only satisfied our voyeuristic desires, he mythologized his subjects. What Weegee did for crime pics, James Ellroy does for the mind's eye. Raymond Chandler's heir returns to his favorite stomping ground in *L.A. Confidential*—Tinseltown in the '50s. When men were dicks with hats, women were gold-hearted hookers who made them spill the beans, and the world was simpler in black and white.

This latest of three neo-noir epics set in L.A. has all the pleasures you'd expect from the genre: double- and triple-crossings, police corruption, sleazoid tabloid leaks, pornography, even a "real" murder. (Remember Lana Turner's guy pal Johnny Stompanato, who was iced by Lana's daughter?) But the LAPD takes center stage. Ellroy believes that hero cops are rare, maybe even nonexistent. The best we can hope for are cops with guilt complexes.

> Marpessa Dawn Outlaw, [Review of *L.A. Confidential*], *Voice Literary Supplement* No. 87 (July–August 1990): 12

MARVIN LACHMAN   Although less than ten years old, the first printing of James Ellroy's *Brown's Requiem* (1981), a paperback original, is rare, and it is appropriate that Avon has reprinted it. The setting is Los Angeles, and Ellroy's hero is former policeman turned private eye, Fritz Brown. As in Ellroy's later work, his protagonist is a driven man, in this case fanatical about many things, especially classical music. Other characters in the book build their lives around old movies and golf caddying. While this is not always a realistic book, Ellroy is good regarding changes in Los Angeles during the 1970s. He provides a succinct, but effective, word picture of a run-down hotel off Hollywood Boulevard, whose lobby is "a thousand years old and bespoke a despair that was almost tangible." You might find the plot scarcely believable and the violence excessive, but its sheer readability will carry you to the end of *Brown's Requiem*.

Marvin Lachman, "Original Sins," *Armchair Detective* 24, No. 1 (Winter 1991): 31

TODD GRIMSON   One after another highly regarded young male American writer takes a shot at writing a hardboiled novel, almost as a rite of passage. The temptation is irresistible. The model is Robert Stone's *Dog Soldiers*, which won a National Book Award in 1975. We have had Denis Johnson's *Angels*, Madison Smartt Bell's *Straight Cut* and Richard Ford's *The Ultimate Good Luck*. The list should also include two of the best writers of this generation, Paul Auster and Steve Erickson, whose most successful work, however surreal, is heavily influenced by the hardboiled tradition and world view.

James Ellroy has earned his place in these ranks, though it must be admitted he did not spring forth fully grown. No, his first several novels were semi-distinguished hackwork, making him a living while he learned his trade. Some of them possess an uncomfortable intensity, but they are so raw, and often so clumsy that his later work is simply in a different class. *The Black Dahlia* was his breakthrough, followed by *The Big Nowhere* and *L.A. Confidential*.

It seems that setting the works in the Los Angeles of the '40s and '50s, the city of his childhood, somehow freed him. Through the profane slang, the dated vernacular, the imaginative connection with black-and-white films like *The Big Heat* and *Underworld USA*—or the well-known parallel of the Black Dahlia case with his own mother's unsolved murder (a hauntingly suggestive biographical element that has been highly publicized)—Ellroy found his voice, which he continues to elaborate and improve.

Todd Grimson, "White-Hot Extreme," *Los Angeles Times Book Review*, 30 August 1992, pp. 1, 9

WENDY LESSER   What the real Los Angeles possesses, amid all its fiery disintegration, is what Mr. Ellroy's latest novel ⟨*White Jazz*⟩ keenly lacks: a coherent narrative line. We may not have been pleased about what was happening this spring, but we knew why it was happening. In *White Jazz* I was lost by page 56—the page on which the author explicitly reveals whatever plot the novel is going to have. ("Instinct—call me bait—a bad cop sent out to draw heat," Klein correctly guesses.) For the next 300 pages it was just a matter of waiting out the body count and wishing for a more interesting variety of subject-verb combinations.

Mr. Ellroy, in order to pack maximo action into minimo pages, has developed what he clearly views as a whiplash telegraphic style. No doubt the violence done to the English language is meant to mirror the violence done to humanity by its fellow humanity (I'm being charitable here). But we can't really begin to care about characters who never even get to inhabit a complete sentence.

Wendy Lesser, "Giving Hate a Bad Name," *New York Times Book Review*, 18 October 1992, p. 40

EMILY WHITE   Ellroy is often grouped with Chandler and Ross Macdonald; like them, he seems to hover between crime fiction and "literary" fiction, using the generic formulas to prop up a singular, poetic vision. Ellroy's voice, however, is unstable. In *White Jazz* he moves from dreamlike italicized sections, through bare, rapid-fire storytelling, into rambling newspaper reports. At its best this method makes room for expertly rendered modes of speech: gangster, journalist, Hollywood, Communist. Sometimes it feels forced, though, an ornate lie masking a smaller, fiercer story. Interrupting itself, *White Jazz* never arrives at any realization—the reader feels broken-off, jarred, breathless.

As Ellroy's voice disperses, what holds constant is the dust of Los Angeles, settling after another demolition clearing the way for an artificial city, another theme park. Constant, too, is relentless, graphic violence, and if *White Jazz* hints at oedipal reckoning, the eyes lost here are ripped clean away: "Biting. Clawing. Ripping at his eyes. Look: One gushing red socket." ⟨. . .⟩

There were times in *White Jazz* when I cared about Klein and his monsters and wanted him to be safe. But it still seems Ellroy's been sidetracked ever since *The Black Dahlia*, exploring complex crime-schemes and form, but never taking real emotional risks. *The Black Dahlia* moved quickly into its hero's worst fears—Bleichert stared his vampires in the face and they were horrible and inescapable and sometimes clumsily written, but never drowned in style. Maybe for Ellroy, as for his detectives, there will always only be One Girl. *The Black Dahlia* possesses the body of his work completely. She still hasn't forgiven him for bringing her back to life.

Emily White, "Fade to White," *Village Voice*, 20 October 1992, p. 70

▨ *Bibliography*

Brown's Requiem. 1981.
Clandestine. 1982.
Blood on the Moon. 1984.
Because the Night. 1984.
Suicide Hill. 1986.
Silent Terror (Killer on the Road). 1986.
The Black Dahlia. 1987.
The Big Nowhere: A Novel of Los Angeles 1950. 1988.
L.A. Confidential. 1990.
White Jazz. 1992.
Hollywood Nocturnes. 1994.
American Tabloid. 1995.

Thomas Harris
b. c. 1940

THOMAS HARRIS was born around 1940 in Jackson, Tennessee. Very little is known about his personal life, as he has kept very much to himself. When Harris was a young boy his family moved to Rich, Mississippi. He began attending Baylor University in Waco, Texas, in 1960 while working as a crime reporter for the *Waco News-Tribune*. He married a fellow student, Harriet; they had one daughter before they divorced in the 1960s. He received a B.A. in English from Baylor in 1964, then worked for the Associated Press in New York between 1968 and 1974.

Harris wrote some short stories during his college years, but his first major work was the novel *Black Sunday* (1975), a thriller about a terrorist attempt to blow up the Super Bowl. The plot was devised by Harris along with two of his colleagues at Associated Press, Sam Maull and Dick Riley, and the three began writing it jointly before Harris took the project over himself. *Black Sunday* received mixed reviews but became a best-seller and was made into a commercially successful film by John Frankenheimer.

After a six-year interval Harris published his second novel, *Red Dragon* (1981), which also became a best-seller. In this novel he introduced the FBI agent Will Graham, who adopts a psychological method in tracking down a serial killer: he attempts to merge his mind with that of the criminal and thereby deduce his identity. This novel was also filmed successfully by Michael Mann as *Manhunter*.

With *The Silence of the Lambs* (1988), Harris achieved his greatest commercial and literary triumph. Also a best-seller, the novel was praised for its depth of characterization and complexity of plot. It involves the highly intelligent and blandly cynical serial killer Dr. Hannibal Lecter, whom Will Graham had earlier captured and who is now serving a life sentence in an asylum for the criminally insane. Lecter seems to know a great deal about another serial killer nicknamed Buffalo Bill, and as a result the young FBI agent Clarice M. Starling, who had been initially ordered to interrogate Lecter so as to produce a psychological profile of serial killers, becomes enmeshed in the case. *The Silence of the Lambs* was filmed by Jonathan Demme and starred Anthony Hopkins as Lecter and Jodie Foster as Starling.

Harris is known for the meticulous research he performs for his novels. For *The Silence of the Lambs* Harris went to the FBI training academy at Quantico and conducted many interviews, and he also studied the biology of moths, which are a critical plot element in the novel. His work has given rise to a lively debate as to whether his work should be classified as horror fiction or as mystery/suspense fiction. His popular success has led to the proliferation of novels about serial killers, although his own work is by no means exploitative or gratuitously violent. Harris has been at work on a fourth novel for some years. In summer he resides with his girlfriend, Pace Barnes, in Sag Harbor, Long Island, and in winter in Miami.

Critical Extracts

NEWGATE CALLENDAR   The Arabs ⟨. . .⟩ are today's universal villains and are celebrated as such in novel after novel, especially in crime novels. *Black Sunday*, in which Thomas Harris asks us to believe that the Black September group of Al Fatah will blow up a stadium during a Super Bowl game (taking the President of the United States along with other spectators), whips the Arab extremists with a leaded knout.

The premise is hard to take. Harris works on the assumption that the American people would withdraw their support from Israel if the caper succeeded. "The United States can't afford to be angry at the Arabs too long," he has the Israeli Ambassador saying. Oil, you know. But how divorced from reality can an author be? If Arab extremists actually did murder an American President, it would be an act of war that would see American troops squatting over those lovely oil fields a week later. And the extremists know that. ⟨. . .⟩

Black Sunday is written in a stolid, expository, unimaginative style in which dialogue is stilted and characterizations are as interesting as an old wad of chewing gum. There is no relieving touch, and Harris grimly plows on to end with conventional last-moment heroics.

Newgate Callendar, "Criminals at Large," *New York Times Book Review*, 2 February 1975, p. 14

JOHN SKOW   *Black Sunday,* a national bestseller by Thomas Harris, supposes an attempt to obliterate a Super Bowl football game (hurrah!) along with (alas!) both teams, the TV play-by-play and color men, beer vendors, pigeons, Pinkertons and some 100,000 spectators, including the President of the U.S. The sociopath who plans this provocation is not an Arab but a defecting American named Lander, who went sour while serving time as a P.O.W. in North Viet Nam. Now he pilots the advertising blimp that floats (aha!) above every important football contest. To get all the plastic explosive he needs, Lander applies to the Palestinians, an alarming people indeed: "Najeer . . . wore a hood of shadow. His hands were in the light and they toyed with a black commando knife. . . . 'Do it, Dahlia. Kill as many as you can.' "

The Gary Cooper role goes to Major Kabakov of the Israeli Secret Service, a tough mensch who (unlike the book's CIA men) is in no danger of stepping on his own necktie. Kabakov's stalking of Dahlia and Lander is competently described, violent, technically interesting and utterly predictable.

> John Skow, "Wild Easterns," *Time,* 26 May 1975, pp. 81–82

JOSEPH AMIEL   At the outset, suspicion should be set to rest that the chromatic titling of Thomas Harris's *Red Dragon* signals merely a louder-hued remake of his vastly successful novel of international terrorism, *Black Sunday.* This is a chilling, tautly written, and well-realized psychological thriller. ⟨. . .⟩

The suspense is sustained by deft characterizations, fascinating crime-lab details, a twisting plot, and understated prose.

> Joseph Amiel, [Review of *Red Dragon*], *Saturday Review,* 8, No. 1 (November 1981): 77

STEPHEN KING   *Red Dragon,* Thomas Harris' novel of a psychopath in the grip of the cannibalistic id-creature who lives inside him, is probably the best popular novel to be published in America since *The Godfather.* ⟨. . .⟩

Red Dragon summons to mind the best of James M. Cain, both in terms of the way the plot is cast and in those of the writing, which has the ferocious focus of a clean white light. Badly written popular novels sometimes work for me if the plot—the *story*—works in a new and fresh way; *Jaws* worked for me on precisely this level. But as important as story is, it can never replace that quality of writing which allows the reader to feel as if he has slipped into the driver's seat of a Rolls Royce, where everything is muted and everything works. Harris has it all working here; the prose ticks in such perfect time that the reader is amazed with delight. ⟨. . .⟩

The book has its flaws (this is the part you never read in any blurb); one admires Harris' research into police and forensic technique, but one finds it impossible to believe that the FBI can operate with such technocratic expertise—one doesn't doubt that they have the equipment, you understand, but just that such agents as Jack Crawford, who hauls Graham back into the game, exist. Reba McClane, the female lead, is a little too much like "the world's champion blind lady" in Frederick Knott's play *Wait Until Dark*—I was a lot more interested in Will Graham's good wife Molly.

But none of this negates the novel's raw, grisly power or its inescapable picture of a society which is on the verge of drowning in nonsensical violence; it does not negate Harris' delineation of Dolarhyde, the psychotic "human monster" who uses his grandmother's false teeth to bite his victims. Like the best popular fiction, the book simply comes at you and comes at you, finally leaving you shaken and sober and afraid on a deeper level than simple "thrills" alone furnish.

Stephen King, "The Cannibal and the Cop," *Washington Post Book World*, 1 November 1981, pp. 1–3

JEAN STROUSE   ⟨In *Red Dragon*⟩ Francis Dolarhyde, now 40, huge and strong, was born with a flat nose and bilateral fissures in his upper lip and palate—he looked "more like a leaf-nosed bat than a baby." Add a horrified mother, an orphange, a grandmother who kept threatening to cut his penis off with a scissors, and the singular cruelty of other children, and you have the perfect formula for pathological revenge. Astonishingly enough, Thomas Harris (author of *Black Sunday*) manages to make you sympathize with both Graham and Dolarhyde as he brings them inexorably to confrontation. Poor old D. fights hard against the hideous monster he becomes, and isn't that the ultimate scare—fear of our own monstrously negative capabilities? Gruesome, appalling, occasionally formulaic and mechanical, *Red Dragon* is guaranteed to terrify and succeed: Tony Perkins should play Dolarhyde in the movie.

> Jean Strouse, "Such a Cutup," *Newsweek*, 9 November 1981, pp. 105–6

THOMAS FLEMING   *Red Dragon* is an engine designed for one purpose—to make the pulses pound, the heart palpitate, the fear glands secrete. This is not immediately apparent. Things stay in first gear for a while. Will Graham, an ex-F.B.I. man who once specialized in finding mass murderers, is lured back to the Bureau to help catch a particularly nauseating madman, who has carved up two families—husband, wife and three children in each case. ⟨. . .⟩

But you begin to sense the engine's power, in spite of the inferior housing. The pistons surge into second gear as Graham prowls the houses of the victims and ponders the almost unbearable details of their meaningless deaths and the even less bearable data, gleaned from diaries and letters, of their ordinary family happiness. Acceleration continues as we meet Hannibal Lecter, a psychotic psychiatrist, also a mass murderer, whom Graham previously caught at the same gruesome game. ⟨. . .⟩

Those who read *Black Sunday*, Mr. Harris's first novel, about a Palestinian plot to inflict mass slaughter on the Super Bowl, may think *Red Dragon* has something to do with Red China. This dragon is apolitical. He emanates from the Apocalypse with an assist from William Blake, who portrayed him in one of his most bizarre paintings. Francis Dolarhyde becomes convinced that he is the dragon incarnate. This leads Mr. Harris to take a few Blakean swings at the nature of evil and the mysterious providence that unleashes mass murderers on the innocent. The philosophy is about as pertinent as Joseph Wambaugh's attempts at constructing a *Weltanschauung* from the cop on the beat, but it does not do any significant damage to Mr. Harris's engine.

> Thomas Fleming, "Hunting Monsters," *New York Times Book Review*, 15 November 1981, p. 14

JOHN KATZENBACH   Thomas Harris constructs his novels from the blackest regions of human experience. In his third novel, *The Silence* *of the Lambs*, the core of the book is the interaction among three characters—two mass murderers and the heroine, a young FBI trainee. Finding herself (not completely by accident) in an emotional vise defined by the two killers, she tries to use the one to find the other before he kills again. ⟨. . .⟩

It is Starling's own turbulent psychology that makes her fascinating to the mad Lecter, and it also is what makes her a gifted hunter. Much the same was true of Will Graham, the protagonist of *Red Dragon*—one difference being that Graham hated his potential as a hunter, while Starling is less aware of hers. A rather plucky heroine, equally undaunted by law enforcement bureaucracy and murderers, Starling is neither as deep nor as fully-realized a character as Graham—who was often at war with himself as much as with external evil.

As always, Harris is first-rate on tactics and equipment, skillfully blending the technical and the psychological. He also understands the nature of politics, especially when it interacts with crime. ⟨. . .⟩

The Silence of the Lambs is fast paced, intriguing and exciting. But those readers who want to clutch at their throats will be better served by Harris' previous book.

> John Katzenbach, "She Hunts for a Killer with a Killer at Her Side," *Chicago Tribune Books*, 14 August 1988, p. 7

DOUGLAS E. WINTER   ⟨*The Silence of the Lambs*⟩ is a superlative mystery, woven in loving detail with strands of psychology, forensic pathology, even entomology; but whether its solution is a matter of rational science is another matter. Harris rejects the conclusions of Dr. Joel Norris, whose recent nonfictional *Serial Killers* sought reassuringly to depict serial murder as a product of quantifiable disease. But let Harris's Dr. Lecter respond for himself: "Nothing happened to me, Officer Starling. *I* happened. You can't reduce me to a set of influences. You've given up good and evil for behaviorism. . . . You've got everybody in moral dignity pants—nothing is ever anybody's fault. Look at me, Officer Starling. Can you stand to say I'm evil?" ⟨. . .⟩

⟨. . .⟩ Harris works with a sparse intensity that often foregoes descriptive scene-setting and atmospherics. His characters live and breathe their surroundings; his prose is so convincing that we know them, and the places they inhabit, without needing to be told very much at all. *The Silence of the Lambs*, like *Red Dragon,* is a virtual textbook on the craft of suspense, a masterwork of sheer momentum that rockets seamlessly toward its climax.

Harris tells his story with the stunning and unflinching eye of a combat photographer. His point of view shifts with nervous irregularity but is drawn back, again and again, to the dark side—asylums, autopsy rooms and, finally, the charnel house of Buffalo Bill. Yet there are moments of sublime lyricism, as deft as poetry: Crawford's tired face "as sensitive to signals as the dished ruff of an owl, and as free of mercy"—or Starling's reaction as a lecherous psychologist proffers a brutal crime photo: "She thought of a thirsty chicken pecking tears off her face."

The Silence of the Lambs proves not so much a sequel as a continuation of *Red Dragon,* as remarkable as its predecessor in mingling the horror story with the police procedural to create some of the most powerful and entertaining fiction of our time. While *Red Dragon* was merciless in its gloom, an inward-spiraling descent into the heart of darkness, *The Silence of the Lambs* offers an optimistic, outward-bound escape from the maelstrom of a world gone mad.

Douglas E. Winter, "Anatomy of a Murderer," *Washington Post Book World,* 21 August 1988, pp. 3, 14

WILLIAM LEITH   *The Silence of the Lambs* is the best book ⟨by Harris⟩. When a fiendishly clever sex-killer goes on a nationwide multiple-murder rampage, the FBI realise that they have only one hope. The one way they can begin to crack the case is to ask the advice of Dr Hannibal Lecter. Lecter will be able to help them, they realise, partly because he is a top-grade psychiatrist. But Lecter's main strength as a consultant is that he is serving life for multiple murder, sex crimes and cannibalism. He is the world's expert.

We find out who the criminal is early on. That's not what keeps us going. The central mystery is *why* he is killing girls in his particular pattern. What does he want from them? They all seem to be quite large, for instance. Why is he flaying skin from different parts of each of their bodies? Why is he putting moths down their throat?

Another thing is that Harris has an excellent sense of how to match the most lurid and twisted activities with very down-to-earth practical details, like how long it would take somebody to drive from Minneapolis to Chicago and how much security there really is in a high-security jail. You find yourself feeling sick with the horror of it all, not because there's so much blood or perversion, but because you actually believe it could happen.

William Leith, "Terror Couple Kill Colonel," *Books* 3, No. 5 (August 1989): 11

CHET WILLIAMSON   *Red Dragon* is not an escape novel, for it refuses to let us escape. Instead, it makes us confront the worst in ourselves. It shows us the monster in the mirror, the one with our own face, smeared not with stage blood but with the naked emotions of hate and lust and murderous rage.

Along with its disturbing theme, *Red Dragon* is full of wicked pleasures. It is an intensely visual novel, rich with sound and color and telling use of small detail to make large points. All of its characters are brilliantly portrayed, and it is filled with gritty verisimilitude. Harris has done his homework, and it shows, but the fascinating investigative procedures never intrude upon the plot or slow the savage pace.

Awful and awesome things happen in this book, but we are not overwhelmed with descriptive and gory detail, for understatement is one of Harris's greatest virtues. He clearly understands the visions already resident in the imagination of his readers, so he tells us, simply and honestly, of the acts of Francis Dolarhyde. Then we move on, and the memories of what Harris may have allowed us to glimpse for only a moment resonate inside us for hours.

Chet Williamson, "Thomas Harris: *Red Dragon*," *Horror: 100 Best Books*, ed. Stephen Jones and Kim Newman (New York: Carroll & Graf, 1988), pp. 185–86

JOHN LANCHESTER   The real substance—somehow 'meat' wouldn't be the right word—of the book ⟨*The Silence of the Lambs*⟩ isn't in the murders and flayings, ⟨. . .⟩ but in the already-famous character of Hannibal Lecter, 'Hannibal the Cannibal', a genius psychiatrist, now incarcerated in the deepest available dungeon after having killed and eaten several of his patients. The bulk of *The Silence of the Lambs* is meticulous, even finicky, about accuracy. Harris is a former crime reporter for the Press Association, and it shows, in the relish with which he lets us know that 'the human skin constitutes about 16 and 18 per cent of body weight,' or when he goes into lepidopteral detail about the kind of moth the killer leaves in the throats of his victims.

Harris has also done his research on serial murderers: his flaying murderer has all sorts of traits and characteristics which come straight out of 'the literature' on the phenomenon. (He lures his victims to him by appearing to struggle with a heavy object while wearing a cast on his arm, a detail borrowed from the case of Ted Bundy, who raped and killed women in Seattle and Utah before being caught and sentenced in Florida; while committing his crimes Bundy also wrote a rape crisis manual for Washington state.) For the character of Lecter, however, Harris manages an even better thing than doing his homework: he simply ignores it. Lecter is straightforwardly a monster, bearing no relation to any murderer who ever lived, but achieving an archetypal quality through his brilliance and inexplicability: his mythic quality is as instantly apparent as, say, Sherlock Holmes's. Perhaps that is because he speaks to what Dennis Nilsen called our being bound together by a collective ignorance of what we are.

John Lanchester, "Strangers," *London Review of Books*, 11 July 1991, p. 5

JOE SANDERS   One frightening thing about Harris's world, lacking supernatural meaning or intent, is that monsters often are more successful initially than normal humans at getting what they want. Most people need the approval of their fellows or the sanction of some moral grace. The mentally abnormal interpret reality by private standards, which makes it much simpler to plan their actions. In *The Silence of the Lambs*, for example, readers soon learn that "Buffalo Bill" is actually Jame Gumb, who tans the skin from his victims into leather so he can stitch together a composite, perfect woman's skin. He believes that once he is finished he will be able to slip into it and become a woman. He is certain that accomplishing this will make him popular; for example, he wants no ugly seam along the spine of his leather garment because "it was not inconceivable that an attractive person might be hugged." Meanwhile, Dr. Frederick Chilton, Dr. Lecter's keeper at the Baltimore State Hospital for the Criminally Insane, is no less lonely, but considerably less practical. Dr. Chilton first imagines that he can sexually entice Starling, then that he can gain fame by manipulating Dr. Lecter into revealing Buffalo Bill's identity. Neither man's goal is achievable in the long term; however, the less "normal" Gumb is happier with himself and sustains his activities longer than Dr. Chilton's foolish attempt to control Dr. Lecter. And even Chilton feels less confused and frustrated than the abnormally fixated Crawford and Starling.

In the long run, though, living without the comfort of deluded certainty may be more productive. Gumb and Chilton eventually fail because they see people around them as merely objects to satisfy their desires. Crawford and Starling, even when they are trying to get someone to do what they want, respect the other person's values and needs. Thus Crawford knows how to manipulate his assistants' emotions to get their loyalty, but he tries not to overwhelm Starling. Even though he would enjoy the role of father/mentor, he realizes that it is not what Starling needs: "He knew that a middle-aged man can be so desperate for wisdom he may try to make some up, and how deadly that can be to a youngster who believes him. So he spoke carefully, and only of things he knew." Difficult as this is, respecting another's independence not only encourages and maintains good social relationships, but it also helps the other person to establish a stable sense of self. During the novel, supported by Crawford (and egged on by Dr. Lecter), Starling realizes how much she still feels pain and anger at the absence of her father, a lawman who was killed when she was a small child. However, she manages to draw on memories of both her parents to put together a mature, integrated understanding of who she is.

Sometimes, however, achieving that kind of realistic but limited self-awareness isn't enough. To locate Buffalo Bill/Gumb, Starling must leave the safety of the self she understands to extend herself into the consciousness of someone whose needs and values are *different*, even horrifying. And that means admitting desires that have been repressed, denied. To put oneself figuratively inside the skin of a person who violates the rules of decent behavior, one must accept that all possibilities are present in oneself. Doing this is extremely dangerous to the manhunter's stability. That was how Will Graham caught Dr. Lecter and the Red Dragon, but doing so destroyed him. Dr. Lecter himself has survived by shedding his human sympathy so that he lives purely for selfish amusement, for satisfying his curiosity about the taste of some novel experience. Consequently, Dr. Lecter does cooperate with Starling in exchange for information about her own life, during which she reveals how much pain she experiences in witnessing suffering. He is especially fascinated to hear how, as a child, she ran away with an old horse that was being fattened to be sold for dog food, and how she was spurred on by hearing spring lambs scream as they were slaughtered. In return, Dr. Lecter gives Starling the clue she needs to find Jame Gumb before he can kill again.

Helping Starling does not make Dr. Lecter less monstrous. It is not so much that he is humanized by contact with her as that giving sympathy is a novel, thus amusing, possibility for Dr. Lecter to entertain. But if he moves no closer to Starling—and, by extension, the readers—he cannot be dismissed either. For we discover that we have extended ourselves to *him*. Having escaped thanks to Chilton's blundering, Dr. Lecter writes a last letter to Starling during which he says, "I have no plans to call on you, Clarice, the world being more interesting with you in it. Be sure you extend me the same courtesy." On the face of it, this is a warning: I won't pursue you if you don't pursue me. However, it also suggests that just as Dr. Lecter is interested by what Starling's character shows about the possibilities of human behavior, so also Starling—and readers—may be interested by what Dr. Lecter's behavior shows about the possibilities of human nature.

Joe Sanders, "At the Frontiers of the Fantastic: Thomas Harris's *The Silence of the Lambs*," *New York Review of Science Fiction* No. 39 (November 1991): 3–4

S. T. JOSHI   *Black Sunday* (1975) is a mere potboiler, with a preposterous premise—terrorists wish to blow up the Super Bowl from a blimp—and stereotypical characters (Dahlia Iyad, the fanatical Palestinian terrorist; Michael Lander, the embittered Vietnam War vet who seeks nothing but death and destruction; David Kabakov, the ruthless Israeli secret service agent who foils the plot). It has only one point of interest: early on a portion of a chapter is devoted to a psychological history of Lander from infancy onward, supplying the inner motives for his actions and desires. It is written in a clinical, almost emotionless manner, but it nevertheless provides the necessary psychological motivation for the entire novel.

Harris developed this idea in a rather ingenious way in *Red Dragon* (1981). The premise of this novel is the attempt by Will Graham, a semi-retired FBI agent, to hunt down a serial killer by adopting the mindset of the criminal. Graham has an unusual sensitivity to other people's minds (it must be emphasized that this idea is not presented as in any way supernatural or occult, and Graham is far from the "psychic detectives" who lumber implausibly through some of the work of Algernon Blackwood, William

Hope Hodgson, and others), and the FBI, stumped in the matter, feel that this may be the only way to capture the killer.

This premise is, as I say, ingenious, but I wonder whether in fact it is actually carried out. That is to say, does Graham really solve the case, or any part of it, by entering the criminal's mind? It seems to me that what Graham really does is simply to interpret the physical evidence more thoroughly, sensitively, and keenly than others have. ⟨. . .⟩ If Harris or his supporters think that he has invented some "new" form of detection, then he and they had better think again.

But this is not what I wish to study here. What (if anything) makes this a weird tale? Chet Williamson, both a sharp commentator and a gifted weird fictionist, has written of this novel that it is "quite simply, the most frightening book I have ever read". I suppose I cannot quarrel with Williamson on what he finds frightening, and it is, I trust, not because I am exceptionally hardened that I did not find anything particularly frightening in this book. The work is highly compelling, but it is a work of detection and suspense and not horror. Much of the novel is given over to a very careful forensic analysis of evidence, until finally sufficient clues are found to identify the murderer. Harris, with unusual restraint for a popular writer, has not even peppered this novel with much overt violence: the murders have already occurred at the start of the book, and we can only infer their loathsomeness from the gradual accumulation of evidence.

It is, I imagine, this whole notion of trying to enter the twisted mind of a serial killer that is supposed to generate horror in this work, and there are occasions when Harris attempts to invest this action with portentous shudders. Graham's great triumph is the capture of Dr Hannibal Lecter, a highly learned but fiercely cynical and misanthropic psychiatrist who sports the charming soubriquet of "Hannibal the Cannibal". Graham actually seeks Lecter's advice on the serial killings, and Lecter delivers a parting shot: "The reason you caught me is that we're *just alike.*" ⟨. . .⟩ This sets the stage for a psychological history of the killer very much like that in *Black Sunday*; and it is here that the parallels to ⟨Robert Bloch's⟩ *Psycho* become striking. The killer, Francis Dolarhyde, was an orphan who was raised by a hideous and tyrannical grandmother who made fun of his speech impediment and who once threatened to cut off his penis with scissors when she found him as a young boy exposing himself to a little girl. Although Dolarhyde certainly does not resurrect his grandmother's body like Norman Bates, he seems to have preserved her false teeth (one suddenly thinks of Poe's "Berenice"), and he pretends to have self-tormenting conversations with his grandmother very similar to Bates'; Dolarhyde fancies that it is the grandmother who is urging him to kill a young blind woman, Reba McClane, who has taken a romantic interest in him:

> "YOU MAY PUT AWAY MY TEETH. YOU PITIFUL LITTLE
> HARELIP, YOU'D KEEP YOUR LITTLE BUDDY FROM ME,
> WOULD YOU? I'LL TEAR HER APART AND RUB THE
> PIECES IN YOUR UGLY FACE. I'LL HANG YOU WITH HER
> LARGE INTESTINE IF YOU OPPOSE ME. YOU KNOW I
> CAN."

But Dolarhyde is tracked down, Reba is saved, and Lecter's plot to have Graham's wife killed is foiled.

S. T. Joshi, "Weird Tales?," *Armchair Detective* 26, No. 1 (Winter 1993): 98–99

▨ *Bibliography*

Black Sunday. 1975.
Red Dragon. 1981.
The Silence of the Lambs. 1988.

Patricia Highsmith
1921–1995

MARY PATRICIA HIGHSMITH was born in Fort Worth, Texas, on January 19, 1921, and grew up in New York. Her parents, Jay Bernard Plangman and Mary (Coates) Plangman, were both commercial artists, as was her stepfather (whose name she adopted after her mother's remarriage), and she herself engaged in drawing and painting before deciding to devote herself to writing. After receiving a B.A. from Barnard College in 1942, she worked as a freelance writer on comic books while publishing occasional short stories. Her first novel, *Strangers on a Train* (1950), provided the basis for one of Alfred Hitchcock's finest films.

Highsmith's second novel, *The Price of Salt,* appeared in 1952. Because of its lesbian subject matter, Highsmith published it under a pseudonym, Claire Morgan. It was reissued in 1984 under her own name, with a new afterword by the author, and in 1990 it was published in England under the title *Carol.*

The Talented Mr. Ripley (1955), Highsmith's fourth novel, was the first in a series of works about the clumsy but likable murderer Tom Ripley. It was filmed as *Purple Noon* (1961) and was followed by four sequels, *Ripley under Ground* (1970), *Ripley's Game* (1974), *The Boy Who Followed Ripley* (1980), and *Ripley under Water* (1991). *Ripley's Game* was filmed as *The American Friend* (1978).

The Ripley novels are, however, not entirely representative of Highsmith's work, which is grim, cheerless, and tautly written, focusing on the psychology of guilt and the effects of crime upon individuals and upon society at large. She encapsulated her theories and practice of suspense writing in *Plotting and Writing Suspense Fiction* (1966).

Highsmith received more recognition in Europe than in America, and after visits in the 1950s she lived in France, England, and Switzerland from 1963 onward. In 1957 she was awarded the Grand Prix de Littérature Policière for *The Talented Mr. Ripley* and, in 1964, the Crime Writers Association of England Silver Dagger Award for *The Two Faces of January.*

In some of her recent work, including *Edith's Diary* (1977) and *Found in the Street* (1986), the crime element was reduced to a minimum.

Highsmith also wrote several volumes of short stories: *The Snail-Watcher and Other Stories* (1970), *The Animal Lover's Book of Beastly Murder* (1975), *Little Tales of Misogyny* (1977), *Slowly, Slowly in the Wind* (1979), *Mermaids on the Golf Course and Other Stories* (1985), and *Tales of Natural and Unnatural Catastrophes* (1987). Many of these stories are not in the crime or suspense field at all but are instead tales of fantasy, horror, and sardonic comedy.

Patricia Highsmith died in Locarno, Switzerland, on February 5, 1995.

◈ Critical Extracts

UNSIGNED   Miss Highsmith's novel ⟨*Strangers on a Train*⟩ is easily one of this year's most sinister items. It has its obvious faults. It is not always credible, and the characters are not entirely consistent. Nevertheless, it is a highly persuasive book. Guy Haines, a young architect, is going back to Texas to persuade his estranged wife Miriam into a divorce. On the train he meets a ne'er-do-well, Charles Bruno, and for some reason tells him his life story. In his turn, he learns that Bruno has a father whom he hates and a mother whom he adores unreasonably, and that his mind verges on the psychopathic. When Bruno proposes that he kill Guy's wife, and that Guy in turn kill Bruno's father, Guy turns the proposition down with disgust and sees no more of him. Then later, Guy's wife is killed, and in a short while he gets a letter which makes it clear that Bruno is the murderer. It is also clear that he now expects Guy to kill for him. The rest of the novel is Bruno's slow and unremitting campaign to force Guy into carrying out his part of their imagined and deadly bargain. Reduced to its skeleton, the plot is exposed in all its incredibility. But as one reads it page by page throughout a full length novel, one is held by an evil kind of suspense. It becomes more believable than one would suppose—a rarely perceptive study in criminal psychology.

Unsigned, [Review of *Strangers on a Train*], *New York Herald Tribune Book Review*, 16 April 1950, p. 26

FRANCIS WYNDHAM   Miss Highsmith writes murder stories which are literally that: stories about murder. They are about what drives people to kill and about what the event of murder is like for the killer and for the people connected with him and his victim. It is rare for death to occur in a Highsmith novel until at least a third of the book is past; often it is reserved for the very end. When it takes place, her readers are made aware not only of the horror, but also of the *embarrassment* following an act of destructive violence; it is as if a person one knows quite well were suddenly killed by somebody else one knows quite well. And although Miss Highsmith makes the most scrupulous psychological preparation for her murders, so that their eruption is never unconvincing, yet the effect on her readers is shocking in the same kind of way as the experience of murder would be in life. For very rarely, in life, can murder be expected; yet it happens.

Guilt is her theme, and she approaches it through two contrasting heroes. These may be simplified as the guilty man who has justified his guilt and the innocent man who feels himself to be guilty. Both appeared in her first and most famous novel, *Strangers on a Train*: the soft, plausible charmer who is really a psychopath and the shy bungler who allows himself to be engulfed in a nightmare from which he is too ineffectual (and perhaps basically unwilling) to extricate himself. Variations on one or other of these mutually attractive figures dominate her later books: *The Blunderer, A Game for the Living* and *The Cry of the Owl* concentrate on the victim of malign events who is hypnotised into immobility by the horror of his situation; while *The Talented Mr Ripley, Deep Water* and *This Sweet Sickness* provide full-length portraits of the well-spoken young man, somehow incomplete and yet not apparently sinister, who slithers into mania and murder. The books in the first group also contain a detective whose behaviour is capricious, irrational yet depressingly dogged; this figure is the more menacing because he is invariably wrong. Miss Highsmith specialises in male characters, but two types of women recur throughout her work: the bitch and the nice girl. The bitch (Melinda in *Deep Water*, Nickie in *The Cry of the Owl*) can be a creature of Strindbergian venom, compensating for some mysterious sexual outrage or disappointment by the total destruction of a man. The nice girl (Marge in *Mr Ripley*, Effie in *This Sweet Sickness*, Jenny in *The Cry of the Owl*) is intense, affectionate, rather arty, and fatally unsuspicious.

Francis Wyndham, "Miss Highsmith," *New Statesman*, 31 May 1963, pp. 833–34

PATRICIA HIGHSMITH   The suspense writer can improve his lot and the reputation of the suspense novel by putting into his books the qualities that have always made books good—insight, character, an opening of new horizons for the imagination of the reader. I do not speak, in this paragraph, about mystery books, because they are out of my line, and it is a characteristic of them that the identity of the murderer is withheld, or at any rate his character as murderer is not deeply explored, if at all. If a suspense writer is going to write about murders and victims, about people in the vortex of this awful whirl of events, he should do more than describe brutality and gore and the gooseflesh in the night. He should throw some light on his characters' minds; he should be interested in justice or the absence of it in the world we live in; he should be interested in the morality, good and bad, that exists today; he should be interested in human cowardice or courage, and not merely as forces to push his plot this way and that. In a word, his people should be real. This seriousness may sound at variance with the element of playing that I mentioned in regard to plot, but it is not, since I am talking of another matter. The spirit of playing is necessary in plotting to permit freedom of the imagination. It is also necessary in inventing characters. But once one *has* the characters in mind, and the plot, the characters should be given most serious consideration, and one should pay attention to what they are doing and why, and if one does not explain it—and it may be artistically bad to explain too much—then a writer should know why his characters behave as they do and should be able to answer this question to himself. It is by this that insight is born, by this that the book acquires value. Insight is not something found in psychology books; it is in every creative person. And—see Dostoyevsky—writers are decades ahead of the textbooks, anyway.

It often happens that a writer has a theme or a pattern in his books, and he should be aware of this, though again not in a hampering way. He should be aware of it so as to exploit it well, and so as not to repeat it without realizing it. Some writers' themes may be a quest for something—a father one never knew, the pot of gold which does not exist at the foot of the rainbow. Others may have a recurrent girl-in-distress motif, which starts them off plotting, and without which they are not exactly comfortable writing. Another is a doomed love or a doomed marriage. Mine is the relationship between two men, usually quite different in make-up, sometimes obviously the good and the evil, sometimes merely ill-matched friends. I might have realized this theme in myself at least by the middle of *Strangers on a Train*, but it was a friend, a newspaperman, who pointed it out to me when I was twenty-six and just beginning *Strangers*, a man who had seen the manuscript of my first effort at twenty-two that I have already mentioned, the book that was never finished. This was about a rich, spoiled boy, and a poor boy who wanted to be a painter. They were fifteen years old in the book. As if that weren't enough, there were two minor characters, a tough, athletic boy who seldom attended school (and then only to shock the school with things like the bloated corpse of a drowned dog he had found on the banks of the East River) and a puny, clever boy who giggled a great deal and adored him and was always in his company. The two-men theme turned up also in *The Blunderer*, *The Talented Mr. Ripley*, in *A Game for the Living*, and *The Two Faces of January*, and raises its head a little in *The Glass Cell* in the curious comrades-in-social-defiance attitude between Carter and Gawill. So in six books out of ten it has turned up, certainly in my "best" books in public opinion. Natural themes cannot be sought or strained for; they appear. Unless one is in danger of repeating oneself, they should be used to the fullest, because a writer will write better making use of what is, for some strange reason, innate.

Patricia Highsmith, *Plotting and Writing Suspense Fiction* (Boston: The Writer, Inc., 1966), pp. 143–46

GRAHAM GREENE   Miss Highsmith is a crime novelist whose books one can read many times. There are very few of whom one can say that. She is a writer who has created a world of her own—a world claustrophobic and irrational which we enter each time with the sense of personal danger, with the head half turned over the shoulder, even with a certain reluctance, for these are cruel pleasures we are going to experience, until somewhere about the third chapter the frontier is closed behind us, we cannot retreat, we are doomed to live till the story's end with another of her long series of wanted men.

It makes the tension worse that we are never sure whether even the worst of them, like the talented Mr. Ripley, won't get away with it or that the relatively innocent won't suffer like the blunderer Walter or the relatively guilty escape altogether like Sydney Bartleby in *The Story-Teller*. This is a world without moral endings. It has nothing in common with the heroic world of her peers, Hammett and Chandler, and her detectives (sometimes monsters of cruelty like the American Lieutenant Corby of *The Blunderer* or dull sympathetic rational characters like the British Inspector Brockway) have nothing in common with the romantic and disillusioned private eyes who will always, we know, triumph finally over evil and see that justice is done, even though they may have to send a mistress to the chair.

Nothing is certain when we have crossed *this* frontier. It is not the world as we once believed we knew it, but it is frighteningly more real to us than the house next door. Actions are sudden and impromptu and the motives sometimes so inexplicable that we simply have to accept them on trust. I believe because it is impossible. Her characters are irrational, and they leap to life in their very lack of reason; suddenly we realise how unbelievably rational most fictional characters are as they lead their lives from A to Z, like commuters always taking the same train. The motives of these are never inexplicable because they are so drearily obvious. The characters are as flat as a mathematical symbol. We accepted them as real once, but when we look back at them from Miss Highsmith's side of the frontier, we realise that our world was not really as rational as all that. Suddenly with a sense of fear we think, "Perhaps I really belong *here*," and going out into the familiar street we pass with a shiver of apprehension the offices of the American Express, the centre, for so many of Miss Highsmith's dubious men, of their rootless European experience, where letters are to be picked up (though the name on the envelope is probably false) and travellers' cheques are to be cashed (with a forged signature).

> Graham Greene, "Introduction," *The Snail-Watcher and Other Stories* by Patricia Highsmith (Garden City, NY: Doubleday, 1970), pp. xi–xii

---

BRIGID BROPHY   Taken (which it could but I don't think should be) purely as a novel of suspense, *A Dog's Ransom* is a virtuoso piece. Miss Highsmith is in such command that she can actually do without mystery and still compel you to read urgently on. ⟨. . .⟩

What *A Dog's Ransom* counts on, to carry the reader, is the soundness of its construction. Before quite renouncing mystery by entering the psychopath's mind, it establishes the strategic centres from which it is going to explore the responses forced from the sane by erratic and lunatic acts of violence. Ed Reynolds is at first unambivalent, concerned simply and reasonably for the safety of his dog. The narrative builds up his plausibility by an engaging circumstantialness about his actions; and by the same token it evokes, without needing to describe, the physical grittiness and social unease of New York: 'He had just come from the office, and as he let the water rinse away the soap, he thought: "I'm washing my hands of the subway and also of that damned letter." ' ⟨. . .⟩

The intellectual effort that goes into (and the intellectual profit that a reader can take from) a novel lies not in the overt statements of the narrative and dialogue but in the power of the thought incarnated in the design. No more than it describes New York does A Dog's Ransom make statements about society and violence. Yet it is a profound act of thought on the theme of violence seducing its opponents into violence. Statistics might affirm that the problem is most acute in New York: A Dog's Ransom can achieve the *imaginative* rightness of being set there. Sociology and reporting, with their wide scatter, can set out contradictions in moral attitudes: A Dog's Ransom performs the indispensable function of fiction by taking the reader deep into the ironies of his own ambivalence.

Brigid Brophy, "Poodle," *Listener*, 11 May 1973, p. 627

LOUIS FINGER   Edith ⟨in *Edith's Diary*⟩ is a well-off, Left-progressive, middle-middle-class housewife, a busy and capable manager, a loyal wife, and a genial and tolerant mother to her only child. When the book opens, the family is packing to leave for a new house in the country, where Brett's salary will be lower but the air less polluted, where there will be space for the boy to grow up in and opportunity for her and Brett to start their own Left-progressive town newspaper and in their small way maybe do some good. It sounds a reliable recipe for a distinctive type of American good life. Edith writes optimistically about the move in the diary she's been keeping for some years.

It's a fairly typical Highsmith opening, so when the packing is interrupted briefly by the sound of the boy Cliffie tormenting the cat, or when Edith reflects idly on an ugly dream she's had a few nights earlier, we settle down to wait for the menace to start building up. And this is more or less where we stay throughout the book. Things happen: Brett's old uncle is moved into the house and proves demanding and irritating; Cliffie grows more and more sullen and disaffected; Brett falls in love with his secretary and goes off with her; there are deaths in the family and quarrels with neighbours;

there are the impinging political upheavals of Vietnam, Watergate, and so on.

Summed up, it's a fairly ordinary sequence of events; and, although the neutral, itemising clarity of Highsmith's prose hints all the time that an eruption is just around the corner, the book's real shock effect is registered precisely through the steady lifelessness of the lives it so inertly charts. Gradually we are made aware that there are two ways of describing Edith's life, and that the second way—the way that sees it as horribly devoured by odious dependents—is the way Edith can't afford to contemplate. Hence her diary, in which she invents a successful career for her son, arranges a satisfactory marriage, two fine children, frequent loving visits to the old homestead. The keeping of the diary and the clinging to the last meticulous, desperate detail of her imprisoning routine is what she hopes will keep her sane; and, of course, if that effort fails, she'll be the last to know. As the pressure intensifies, the most mundane domestic function is made to seem like an icy little melodrama. It's not going to be easy from now on for Miss Highsmith to scare us with mere murder.

Louis Finger, "Mere Murder," New Statesman, 1 July 1977, pp. 23–24

ERLENE HUBLY   Patricia Highsmith's artists, those characters who create works of art and often themselves in the process, form, even when compared to some of her other protagonists, a unique group of characters. There is Sydney Bartleby, the writer-hero of A *Suspension of Mercy*, who in order to stimulate his imagination, plans the imaginary murder of his wife, an endeavor which he then proceeds to act out as though it were so. His ruse is so successful that both his friends and the authorities think he has murdered his wife, as does he himself at times. There is Howard Ingham, the writer-hero of *The Tremor of Forgery*, who, again, in order to excite his imagination, deliberately lives in a dangerous place, Tunisia, in order to undergo new and dark passions, committing, possibly, even a murder, so that he can write about his experiences. And there is, above all others, the character of Tom Ripley, who if he is not a writer, is an actor, a master of the art of impersonation. It is this art, when coupled with the act of murder, that enables Ripley not only to kill a wealthy young American, Dickie Greenleaf, and then to pose as him, but also to provide for his own future security as well, Ripley producing, after Dickie's death, a will, forged, of course, by him, in which Dickie Greenleaf leaves all his money to his good friend, Tom Ripley. Indeed, Highsmith's artists display her ingenuity at its best, allowing her to fashion plots that dazzle the reader with their inventiveness. In addition, Highsmith's artists get the reader closer to the heart of her fictional world perhaps better than any other of her characters. For by examining her artists, we explore some of her major themes: the nature of identity; homosexuality; the real versus the imagined world; the effect of a foreign country on the Americans who live there. ⟨. . .⟩

If murder stimulates Highsmith's writers' imaginations, it can do so because of their peculiar view of reality. For Highsmith's artists, having manipulated reality for so long through the act of writing, masters at turning the real into fiction, live in a fluid world where few things are clearly defined. Sydney Bartleby, for example, often has difficulty distinguishing the real from the imagined and at times thinks that real conversations he is having with real people are imaginary ones, the words being spoken sounding "like lines in a play they were performing." His efforts at creating fiction, of acting out and experiencing the murder of Alicia, are so successful that he convinces himself that she is dead. And at the height of his difficulties with the police, when asked by Inspector Brockway if he did kill his wife, Bartleby can barely answer "no," feels as if his imagined murder of her is real, that he has "only hours more of freedom" before he is arrested for the crime of murder. The line between the real and the imagined becomes so blurred in Bartleby's mind that later, when he commits a real murder, that of Edward Tilbury, the man with whom Alicia had lived while she was at Brighton, he does so with less effort and with fewer feelings of guilt than he experienced when he committed the imaginary murder of Alicia. Indeed, it is his imagined murder that affects him most deeply.

Erlene Hubly, "A Portrait of the Artist: The Novels of Patricia Highsmith," *Clues* 5, No. 1 (Spring–Summer 1984): 115–17

KATHLEEN GREGORY KLEIN   A key to both *Strangers* ⟨*on a Train*⟩ and Highsmith's inversion of the standard techniques of the genre can be found in Guy Haines' profession. As an architect he is concerned with design, order, harmony and honesty. When he rejects a beach club commission because of Miriam's new entanglement in his life, Guy is genuinely pained to think of the imitation Frank Lloyd Wright building which will replace his perfect conception; in designing his own Y-shaped house, he refused necessary economies which would truncate the building. His work is, for him, a spiritual act, defined by unity and wholeness; it rejects disorder, fragmentation and shallowness. Contrasted in the two sections of the book are his description of the bridge he hopes to build as the climax of his career and his inability to accept the commission when telegraphed an offer. His dream of a great white bridge with a span like angels' wings is shattered when his feeling of corruption keeps him from his talent.

In Highsmith's fictional world, issues of order, harmony or civilization—whatever it is called—are seldom so simple and traditional. Contrasted with the more stereotyped perspective which Guy accepts is her series character Tom Ripley. His notions of order are equally predictable; Bach, or classical music in general, provides the right stimuli to focus his attention, distill and concentrate his mind. Ripley uses these devices, however sincerely he may value them as entities in themselves, as personal preparations for crime: fraud, theft, murder. Not so amoral, Guy uses them as avoidance mechanisms; he refuses to consider trying to create perfect order out of his own disordered mind. These attitudes toward order mark Highsmith's vacillating and threatening challenge to oversimplified theories of order and disorder, harmony and chaos. Never committing her fiction to either the triumph of order or the inevitability of chaos, she creates worlds which misuse both, locations in which both are equally and simultaneously present; in fact, she suggests that they may be indistinguishable. Highsmith's manipulation of these dualities suggests closer parallels with contemporary absurdists and existentialists than with her colleagues in crime or suspense fiction. Challenging the either/or structure of human thinking in a work ostensibly about a pair of murders and murderers is part of Highsmith's conscious expansion of an established genre into a new and provocative form.

> Kathleen Gregory Klein, "Patricia Highsmith," *And Then There Were Nine . . .: More Women of Mystery*, ed. Jane S. Bakerman (Bowling Green, OH: Bowling Green State University Popular Press, 1985), pp. 176–77

SUSANNAH CLAPP   *Carol* is a novel about a lesbian love-affair, and was written shortly after *Strangers on a Train*, which was branded by Harper as 'A Harper Novel of Suspense'. Anxious not to be relabelled as 'a lesbian-book writer', Highsmith submitted the manuscript under a pseudonym: Harper turned it down. She changed publishers, and the book appeared in 1952. It was called 'The Price of Salt' and was said to be by Claire Morgan; it received 'respectable' reviews, piles of fan mail, and sold a million copies in paperback. It is a romance which reads almost exactly like a Patricia Highsmith thriller.

Highsmith got the idea for *Carol* in 1948, when she was 27. She had finished her first novel, was broke and fed up, and had taken a job in a Manhattan department store. She was sent to work in the toy department, on the dolls' counter—where all those floppy or morbidly stiff little limbs and those rows of glassy eyeballs must have appealed to her. One day a blonde woman in a mink coat came into the store. She was elegant and a little uncertain. She bought a doll, gave a delivery name and address, and left. 'It was a routine transaction . . . But I felt cold and swimmy in the head, near to fainting, yet at the same time uplifted, as if I had seen a vision.' Highsmith went home and wrote out the entire plot of *Carol*, which begins with a meeting between a salesgirl and a glamorous older woman in the toy department of a large store, spills out across the North American continent, as the two women decide to go travelling together (at first simply as friends, later as lovers), and ends with the couple looking as if they will try to settle down together. ⟨. . .⟩

Like her murderers, Highsmith's lovers make their dreams come true. In *Strangers on a Train* Bruno imagines committing the perfect murder ('the idea of my life'), and then does it. In *Carol* the 19-year-old shop assistant fantasises about kissing the beautiful older woman—who has money, a husband, a child and a huge house—and ends up running off with her. In many novels such success would be punished, but in Highsmith's fiction people get away with things. Tom Ripley begins a murderous career by drowning one acquaintance and battering another—and then swans off to a Greek island. Therese and Carol are vilified and threatened by husbands, lovers and lawyers, but finally decide they can manage a future together. It was this glimmer of a happy ending that attracted early readers of *Carol*. 'Prior to this book,' Highsmith reflects, 'homosexuals male and female in American novels had had to pay for their deviation by cutting their wrists, drowning themselves in a swimming-pool, or by switching to heterosexuality (so it was stated), or by collapsing—alone and miserable and shunned—into a depression equal to hell.'

Susannah Clapp, "Lovers on a Train," *London Review of Books*, 10 January 1991, p. 19

NOEL DORMAN MAWR   In her *The Glass Cell* (1964), Highsmith
depicts a naïve protagonist first victimized by criminals, then corrupted by
the prison environment in which he is unjustly confined. That Highsmith's
focus on society begins to usurp her earlier vision of isolated criminality is
underlined by her using *The Glass Cell* as the one extended example of her
creative process in her 1966 how-to book, *Plotting and Writing Suspense
Fiction* (wherein she speaks of one of the "elements" of the story as "the
deleterious effect of exposure to brutality in prison, and how this can lead
to anti-social behavior after release"). Her next two novels, excluding the
1970 *Ripley under Ground* and the 1974 *Ripley's Game*, continue the new
interest in social forces: *The Tremor of Forgery* (1969) depicts the effects of
the alien view of criminality in Tunisian society on an American, and *A
Dog's Ransom* (1972) is an obsessive portrait of a crime-ridden New York
City which corrupts and destroys decent human beings. Three of Highsmith's
four most recent novels (*The Boy Who Followed Ripley* is the exception) are
set in the United States (and the latest Ripley novel ends there), and none
focuses primarily on criminals. All (*Edith's Diary*, 1977; *People Who Knock
on the Door*, 1983; and *Found in the Street*, 1986) depict a society in which
most people are either obsessed with fanatical religious or political beliefs or
are turned inward toward totally self-serving, socially irresponsible behavior.
Both orientations can lead to criminality, and they do so in these books.
The evolution of the picture of crime and society which occurs in the Ripley
novels is consistent with the evolution occurring in Highsmith's other works.
But, while Ripley's perception of society seems to parallel Highsmith's, his
perception of himself does not.

One must remember the irony: Tom Ripley may be right about the world,
but he is still thoroughly lacking in insight into Tom Ripley. His motives
are, ultimately, the strictly personal ones of his need for the stimulation of
danger and, still, for occasionally losing his identity in a masquerade of
some kind. These last Ripley novels are not works of social criticism. Patricia
Highsmith remains the novelist of the psychological portrayal of criminal
behavior. She has simply moved, over the years, toward a more social
orientation—to a greater awareness of the effects of society on behavior.

Noel Dorman Mawr, "From Villain to Vigilante," *Armchair Detective* 24, No. 1
(Winter 1991): 38

PAT DOWELL   *Ripley under Water* finds Tom settling down to enjoy the fruits of his labor in the lovely little house called Belle Ombre near Fontainebleau. Ever polite in his nippy, slightly aggrieved way, Tom is still studying the harpsichord and puttering about his garden, when the past is deposited on his doorstep by a couple of twitchy neighbors, the Pritchards. They are Americans, of course, who have fixed on Tom as a shady character. A chilling game of cat and mouse ensues, involving an old bag of bones, a pretty little pond and a trip to Morocco.

Once past some surprisingly clumsy paragraphs recapping Tom's past accomplishments, *Ripley under Water* is a satisfying example of Highsmith's special talent for inhabiting the anxious, self-absorbed world of a mind that has never quite internalized society's rules. Tom is always calculating even the most casual act of *politesse*, and when violence comes, as it must, it is often realistically improvised, a kind of grisly faux pas that Tom diligently shrugs off. Passion is not a part of his makeup, but he's compelling all the same. A Ripley novel is not to be safely recommended to the weakminded or impressionable.

Highsmith, an expatriate Texan who now lives in Switzerland, is much admired as a modern novelist in Europe, and yet she is still consigned here to the secondary rank of mystery writers. *Ripley under Water*, which doesn't depart radically from her previous two dozen books, probably won't change that. It falls somewhere in the middle of the Ripley books in terms of quality, but that makes it a cut above almost everyone else.

Pat Dowell, "Gentleman with a Past," *Washington Post Book World*, 18 October 1992, p. 9

◈ *Bibliography*

Strangers on a Train. 1950.
The Price of Salt ⟨Carol⟩. 1952.
The Blunderer. 1954.
The Talented Mr. Ripley. 1955.
Deep Water. 1957.
A Game for the Living. 1958.
Miranda, the Panda, Is on the Veranda (with Doris Sanders). 1958.
This Sweet Sickness. 1960.

The Cry of the Owl. 1962.

The Two Faces of January. 1964.

The Glass Cell. 1964.

The Story-Teller (A Suspension of Mercy). 1965.

Plotting and Writing Suspense Fiction. 1966, 1981.

Those Who Walk Away. 1967.

The Tremor of Forgery. 1969.

The Snail-Watcher and Other Stories (Eleven). 1970.

Ripley under Ground. 1970.

A Dog's Ransom. 1972.

Ripley's Game. 1974.

The Animal Lover's Book of Beastly Murder. 1975.

Edith's Diary. 1977.

Little Tales of Misogyny. 1977.

Slowly, Slowly in the Wind. 1979.

The Boy Who Followed Ripley. 1980.

The Black House. 1981.

People Who Knock on the Door. 1983.

The Mysterious Mr. Ripley (The Talented Mr. Ripley, Ripley under Ground, Ripley's Game). 1985.

Mermaids on the Golf Course and Other Stories. 1985.

Found in the Street. 1986.

Tales of Natural and Unnatural Catastrophes. 1987.

Folie à Deux: Three Novels (Strangers on a Train, The Talented Mr. Ripley, This Sweet Sickness). 1988.

Ripley under Water. 1991.

John le Carré
b. 1931

JOHN LE CARRÉ is the pseudonym of David John Moore Cornwell, who was born in Poole, Dorset, on October 19, 1931. His early family life was troubled: his father, Ronald Cornwell, was sentenced to prison for fraud, and shortly thereafter his mother, Olive Grassy, deserted her husband. David spent his youth shuttling between various relatives. Though he began his education in England, he persuaded his father to let him attend the University of Bern in Switzerland, where he spent a year learning German, French, and skiing.

Returning to England in 1949, Cornwell entered military service with the Army Intelligence Corps and was stationed in Austria. He then studied modern languages at Lincoln College, Oxford, graduating with first-class honors in 1956. He was a tutor at Eton College for two years, then in 1960 joined the British Foreign Office and was posted to Bonn and Hamburg.

Since Foreign Service officials were discouraged from publishing under their own names, Cornwell adopted a pseudonym when he published his first novel, *Call for the Dead*, in 1961. This was a fairly conventional spy novel, and it was followed by a routine detective story, *A Murder of Quality* (1962). Le Carré's next novel, however, *The Spy Who Came In from the Cold* (1963), won him the Somerset Maugham Award and the Crime Writers' Association Gold Dagger and enabled him to resign from the Foreign Office in 1964. Both a critical and a popular success, *Spy* was praised by Graham Greene as "the best spy story I have ever read" and was the first espionage novel to dominate the American best-seller list for a year. An effective film version, starring Richard Burton and Claire Bloom, came out in 1965, and several of le Carré's other novels have been adapted as films or as miniseries for British and American television.

After writing two further spy novels—*The Looking Glass War* (1965; winner of the Edgar Allan Poe Award from the Mystery Writers of America) and *A Small Town in Germany* (1968)—and an unsuccessful mainstream novel, *The Naive and Sentimental Lover* (1971), le Carré wrote *Tinker, Tailor,*

Soldier, Spy (1974), whose hero is the "breathtakingly ordinary" secret agent George Smiley, a character who had been featured in le Carré's first two books and had a minor role in the next two. Smiley subsequently appeared in two further novels: *The Honourable Schoolboy* (1977; winner of the James Tait Black Prize and the Gold Dagger from the Crime Writers Association) and *Smiley's People* (1980). These three novels were subsequently reissued in an omnibus entitled *The Quest for Karla* (1982).

With *The Little Drummer Girl* (1983) le Carré stirred up considerable controversy by writing about the struggles between the Israelis and the Palestinians and clearly taking the Palestinian side on the issue. After publishing *A Perfect Spy* (1986), an introspective novel about a spy writing his autobiography, and *The Russia House* (1989), a prophetic novel that suggests that Russian military capability has been vastly exaggerated by the West, le Carré issued *The Secret Pilgrim* (1991), in which George Smiley returns only to deem himself supernumerary with the end of the cold war. Le Carré's most recent novel, *The Night Manager* (1993), shifts gears radically, involving the secret services of both the United States and England battling a drug cartel.

Le Carré married Alison Ann Veronica Sharp in 1954; they had three sons before being divorced in 1971. The next year he married Valerie Jane Eustace; they have one son. Le Carré was made an honorary fellow of Lincoln College in 1984, received the Grand Master Award from the Mystery Writers of America in 1986, and was awarded the Diamond Dagger from the Crime Writers Association in 1988.

▨ *Critical Extracts*

ROBERT M. ADAMS   Contemporary redactions of the old good-guys-versus-bad-guys story are rarely so tough and able as John le Carré's well-heralded whizzer, *The Spy Who Came In from the Cold*. The author whose square pseudonym masks a first-rate narrative architect has provided us with a tightly plotted, non-episodic, controlled action, worked out with few theatrical flamboyances, no picturesque rhetoric, and very little political folderol. In a novel about the so-called cold war, these omissions alone occasion considerable relief. On Mr. le Carré's showing, the world of the professional spy is cold, gray, impersonal, and contrived; now and then, it gives way beneath one's feet. The indigenes, who live by angling desperately for information they cannot assess, are almost schizoid mixtures of cynicism and loyalty. Practiced professional deceivers, they may be deceived even about the reasons for their deception. Humanity itself is compromised, outraged, divided; the arch-plotters become victims of their own plots. Out of these paradoxes grows the intricate and moving climax of the novel.

⟨. . .⟩ Circumstances of the action don't permit much character portrayal; a man as complexly drawn as Leamas passes major parts of his character under the hot iron. But the story is told in terse, cutting prose, and it leads inward as well as outward; Mr. le Carré has given more thought to the problem of ends and means than our usual cheap formularies provide. His book will not yield the less food for thought because it ends on a note of unaccustomed bitterness. It's a cold world, not just for spies but for humanity, and there doesn't seem to be more than one way out of it.

Robert M. Adams, "Couldn't Put It Down," *New York Review of Books*, 5 March 1964, p. 13

JOHN KENNETH GALBRAITH   ⟨*The Looking Glass War*⟩ is still, in a manner of speaking, about spies and part of the setting is the same repellent north German countryside ⟨as *The Spy Who Came In from the Cold*⟩. He has still to prove he isn't a one-subject, one-landscape man. But while his earlier book took Cold War operations very, very grimly, this one is a magnificent, contemptuous and yet wonderfully plausible spoof. Some exotically mismanaged events in recent times have given the public a sounder perspective on the intelligence profession and have taught it, in particular, that average bureaucrats do not become supermen by becoming secret. Mr. le Carré now gets deflation into fiction. ⟨. . .⟩

I expect that among Mr. le Carré's purposes was the intention to tell a highly entertaining story. In this he has succeeded. Perhaps he also wished to prove, with forgivable chauvinism, that the highly regarded British intelligence system could match any offering of ours in intricately designed insanity. Here too he has succeeded. But perhaps he also intended to show that spies, like soldiers, must always be subject to a firm and courageous control by the civilial political authority which should never easily be satisfied with their answers. Here also he has succeeded and a best-selling novel will not be a bad way of driving home the point.

John Kenneth Galbraith, "Spies Who Never Came In," *New York Herald Tribune Book Week*, 25 July 1965, p. 3

RICHARD LOCKE   John le Carré's new book ⟨*Tinker, Tailor, Soldier, Spy*⟩—his seventh in thirteen years—is a thoroughly enjoyable English spy novel about the discovery of a double agent at the highest level of the British Intelligence bureaucracy. It reconfirms the impression that le Carré belongs to the select company of such spy and detective story writers as Arthur Conan Doyle and Graham Greene in England and Dashiell Hammett, James M. Cain, Raymond Chandler and Ross Macdonald in America. There are those who read crime and espionage books for the plot and those who read them for the atmosphere; the former talk of "ingenious puzzles" and take pride in "pure ratiocination"; the latter think themselves more literary, worry about style and characterization, and tend to praise their favorite writers as "real novelists." Le Carré's books—like those of the six authors just mentioned—offer plenty for both kinds of readers.

Tinker, Tailor, Solder, Spy is fluently written; it is full of vivid character sketches of secret agents and bureaucrats from all levels of British society, and the dialogue catches their voices well. The social and physical details of English life and the day to day activities of the intelligence service at home and abroad are convincing. Unlike many writers le Carré is at his best showing men hard at work; he is fascinated by the office politics of the agency since the war. He even has a go at such "novelistic" effects as interlocking themes of sexual and political betrayal. Yet the plot is as tangled and suspenseful as any action fan could require, and the inductive skill of the diffident, intellectual hero should bring joy to the hearts of the purists. The scale and complexity of this novel are much greater than in any of le Carré's previous books. It marks a happy return to the spy genre for le Carré; his last book, *The Naive and Sentimental Lover* (1971), was a pretentious, romantic story about a businessman, a writer and the woman they share—an inept psychosexual portrait of the bourgeois and the bohemian soul. ⟨. . .⟩

Le Carré's originality and distinction as a popular novelist lie in his use of the conventions of the spy novel for purposes of social criticism. In his introduction to The London Sunday Times Insight Team's study of *The Philby Conspiracy* (1968), le Carré remarked that the career of the double agent Kim Philby—who is a prototype of the double agent in *Tinker, Tailor, Soldier, Spy*—illustrates the "capacity of the British ruling class for reluctant betrayal and polite self-preservation." The British secret services are "microcosms of the British condition, of our social attitudes and vanities."

> Richard Locke, [Review of *Tinker, Tailor, Soldier, Spy*], *New York Times Book Review*, 30 June 1974, pp. 1–2

T. J. BINYON   *The Honourable Schoolboy* has two centres of action. On the one hand, the Circus ⟨Secret Service⟩ in London, full of old acquaintances, Connie Sachs, Peter Guillam, Toby Esterhase, Sam Collins, who have never been portrayed at such length before, feverishly active as the researchers try to trace the burrowings of the mole (le Carré can get more excitement out of an archive than most writers can out of a squadron of tanks). On the other, Jerry Westerby, large and cheery in his old blue suit and dirty buckskin boots, moving round South-East Asia, through scenes of war and destruction, from Hongkong to Bangkok, from Phnom Penh, to Saigon and Vientiane on the orders of his superiors, falling in love with Lizzie Worthington, "nightclub hostess, whiskey saleswoman, high-class tart", and finally rebelling, entering the contest on his own accord as a maverick, a wild card.

The contrast between the two narrations emphasizes the conflict in the novel: a conflict which is inherent in all le Carré's thrillers, and which gives them their inner tension. It is that, as he puts it elsewhere, between aims and method, between the claims of the individual and those of the service. In *The Spy Who Came In from the Cold* the issue is discussed at length by the hero, Leamas, and his East German interrogator, Fiedler, and then again by Leamas and his girlfriend, Liz. Here Smiley sums it up, to the embarrassment of his colleagues, when he describes the requirements confronting the intelligence officer: "to be inhuman in defence of our humanity ... harsh in defence of compassion. To be single-minded in defence of our disparity." ⟨...⟩

At a time when, in the West, simple loyalties are no longer possible (Haydon, in *Tinker, Tailor, Soldier, Spy*, it is hinted, becomes a traitor because he cannot be an Empire-builder), le Carré seems to suggest that the only alternative to the amorality, the refusal to adopt a moral stance of the Deighton hero (indicated by his namelessness), is both to question and to accept; to see the dilemma but not to resolve it. His characters— Smiley above all—are torn between their inclinations and their duty; though they might wish to stand by Forster's dictum, in the last resort they will betray their friends rather than their country. In *Call for the Dead* Smiley kills Dieter Frey, a former pupil and close friend; in *Tinker, Tailor, Soldier, Spy* Haydon sets up his best friend (and possibly former lover), Jim Prideaux, to be captured by the Russians so that he himself may remain undetected. Only in *The Honourable Schoolboy* is there a break in the pattern: Jerry disobeys orders and returns to Hongkong to try to save Lizzie, wishing he could have a word with Smiley "about the selfless and devoted way in which we sacrifice other people". But his intervention achieves nothing; he can save neither Lizzie nor himself. In any case, he is only an Occasional; Smiley, the professional, the last of the Empire-builders, remains true to his code, even though he knows he will be stabbed in the back.

T. J. Binyon, "A Gentleman among Players," *Times Literary Supplement*, 9 September 1977, p. 1069

V. S. PRITCHETT   Spy stories have a good deal of the farrago in them even when they are as accomplished as le Carré's and it would be impossible and unfair to give away his elaborate plot ⟨in *Smiley's People*⟩. Le Carré creates a manner which moves by suggestion, leaking a little at a time and gradually gathering all in, without reducing it all to a flat intelligence test or conundrum. He has got to make his implausible people plausible in their dirty and shabby game. In part he belongs to the romantic school of spy literature, and has a blokey, speculative, disabused yet fateful manner which recalls Conrad's use of Marlow; he is good at loud talk, with an occasional apologetic leaning to the metaphysical. Le Carré is a romantic, for example, in joining the General and Smiley as the chivalrous and the good men, faced with the archfiend—discreetly referred to eventually as the Sandman—the legendary Baltic figure who puts even the strongest to sleep. He must convey that Smiley is sad, lonely, and haunted by a gnawing sense of failure, whereas the enemy has never failed and has indeed once gypped him, has once even inserted a defector in the British Service and into Smiley's private life.

V. S. Pritchett, "A Spy Romance," *New York Review of Books*, 7 February 1980, p. 22

JOHN HALPERIN   John le Carré is the only writer of espionage "thrillers" today who is also a writer of literature (the feeble efforts of the later Graham Greene may be gauged by a reading of *The Human Factor*, recently published). Few writers of thrillers have been as skillful as le Carré in placing their stories in a world recognizable as our own and yet stamped with a character that makes it unique. Not the least interesting aspect of le Carré's stories—which seem so tuned to the present, the modern note— is that they are in many ways old-fashioned, even Victorian, in cast, set as all of them are in the recent past and in a world as atmospherically familiar from book to book as those created and populated by George Eliot or Trollope or Conrad. The "literary" quality of le Carré's work resides largely in this familiarity of texture and atmosphere, and in the repetition of themes and characters as in a saga by Galsworthy or Arnold Bennett. Indeed, le Carré's novels provide the sort of critical analysis of modern life and values that Matthew Arnold and Camus and T. S. Eliot undoubtedly would have found congenial and embody a pathology of contemporary existence instantly recognizable to, say, the scholar-gypsy, Sisyphus, or Prufrock. The absurdist, wasteland quality of modern international politics is le Carré's subject; the world he describes is as deeply divided by allegiance to the past, distaste for the present, and inability to fathom the future as the visitor to the Carthusian monastery in Arnold's "Stanzas from the Grande Char- treuse," who saw modern man, remember, as "Wandering between two worlds, one dead, / The other powerless to be born."

The "two worlds" of le Carré's novels are East and West as often as past and present (the relation between the "two worlds" of fact and fiction is also a relevant concern ⟨. . .⟩). It is no accident that Kipling's *Kim*, an early—perhaps the first—spy novel whose very subject is the bifurcation of East and West, is quoted copiously throughout le Carré's work. *Kim* articu- lates a theme (contained in a verse by Kipling) that most of le Carré's books are written around:

> Something I owe to the soil that grew—
> More to the life that fed—
> But most to Allah, who gave me two
> Separate sides to my head.

The last chapter of le Carré's *Call for the Dead* is entitled "Between Two Worlds." In the book's final paragraph the hero, embroiled in rivalry with an old-friend-turned-enemy-agent, glimpses an "eternity between two worlds." Leo Harting, the elusive hero of *A Small Town in Germany*, is ultimately "crushed . . . between . . . worlds" which cannot be reconciled. Many of le Carré's fictional agents are split personalities, having "separate sides to their heads" and being subject to arrested development in the matter of political loyalties. In the novel in which this problem is most minutely scrutinized—*Tinker, Tailor, Soldier, Spy*—the central character is based on a real spy who himself was named for Kipling's hero.

> John Halperin, "Between Two Worlds: The Novels of John le Carré," *South Atlantic Quarterly* 79, No. 1 (Winter 1980): 17–18

DAVID PRYCE-JONES   Le Carré's opinion of Israel ⟨. . .⟩ is a matter of record. In *The Observer* of June 13, 1982, he laid the foundation for a comparison between Israelis and Nazis. The Israeli invasion of Lebanon, he wrote, was "a monstrosity, launched on speciously assembled grounds." Too many Israelis, he went on,

> have persuaded themselves that every Palestinian man and woman and child is by definition a military garret, and that Israel will not be safe until the pack of them are swept away. It is the most savage irony that Begin and his generals cannot see how close they are to inflicting upon another people the disgraceful criteria once inflicted upon themselves.

Generally speaking, people of independent mind can acquire adequate information to measure agitprop against what actually happens in the Middle East. Lies and distortions, even in newspapers or on television, are open to correction. But *The Little Drummer Girl* matters very much indeed, because in it the contemporary image of Israel as an unutterable, indeed Nazi, evil is crystallized, and this portrait will go round the world with the authority of a best seller. Statements in fiction are immune to the truths of real life. A novel lives in the imagination, after all, and it is there, for the credulous, that the image of an evil Israel will be fired and sustained. And an imagination like le Carré's, when out of control, is a thing that will impress those who want to believe in a demonological vision, or perhaps cannot judge it for themselves, and it will scarify a good many others.

> David Pryce-Jones, "A Demonological Fiction," *New Republic*, 18 April 1983, pp. 29–30

DAVID MONAGHAN   The shape of le Carré's fictional world is not ⟨. . .⟩ drastically altered by *The Little Drummer Girl*. His social landscape is broadened and enriched by the introduction of Israel and Palestine, passionate societies which contrast so sharply with the sterile communities to be found in earlier novels, but its dark contours are in no sense lightened. And while Charlie comes much nearer to achieving personal resolution than any previous le Carré hero, the special circumstances in which she is placed and the closeness of her approach to the precipice of disaster lessen the impact of the novel's emphatically romantic ending. The story of this new heroine has a good deal to say about the positive function of role-playing in the individual's struggle to bring into harmony the warring elements of personality. However, as with the glimpses he allows his readers to catch of the ways in which a close relationship to society can sustain the individual, le Carré is as far as ever from allowing that such experiences might be possible for the great majority of us.

It is, of course, dangerous to offer conclusions about a writer who is in mid-career and who shows every sign of producing further novels. Nevertheless, the ease with which *The Little Drummer Girl*, a work which differs in so many respects from its predecessors and which breaks so sharply away from the *Quest for Karla* trilogy, can be accommodated within a canon that includes nine novels written over a period of more than twenty years, clearly suggests that le Carré's vision of the world is not an evolving one and that his concern in the future is likely to be, as it has been up to now, with the elaboration, development and modification of this vision rather than with the search for new perspectives.

David Monaghan, *The Novels of John le Carré* (Oxford: Basil Blackwell, 1985), p. 201

HAROLD BLOOM   As the literary son of Graham Greene, John le Carré has no true contemporary rival, unless it be Greene himself. This is the Greene of the "entertainments" from *The Man Within* onwards, including two powerful achievements, *This Gun for Hire* and *Brighton Rock*. Le Carré, it seems to me, resembles Greene more and more, which may not be an altogether good thing, particularly in the recent novels, *The Little Drummer Girl* and *A Perfect Spy*. The image of fatherhood is at best an ambivalent, perhaps even an ambiguous one in *A Perfect Spy*, which begins with a phone call from a man named Jack Brotherhood, calling from London, to a man in Vienna named Magnus Pym. The call is to tell Pym that his father has died, information that Pym welcomes as setting him free. Pym's father, a sublime crook, has shadowed and inhibited his son's life, and in the moment of liberation Pym resolves to write out the story of his own life so as to instruct his own son.

That Pym is a surrogate for le Carré seems clear enough, both in the relation to an actual father and to "the Firm," now called SIS. Axel, Pym's undeserving friend, condemns Pym for a lack of authenticity or originality, as someone put together from bits of other people. Is this le Carré's own anxiety, despite his vast audience and his growing critical acclaim? Are le Carré's novels put together out of Joseph Conrad and Graham Greene, or does he justify Noel Annan's praise? Annan insists that "Le Carré is a natural writer with an unmistakable voice and a vitality that bounces off the page." The vitality can be granted, but the voice sometimes can be mistaken for that of Conrad or Greene. Le Carré's overtly allusive counter-pointing of Conrad and Greene against popular spy fiction formulae, from Buchan, Oppenheim, and even Fleming, seems to me a defense against the enormous influence upon him of Conrad's *The Secret Agent* and Greene's spy novels, particularly *The Quiet American* and *Our Man in Havana*.

Harold Bloom, "Introduction," *John le Carré*, ed. Harold Bloom (New York: Chelsea House, 1987), p. 1

TREVOR ROYLE   Treachery, not deception, lies at the heart of John le Carré's view of the espionage game. Certainly, the players are deceivers all, and certainly, the rules are governed by deceit, but the hidden goal of all the actors is treason. What is there to say then about a man who acts the traitor, who betrays not only his country but also those who trust him? That is the central question which le Carré has been addressing ever since he published *The Spy Who Came In from the Cold* in 1963. In *A Perfect Spy* (1986) he goes some way to illuminating, if not the complete solution to the conundrum, then at least a glimmering of his own thinking on the matter.

On the surface, *A Perfect Spy* contains several features which le Carré has marked out as his own territory. The central character, Magnus Pym, an agent not quite burned out but badly singed by a lifetime's work in espionage, goes to ground taking with him a curious collection of biographies, unintelligible secrets and more than an ample supply of disgust and self-hatred. The pattern of insinuation, of making himself indispensable, of using others, emerges as le Carré builds up a comprehensive picture of Pym's lost life. We learn that he has been something of a star turn in the nation's intelligence service, a public schoolboy and an Oxford man, a linguist with an eccentric, though vaguely upper-class, English background; in other words, he possesses the virtues which our intelligence services find intensely exciting in their recruits. ⟨. . .⟩

In the foreground, meanwhile, the shadows begin to take on some sub-stance. Through an autobiography he is writing for his son, we can piece together the hidden story of Pym's life: his eccentric con-man father, his fears and fantasies, his sexual hang-ups, his earnest craving to be honoured and respected, the fatal flaws which lead him—the casual player—into the game of spying. No other writer has drawn such a sympathetic, though unnerving, picture of intelligence work, or has felt so intensely the problems of idealism, innocence and practical politics which serve as the ground rules. The conclusion of this remarkable novel is all too dreary and predictable, but Pym's end matters not; the main concern is what has gone before, the feeble motives and faulty ideals, the wishful thinking and the absence of love.

A Perfect Spy is a well-nigh flawless novel about the seedy world of intelligence gathering and the corruption of human values that it encom-passes. Whereas earlier novels like The Spy Who Came In from the Cold and The Looking Glass War were more concerned with the minutiae of the world of espionage, the training of spies and the beastly undercurrent of fear that runs through their lives, A Perfect Spy addresses itself to the idea of espionage. In that sense it is more about the creation and the raison d'être of the spy than it is about the preparations which turn an ordinary man into a man capable of betraying those he loves and that which he holds most dear.

Trevor Royle, "Le Carré and the Idea of Espionage," The Quest for le Carré, ed. Alan Bold (New York: St. Martin's Press, 1988), pp. 87–89

CONOR CRUISE O'BRIEN   Why is it that writers who take the bleakest view of the human condition—Pascal, Swift, Graham Greene, John le Carré—make such excellent entertainers? The Russia House, though bleak in its political implications, is essentially an "entertainment" in the Graham Greene sense. That is to say it is an exciting spy story, which is at the same time a lively international comedy of manners. The comedy is black, most of the manners being those of spies. The book is also a well-informed, up-to-the-minute political parable, incisive and instructive. In short, vintage le Carré, by which I mean that it is more like *The Spy Who Came In from the Cold* than *The Naive and Sentimental Lover* or *The Little Drummer Girl*. In other words, the vein of the portentous, always present in a le Carré novel, is not allowed to get out of control in *The Russia House*.

At the center of the novel is a Soviet physicist, known as Goethe (code name: Bluebird), who smuggles out to the West a document revealing that Soviet military technology is a sham and a mess. Goethe is an idealist, and a rather wooden one. Mr. le Carré is less good at portraying idealists than at portraying cynics, and Goethe's real function in the novel is to provide the cynics—who are here the professional spies—an apple of discord over which they plausibly contend. ⟨. . .⟩

A poignant sense of ⟨. . .⟩ comedown pervades *The Russia House*, as it does other le Carré novels. And it is possible that the sense of national comedown contributes to the general disillusionment about the usefulness of any intelligence that le Carré characters so often signal in their various ways. The grapes that were once so sweet have rotted, and the ones that are left are sour. That taste may perhaps underline Mr. le Carré's acrid, astringent style.

As in earlier le Carré novels, the world of "intelligence" appears as intellectually fascinating, morally degrading and inherently pointless. The Russian and the British heroes come eventually to the same conclusion, that each had stood on his own side "of a corrupt and anachronistic equation."

Conor Cruise O'Brien, "Bad News for Spies," *New York Times Book Review*, 21 May 1989, p. 3

GEORGE KEARNS   This ⟨*The Secret Pilgrim*⟩ is not just a rich evening of story-telling, the latest book in a fabulous series, but the swan song, the elegy for a genre, and in some sense its revision from another, perhaps incommensurable perspective as well. ⟨. . .⟩

⟨. . .⟩ The suspense in this novel is displaced more than slightly, indeed, almost entirely, onto another narrative level than the one on which we conventionally read le Carré. The issue here is not who will betray whom, but will Smiley betray himself and his author. Will he, now that the cold war is over, look back on all he has done and make the elegant recantation of which he is no doubt eminently capable? Because what *was* it all about, in the end, the double- and triple-crossing of friends and lovers and the pathetic deaths of the "little people" whose bodies are strewn about so frequently in those shabby East European rooms and suspiciously similar cheap hotels? Ned's stories, interwomen with Smiley's after-dinner *causerie*, raise this issue repeatedly, from the first betrayal of his dearest friend, whose life of subsequent self-punitive disempowerment shadows the whole series, to the last supremely cruel and achingly deliberate unmasking of a pathetic and duped old Brit who has been emotionally suckered into sending crypto-gram codes to the Russians, with all the clanking apparatus of the trade and genre much in play, including double messages over the radio and concealed headsets and crystals.

Smiley, it seems, neither wishes to recant nor to revise, though perhaps to mitigate. "Quizzed" by a young idealist about British colonialism and its indifference to its victims, he remarks that he rather agrees. Asked whether spying is not an anachronistic choice of vocation, he laughs the laugh of Tiresias. His support for the new recruits and their decision to embark on a lifetime of spying never wavers, even under the impact of tale after tale of idiocy, folly and deceit. His sense of what, for lack of a more modest word, we must call their "mission" remains. It merely takes a new form.

And that new form is in part the logical culmination of all the self-betrayals and self-interrogations, the workings of moles and mole-chasers within the Circus itself that have helped to lay the clever devices and cunning traps of the le Carré world, and yet it is also in part the mark of their final destruction. For what Smiley enjoins upon the young is their duty not to the state but to its necessary subversion, subversion not in the name of some political stance or ideology, but in the name of common decency, of humanity. "We've given up far too many freedoms in order to be free," Smiley concludes. "Now it's time to take them back." Then, pausing at the door, "Tell them to spy on the ozone layer, will you, Ned?" Exit, stage left. And a great exit it is, too. The final pages are gorgeously sentimental, valedictory, and novelistically self-reflexive: "It's over, and so am I. Abso-lutely over. Time you rang down the curtain on yesterday's cold warrior. And please don't ask me back, ever again."

George Kearns, "Fiction: In History and Out," *Hudson Review* 44, No. 3 (Autumn 1991): 497–99

DAVID REMNICK   With *The Night Manager*, the world has changed completely. There are no Russians. In fact, the enemy, the head of an enormous drugs and arms cartel, is English by birth, but almost stateless, a free-floating, untaxable embodiment of all things evil, who sometimes lives on a private island and is frequently at sea. For le Carré, such an enemy represents the sort of state-of-the-art corruption that secret services have done little to combat; in fact, as the Iran-contra scandal underscored, the worst are ready to trade in arms for national interests real or imagined.

The Night Manager is as taut a spy novel as one could hope for, full of le Carré's signature plot swerves and ironic glimpses of the bureaucratic conflict in Whitehall and the United States. As always, he is incapable of writing a superfluous scene, and his dialogue still manages to combine cheek and threat, as if Nick and Nora had gone to Eton and Oxford then graduated to MI5:

> "My name's Leonard," Burr announced, hauling himself out of
> Quayle's office chair like someone about to intervene in a brawl.
> "I do crooks. Smoke? Here. Poison yourself."

But for all the customary skill and smart talk, the truth is that le Carré is having no less difficulty finding his bearings in the new world than the aristocrats and politicians he has always skewered. So much of the pleasure of le Carré's cold war novels lay in the way he created a shadow world that the reader imagined, somewhere, to exist. Now it has cruelly and suddenly disappeared. I can think of no other novelist associated with a specific atmosphere—not Faulkner, not Waugh—who ever had to deal with such complete and instantaneous obliteration. ⟨. . .⟩

Part of what made le Carré's version of the cold war so fascinating was the way it rejected or manipulated the conventions of the spy novel and the political propaganda on both sides. Shading, ambiguity, and doubt: these were never much present in Le Queux or Buchan. But only the most programmatic reader could have ignored, for example, how alike Smiley and Karla were, secret sharers on either side of the Iron Curtain. Smiley represented the better side, and yet the bureaucracy that employed him was heartless, soft, frequently stupid. Karla represented a brutal tyranny and yet he defected for the love of his lost daughter. In many ways, Karla appeared to be the superior spy and his the superior service. ⟨. . .⟩

Le Carré is undoubtedly not going through a "premature demise," as he said ⟨in a lecture⟩ in Boston. He still has important things to say even as he exploits and subverts the conventions of the spy novel. Recently, he argued in an interview with Charlie Rose of PBS that the United States and the UN must now engage in "altruistic colonialism," intervening around the globe whenever moral necessity demands. That bit of politically incorrect thinking may be the stuff of a new novel. But for the moment le Carré seems like the rest of us, in a state of transition, still trying to get his bearings in the new world beyond the old secret world. *The Night Manager* is the novel of his post–cold war disorientation.

David Remnick, "Le Carré's New War," *New York Review of Books*, 12 August 1993, pp. 22–23

▩ *Bibliography*

Call for the Dead. 1961.

A Murder of Quality. 1962.

The Spy Who Came In from the Cold. 1963.

The Looking Glass War. 1965.

A Small Town in Germany. 1968.

The Naive and Sentimental Lover. 1971.

Tinker, Tailor, Soldier, Spy. 1974.

The Honourable Schoolboy. 1977.

Smiley's People. 1980.

The Quest for Karla ⟨*Tinker, Tailor, Soldier, Spy, The Honourable Schoolboy, Smiley's People*⟩. 1982.

The Little Drummer Girl. 1983.

A Perfect Spy. 1986.

The Clandestine Muse: The Harry G. Pouder Memorial Lecture. 1986.

The Russia House. 1989.

The Secret Pilgrim. 1991.

The Night Manager. 1993.

Elmore Leonard
b. 1925

ELMORE JOHN LEONARD, JR., known as "Dutch," was born on October 11, 1925, in New Orleans, Louisiana. After several moves, his family settled in Detroit. After high school he was drafted into the navy, where from 1943 to 1946 he served with the Seabees in the Pacific. He received a Ph.B. from the University of Detroit in 1950. In that year Leonard began work as an office boy at the Campbell-Ewald Advertising Agency in Detroit, where he later became a copywriter.

Leonard's first story, "Trail of the Apache," appeared in *Argosy* in 1951, and he subsequently published many other stories in such magazines as *Dime Western*, the *Saturday Evening Post*, and *Zane Grey's Western Magazine*. His first novel, a Western entitled *The Bounty Hunters*, was published in 1953. Other Westerns followed, including *Hombre* (1961; later named as one of the twenty-five best Western novels of all time by the Western Writers of America) and *Valdez Is Coming* (1970). After quitting his advertising job in 1961, Leonard worked as a freelance copywriter and writer of educational and industrial films for Encyclopaedia Britannica Films; between 1963 and 1966 he operated his own company, the Elmore Leonard Advertising Company. The sale of film rights to *Hombre* in 1965 allowed him to become a full-time writer.

Although he continued writing Westerns sporadically into the late 1970s (his last was *Gunsights*, 1979), by the late 1960s Leonard decided that the Western market was drying up, so he turned his attention to crime novels. His first, *The Big Bounce*, appeared in 1969 and was filmed later that year. Over the next decade his novels in the genre met with critical acclaim, but only in the early 1980s did he begin to reach a wider audience. Every novel since *Stick* (1983) has made the best-seller lists. Readers and critics alike admire Leonard for his realistic dialogue and his ability to efface himself from his prose. He has said in interviews that he was influenced by the lean, unadorned styles of such writers as Ernest Hemingway, John Steinbeck, and John O'Hara.

Among Leonard's most recent novels are *Glitz* (1985), *Freaky Deaky* (1988), *Get Shorty* (1990), *Rum Punch* (1992), *Pronto* (1993), and *Riding the Rap*, scheduled for publication in 1995. Leonard has written or cowritten a number of screenplays, including adaptations of his own works. *LaBrava* (1983) received the Edgar Allan Poe Award for best mystery novel of the year in 1984.

In 1949 Leonard married Beverly Cline, with whom he had five children. His first marriage ended in divorce in 1977; he married Joan Shepard in 1979.

◈ *Critical Extracts*

JEAN M. WHITE   Several crime mystery novels recently published reflect the range of offerings in a field so often stereotyped as populated only with tough private eyes, gentlemanly English inspectors, or hardpressed homicide cops. Take *Fifty-two Pickup* by Elmore Leonard. At first glance, it is vintage hard-boiled Detroit in the '70s, but there is a twist: instead of a private-eye hero, we have Harry Mitchell, a self-made businessman who fights back on his own when three psycho punks try to blackmail him with home movies. One film segment shows how the blackmailers ingeniously arranged to have Harry's young mistress shot to death with his gun. Harry does love his wife of 22 years despite the indiscretion, and Leonard sensitively explores their relationship as they are forced into a world of porno flicks and nude model studios far removed from their suburban Detroit home. Amid the fast-moving action, Harry, who is accustomed to handling things himself, deals with the blackmailers and, in the end, when some one wants to call the cops, can ask: "But who are they going to arrest?"

Jean M. White, "The Plot Thickens . . . ," *Washington Post Book World*, 19 May 1974, p. 6

ROBIN WINKS   Elmore Leonard has written his toughest book in *City Primeval: High Noon in Detroit*. It's too bad Leonard felt he needed a subtitle, for the theme is obvious enough: how one vicious killer and one committed cop come to see themselves as locked in a classic shootout in the OK Corral of modern America, the city in which the lone hero climbed down from his mustang to climb into his Mustang and do battle once again for the cowardly, blind populace. This is rough stuff: the language, the attitudes, and the people are all unpleasant, products of the city that has grown up over the primeval forest. Theme, plot, writing are obvious, yet compelling.

Robin Winks, "Mysteries," New Republic, 13 December 1980, p. 40

KEN TUCKER   Elmore Leonard strikes me as being the finest thriller writer alive primarily because he does his best to efface style, and has done this so successfully that few readers know about him at all. Since 1953, Leonard has written a remarkable series of novels, Westerns as well as thrillers, the latest of which is *Split Images*. There are no wisecrack-eloquent detectives or overwrought similes in Leonard's writing. His characters are often lower-middle-class people who fall into crime because it's an easier way to make money than that tedious nine-to-five. Leonard's favorite plot is the revenge story—someone exploited by criminals commits a bigger, better crime that ruins his or her victimizers.

In *Fifty-two Pick-Up*, beetle-browed business-and-family-man Harry Mitchell is blackmailed by three men on the fringe of the porno industry. They kidnap Mitchell's lover and make her the object of a snuff film. Instead of backing down, Mitchell tells his wife about both his affair and his predicament, and the two of them go after the thugs. The novel is as much about a strained-but-surviving marriage as it is a tightly wound thriller with a smash-up climax. In *The Switch*, a woman is abducted and held for ransom, but this bored restless housewife, embittered by a lifetime of her husband's petty cruelties, joins forces with her captors to dupe her ratty mate, relishing her revenge—it's a female Walter Mitty tale played for keeps. ⟨. . .⟩

Leonard resists mannerisms instinctively; it's one reason he ditches his heroes from book to book, always inventing new crooks and detectives who weight the balance between good and bad in quirky disproportion. Early on in Leonard's best novels, there's always a disorienting, exhilarating period when you can't tell where your sympathy is supposed to fall; the first few chapters not only offer up the donnée of the thriller plot, but also spend a while picking, choosing, and discarding people—a cop who looks like a pip of a fellow in chapter one gets blown away in chapter three, so that a seedy hood flitting around the back alleys of the story can step into the glare of Leonard's admiring prose. The best thing about *Split Images,* in fact, is that initially it looks as if we'll have to work up a fondness for rich, twitchy Robbie Daniels; what a relief it is when Bryan Hord, as unassuming a gumshoe as you'll find this side of Jim Rockford, comes forward to mull over Daniels's nastiness.

This lovely trick of Leonard's—the ability to keep you in the dark about not only where the story is going, but also who its hero is—adds great force to the violence that rears up regularly; it permits the author to dispatch characters you may have been convinced were central to the drama. In all of this there's a kind of wicked amorality. Thriller writers can be the cruelest of artist-gods, lopping off heads in cynical, mean ways, as if envisioning the colorful scenes they'll make in the movie version. But Leonard is much more skillful, more scarily witty, than that. The violence in his books is quick, quiet, and brutal; it's the kind that can strike you as being true and realistic even though the actions are utterly beyond your experience. Can an artist receive a higher compliment than that?

Ken Tucker, "The Author Vanishes: Elmore Leonard's Quiet Thrillers," Village Voice, 23 February 1982, p. 41

JOEL M. LYCZAK   *Interviewer:* What are the characteristics of your style?

Elmore Leonard: The style is naturalistic, I suppose; it avoids images and purple passages. It requires that the characters move the story and that I keep my nose out of it. My sound is the sound of the individual characters. I stick to third person and wrote only one story in the first person, *Hombre;* a minor character tells the story. But I like to use different points of view; so first person is too restrictive.

I: You switched from the Western novel to those with a contemporary setting with *The Big Bounce* in 1968. What caused you to change genres? Was any prejudice shown towards the acceptance of *The Big Bounce* due to your background as a Western novelist?

EL: During the 'sixties the Western book market dried up to the point the advances weren't worth the effort. I freelanced from '61 to '65 writing industrial and educational films, finally sold *Hombre* to Fox and had enough to live on for a time while I wrote another book. It was time to leave Westerns, and I wasn't that well known as a Western author that it would hinder my branching out. *The Big Bounce* was rejected 84 times, counting Hollywood and New York, but finally sold as a movie to Warner Bros. before Gold Medal picked it up.

I: Critics tend to categorize you as a mystery/suspense writer. What is your opinion of this and the books currently published in the mystery/ suspense field?

EL: I don't mind being categorized as a suspense writer; I hope my books are suspenseful. But I do object to being called a mystery writer. I don't write mysteries. I'm reading John D. MacDonald again because he influenced me in the '50s and because I think he keeps getting better, a master at writing in the first person and keeping the first person pronoun almost hidden from view. He works at making his prose more readable and interesting, just as I do. I don't read mystery/suspense regularly because most of the stories sound alike. Authors in the suspense field I enjoy are Donald E. Westlake, Ed McBain, Ira Levin, and William Goldman.

I: Do you have a particular starting point when preparing to write a novel?

EL: For the most part I begin with characters. An ex-con goes to work for a millionaire investor who thinks he's a stand-up comic. Add a few more characters, inside and outside the law, throw in a few things I know about Hollywood and how movie deals are made, and see what happens. I don't know myself what's going to happen until I'm well into the story and I see how the characters interact. In *Cat Chaser*, Jiggs Scully shoots Andres De Boya. It could have been the other way around. But which character would provide a more interesting confrontation with Moran in the end?

I: Have you ever based a character on a living individual?

EL: Sometimes a character comes out of a news story—the judge in *City Primeval*—but most often, 99 per cent of the time, I begin with the basic idea of a character and then research to provide the character's background. Chichi, the victim in *Split Images*, was based on Porfirio Rubirosa, after searching around to give him a suitable Latin American background.

Joel M. Lyczak, "An Interview with Elmore Leonard," *Armchair Detective* 16, No. 3 (Summer 1983): 236–37

JEFFERSON MORLEY   Leonard is too interested in the flaws in his characters and in the details of the world they live in to be classed with three-chord crime hacks like John D. MacDonald and George V. Higgins. His company, for better or worse, is Bobbie Ann Mason and John Updike. The restlessness, the insecurities, the private resentments, the quiet ambitions, the best-laid plans that Mason and Updike evoke are all there in Leonard—and often with less posturing. When a Bobbie Ann Mason character opens the refrigerator and sees a ham, it is bathed in the soft fluorescent glow of the Iowa Writer's Workshop and we're supposed to hear the bell of Meaning go ting-a-ling. When Stick goes to the fridge for a Stroh's, it's because he's thirsty.

Leonard's chief flaw is that no matter where he drives you, you still go through familiar intersections. The trouble isn't that he relies on a prototypical hero. There's no harm in knowing that the central character of a Leonard book is likely to be a shrewd operator with a yearning for a good woman (or two). He'll be decent, divorced, smart, and, once in a while, a son of a bitch. In the same way it's not bothersome that he's likely to live or be from Detroit. But I find it a little distracting when the mechanics of plot and character recur from book to book.

This kind of perfunctory writing compounds the self-consciousness of *Glitz*. In *Stick* Ernest J. has a memorable yet deflating evening in the successive company of a *Playboy*-type knockout, an unhappily married woman, and the working girl of his dreams. The situation is faintly echoed in *Glitz*, where the same three types wind up awkwardly face-to-face in Mora's hotel room. Mora also has exactly the same instantaneous rapport with the married woman in this trio as the hero of *Cat Chaser* (1982) has with the wife of an exiled Latin torturer. Both women have self-made, stolid, dense husbands, and both first meet the hero in connection with a nubile prostitute, whom the hero has befriended. These recycled devices drag *Glitz* to a flat conclusion. Toward the end, you get the sneaking suspicion Mora's just cruising Leonard country in search of a plot twist.

Jefferson Morley, "Middle-Class Hustlers," *New Republic*, 25 March 1985, pp. 39–40

WALKER PERCY   The question here is, Why is Elmore Leonard so good? He is. He is as good as the blurbs say: "The greatest crime writer of our time, perhaps ever," "Can't put it down," and so on. It's true enough.

But how does he do it? Because it looks like he's thrown away the rules of a noble genre. He doesn't stick to the same guy or the same place. I had thought Raymond Chandler wrote the book when he set down Philip Marlowe in Los Angeles, in his lonesome house up Laurel Canyon, stoic and pure-hearted amid the low life of Sunset Boulevard and the bad crops of Bay City, a tough Galahad pitted against some very sleazy barbarians.

But look at what Mr. Leonard is doing. Here ⟨in *Bandits*⟩ he is now in New Orleans. I haven't read many of his books, but, as I recall, he's taken on Detroit, Miami Beach, Bal Harbour, Jerusalem, with a different cop or a different tough guy in each place. His New Orleans is done up with meticulous accuracy. The restaurants, streets, bars, hotels are just right—especially a lovely neighborhood restaurant, Mandina's, which tourists have never heard of, and even the funeral home across the street. One imagines Mr. Leonard moving into a city for a couple of weeks, yet doing his research as exhaustively as John Gunther doing another "Inside" book. Yet Mr. Leonard's New Orleans lacks the authenticity of Chandler's L.A., which works for Marlowe—and for us—as his very soul's terrain. ⟨. . .⟩

Here's an item for the next doctoral thesis on Mr. Leonard: he often drops the word "if" in dialogue—and uses hardly any conjunctions. "I had a tire iron we could find out in ten minutes." This sentence could use an "if" and a comma and would be worse for it.

Yes, Mr. Leonard knows what he's doing. In the end he senses ⟨in *Bandits*⟩ that Nicaragua and the gun-toting ex-nun may not be working out here. He backs off. Says Roy, mystified: "I want to know, for my own information, which are the good guys and which are the bad guys." Jack doesn't know either. Mr. Leonard's instincts are good. Nicaraguan politics, in turns out, may be a bit too heavy to be carried by the graceful pas de deux of Mr. Leonard's good guys and bad guys. For this reason, *Bandits* is not quite of a piece, like *Glitz*.

But it will do. Mr. Leonard has got his usual diverting cast of grifters and creeps up his sleeve and action as Byzantine as ever Chandler himself thought up. In fact, reading it, I felt like William Faulkner when he was writing the screenplay for the film version of Chandler's novel *The Big Sleep*. The story is that he had to call up Chandler to find out what was going on. Chandler wasn't sure.

Yes, it will do.

Walker Percy, "There's a Contra in My Gumbo," *New York Times Book Review*, 4 January 1987, p. 7

DAVID GEHERIN   Leonard's literary excellence is the result of artistic genius coupled with an approach to writing that can be expressed in three main tenets: (1) Get It Right; (2) Let It Happen; (3) Be Natural.

1. GET IT RIGHT: For Leonard this means doing research. Research has played an essential role in his fiction since his earliest westerns. Often the purpose of the research is simply to gather specific information: how do the local police investigate a killing? how does a drug dealer launder money? how does a casino surveillance system work? how do you make a bomb? Research of this type enhances the realism of the fiction by ensuring authenticity down to the smallest detail.

Leonard is not the sort of writer (like James Michener, for example) who does an enormous amount of research and then tries to incorporate as much of it as possible into his novel. He uses only what is appropriate, and what he uses he works in very unobtrusively. The factual information is never allowed to impede the flow of the story. A reader of *Bandits,* for example, won't be given every detail about how to conduct an embalming (which, based on his eyewitness research, Leonard could give); but because Jack Delaney is a mortician's assistant, the reader will be given enough details to convince him of the authenticity of the scenes of him at work. ⟨. . .⟩

2. LET IT HAPPEN: Once Leonard begins writing his book, he switches to an entirely different approach. Instead of depending on research, he now relies on instinct. To borrow a phrase uttered by several of his characters, Leonard's philosophy of composition can be described as "letting it happen." As intimately as he knows his various characters, he never knows in advance what they'll do. Once he begins a book, he lets them "tell" him what will happen next.

"I hate to plot," Leonard concedes. He used to plot out his books very carefully; in fact, some of his early novels were based on detailed screenplay treatments he had first written. Now he no longer worries about plot. He knows one will take shape once he creates interesting characters and comes up with a situation that forces them to rub against each other. (He also concedes it is useful to have a gun somewhere in his story. "I don't have any desire to fire a gun," he says, "but they come in handy in a book.") ⟨. . .⟩

3. BE NATURAL: A corollary to his philosophy of "letting it happen" is "let it happen naturally." Leonard avoids situations that are artificial, contrived or clichéd. His readers will not get what convention dictates but what develops naturally out of the characters and the situation. He was

inspired to write *Hombre*, for example, because of his impatience with all those "white flag" situations he was used to seeing on TV, where gunfighters followed the rules of polite gentlemen. In his novel, after John Russell's opponent approaches waving the white flag of surrender, Russell shoots him in the back as he walks away. One gets the sense that this is exactly how such a scene would be played out in real life.

Leonard's novels have such a natural quality about them because he rigorously avoids stereotypes and clichés. In his books personal confrontations between characters don't always result in fisticuffs or gunplay, as they invariably do in the works of lesser writers who lazily depend on formula. Leonard likes to avoid the expected. He also likes the unexpected when it comes to violence in his books. In *Bandits*, for example, Franklin de Dios walks up behind Jerry Boylan and shoots him in the head while he's standing at a urinal. His action is shocking simply because it is so surprising. And so realistic.

> David Geherin, *Elmore Leonard* (New York: Continuum, 1989), pp. 126–27, 130, 132

MARC BALDWIN   In the beginning of *Glitz*, one of Elmore Leonard's finest crime novels, Vincent Mora, a Miami Beach cop, is shot by a mugger he subsequently kills. In the end, Vincent is shot by Teddy Magyck, a psychopathic rapist and murderer whom Vincent had arrested and sent to prison seven years before. Teddy, having sworn revenge, stalks Vincent throughout the book, only to fail thanks to Vincent's girl friend, Linda Moon. Linda shoots Teddy before he can finish Vincent off. Vincent lives. Teddy dies.

Within this frame Leonard presents an underworld in search of itself, a Great Wrong Place (as W. H. Auden said of Raymond Chandler's novels) where the difference between the good, the bad, and the marginal is how they read and react to the signs of society and language. The roles people play are as unstable as the characters themselves. Leonard explores the subjectivity with which people assign value to the conventional trappings of society, such as power, money, and appearances. The significance of these conventions shifts along with the alternating narrative perspectives which Leonard employs. Throughout the novel, the conventions and signs are as contingent as the contexts which determine their meaning. Characters and the signifiers which define them derive their meaning extrinsically, through their difference.

In their quest for a stable identity, the self-reflexive characters (Vincent and Linda) are aware of the roles in which society has cast them, and thus wrestle constantly with the questions of seeming and being, what is and what is not reality. Ultimately, Vincent, the cop-in-doubt, must engage Teddy, the psycho-killer, in a duty dance, a hermeneutic circling around each other, if you will, wherein cop and criminal share ever alternating roles of author/reader, at once creating and interpreting each other's thoughts and actions. And though Leonard effects a closure of sorts with Teddy's eventual demise, it is a closure only of one criminal's spree. The cop knows no great peace, experiences no transcendent triumph. The Great Wrong Place thrives obliviously on. Crime's unsolvable underworld survives.

Marc Baldwin, "The Conventions of Crime and the Reading of Signs in Elmore Leonard's *Glitz,*" *Clues* 11, No. 1 (Spring–Summer 1990): 85–86

JOSEPH HYNES   Leonard is an equal opportunity writer, one whose women characters evolve from being extreme instances of gold-diggers, tramps, or sainted virgins (see, for instance, *The Big Bounce, Escape from Five Shadows, Forty Lashes Less One, Hombre*) to heavier and more complex involvement in the action as well as to richer and more ambiguous character-ization—as in *52 Pick-Up, Mr. Majestyk, The Switch, Gold Coast, City Primeval, Stick, LaBrava, Glitz, Bandits,* and *Killshot.* In much the same way, Indians and Mexicans are typically put-upon collectively in the Westerns, but in the city can be deadly gunmen—like any other person of whatever ethnic origin—as in *Killshot.* Blacks, too, gravitate from being somewhat improbable victims in the Westerns to being just part of the racial sprawl in urban novels, where they may be good or bad, cops or not, and mixed of motive like others. Instances of this increasingly all-around character fullness include Karen DiCilia in *Gold Coast,* Linda Moon and DeLeon Johnson in *Glitz,* Margaret Dawson in *The Switch,* Armand Degas and Carmen Colson in *Killshot,* Donnell Lewis in *Freaky Deaky,* and Lucy Nichols and Franklin de Dios in *Bandits.* Perhaps the richest case of the minorities' acting outside the law to achieve justice is that of *Forty Lashes Less One,* where two convicts—Raymond San Carlos (Apache) and Harold Jackson (black)—collaborate with the warden to kill a number of outlaws and escaped convicts who have mistreated them, to return to prison the boss of the prisoners' syndicate and his doxy, and then to head south for the freedom offered by Mexico.

Leonard's protagonists, then, whether men or women, minorities or not, tend to operate alone as a rule, or at least without formal substantial assistance from the law. This persistent trait helps to solidify Leonard's comment that he thinks himself influenced not so much by the likes of Raymond Chandler as by movies such as *The Plainsman, My Darling Clementine*, and *Red River*, and especially by Hemingway's *For Whom the Bell Tolls*. The situations in which Leonard places his protagonists accentuate the inefficiency or incompetence or ignorance or crookedness or obtrusiveness or indifference of sheriff or police force (that is, of Western or urban lawkeepers) and the consequent need for individuals to prove their personal mettle. ⟨. . .⟩

In the long run, what makes these central figures tick? What spurs them on? Sometimes they may appear to be moved by selfishness or by a cynical despair in the face of overwhelming moral evil. Undoubtedly Leonard is aware of original sin and its effects. But his protagonists never despair. On the contrary, like Hemingway and ⟨Henry⟩ James, Leonard is a romantic who believes in free will to some extent. At heart he believes in the possibility and desirablity of achieving good ends, although he is profoundly skeptical of doing so through channels. More specifically, despite Leonard's obvious sense that we've all eaten of the apple, he also believes that isolated, ordinary individuals, like his protagonists, can surmount their own weaknesses and criminal records in order to do right. Because such people can show up not only in detective fiction but anywhere, it matters not whether they do their work in the Arizona Territory or Detroit: Mr. Smith goes to Washington while Natty Bumppo saves the wilds.

Joseph Hynes, " 'High Noon in Detroit': Elmore Leonard's Career," *Journal of Popular Culture* 25, No. 3 (Winter 1991): 183–84, 186

MICHAEL DIRDA   Beneath its fast-moving surface, *Rum Punch* is a novel about growing old, about the way that time changes us, about the old dream of starting over again and its cost. In *The Switch*, Ordell and Louis were a couple of amiable ex-cons, reminiscent of Angel Martin and Jim Rockford; they talked like tough guys but neither could ever blow anyone's head off. Louis, especially, was so likeable that the unhappily married woman he and Ordell kidnapped turned to him for sympathy and affection. In the 13 years since then he's become a sorry, burned-out shell, the humanity leached out of him. Ordell has learned to kill with a casualness that takes the breath away. Melanie, once as smart as she was gorgeous, has grown into a pouty, going-to-fat, nagging bimbo.

Getting old. At 57 bail-bondsman Max Cherry looks back on 27 meaningless years of marriage and a life dealing with sleazoids and no accounts; he sees Jackie—still a stunner even though she's 44—as a last chance for happiness. Jackie, after three marriages and a career of phony smiles, naturally figures that Ordell's half a million might just be the ticket she needs to a shiny future. But does that future include Max? ⟨. . .⟩

There are no heroes in *Rum Punch*, only survivors. Even Max is passive, henpecked, almost a schmuck; Jackie remains a little unfocused, partly because we need to be kept in the dark about her real loyalties. All the old values—devotion, love, honor—fade in the South Florida sunshine, in the brightly lit designer shopping malls. No one knows who can be trusted; no one, in fact, can be trusted. Like many of Leonard's other books, this is not so much a whiz-bang boy's adventure as a hypnotic dance of death.

Michael Dirda, "Dreams Die Hard," *Washington Post Book World*, 19 July 1992, p. 2

DICK LOCHTE   It's a mistake to categorize Leonard's novels as mysteries or thrillers. Murderers are not announced in their final chapters, secrets are not revealed, the fates of nations do not hang on their outcome. They are tales of heroes and villains engaged in mortal and moral struggle. What distinguishes them is Leonard's ability to create characters, conversations and situations that are as natural and convincing as they are unique. He seems to know the hustlers, con men, killers and especially the good guys firsthand, and he passes along this knowledge in an understated way that suggests we readers are his equals in awareness. ⟨. . .⟩

It should be noted that Leonard began his career as an author with yarns about cowpokes and villains. His 1981 contemporary police novel, *City Primeval*, was constructed very much like a Western, complete with shootout in the street; and in case the point was not made, it carried the subtitle "High Noon in Detroit." This new book ⟨*Pronto*⟩, with its thoughtful, mild-mannered lawman protagonist looking a bit silly and out of place in Italy wearing his Dallas special Stetson (think Joel McCrea in his prime), is another of his wild West/urban crime melds. It mixes the romantic notions of the past, when honor and justice and a woman's love were things to be cherished, with Leonard's particularly adroit insight into the harsh realities and tensions of today. The mixture works beautifully.

> Dick Lochte, "When Honor and Justice Were Things to Be Cherished," *Los Angeles Times Book Review*, 24 October 1993, p. 8

◈ Bibliography

The Bounty Hunters. 1953.

The Law at Randadao. 1954.

Escape from Five Shadows. 1956.

Last Stand at Saber River. 1959.

Hombre. 1961.

The Big Bounce. 1969.

The Moonshine War. 1969.

Valdez Is Coming. 1970.

Forty Lashes Less One. 1972.

Mr. Majestyk. 1974.

52 Pickup. 1974.

Swag ⟨Ryan's Rules⟩. 1976.

The Hunted. 1977.

Unknown Man No. 89. 1977.

The Switch. 1978.

Gunsights. 1979.

City Primeval: High Noon in Detroit. 1980.

Gold Coast. 1980.

Split Images. 1981.

Cat Chaser. 1982.

Stick. 1983.

LaBrava. 1983.

Glitz. 1985.

Elmore Leonard's Dutch Treat ⟨The Hunted, Swag, Mr. Majestyk⟩. 1985.

Elmore Leonard's Double Dutch Treat ⟨City Primeval, The Moonshine War, Gold Coast⟩. 1986.

Bandits. 1987.

Touch. 1987.
Freaky Deaky. 1988.
Killshot. 1989.
Get Shorty. 1990.
Maximum Bob. 1991.
Rum Punch. 1992.
Pronto. 1993.
Riding the Rap. 1995.

Robert Ludlum
b. 1927

ROBERT LUDLUM was born on May 25, 1927, in New York City. He spent the years 1944–46 in the U.S. Marine Corps, then began attending Wesleyan University. He received a B.A. in 1951, the same year he married Mary Ryducha, an actress, with whom he had three children. Ludlum spent the next twenty years as an actor and producer in New York and New Jersey. He enjoyed some success in these professions: a New England Professor of Drama Award in 1951 helped to launch his acting career, and he subsequently received grants from the American National Theatre and Academy (1959) and the Actors' Equity Association and William C. Whitney Foundation (1960), and the Scroll of Achievement from the American National Theatre and Academy (1960).

Ludlum was a producer for the North Jersey Playhouse in Fort Lee, New Jersey, from 1957 to 1960. He then founded the Playhouse-on-the-Mall in Paramus, New Jersey (the first theatre in a shopping mall), and produced Bill Manhoff's *The Owl and the Pussycat* with the then-unknown actor Alan Alda. During the 1960s he also produced plays in New York.

By 1970 Ludlum had become frustrated with the pressures of working in the theatre and took up his wife's suggestion to attempt writing. His first novel, *The Scarlatti Inheritance* (1971), was well received, but it was his second book, *The Osterman Weekend* (1972), that launched his career. Since then nearly every one of his novels has reached the best-seller lists, and through the 1970s Ludlum's ever-increasing cadre of readers could count on a novel every year; among them were *The Matlock Paper* (1973), *The Rhinemann Exchange* (1974), *The Road to Gandolfo* (1975; first published under the pseudonym Michael Shepherd and later reprinted under his own name), and *The Matarese Circle* (1979).

Most of Ludlum's novels focus on a conspiracy by powerful foreign military or political figures to destroy civilization or to gain world supremacy, a conspiracy that is foiled in the nick of time by intrepid Americans usually operating alone and outside the recognized channels of law and government.

Ludlum has been vigorously attacked by critics for his seeming paranoia as well as for his leaden prose, implausible scenarios, and bewilderingly convoluted plots; but millions of readers have found his work compulsively readable.

The Bourne Identity (1980) is the first of a trilogy of novels involving the character Jason Bourne (also known as David Webb and Cain), the others of which are *The Bourne Supremacy* (1986) and *The Bourne Ultimatum* (1990). *The Bourne Identity* also represented a slowdown on Ludlum's part, so that during the 1980s he produced only one novel every two years. At this time, however, his novels were being increasingly adapted for television and film. The first such adaptation had occurred in 1977, when *The Rhinemann Exchange* was made into a miniseries on NBC, and several others have followed. As with his previous works, such novels as *The Parsifal Mosaic* (1982), *The Aquitaine Progression* (1984), and *The Icarus Agenda* (1988) dominated the best-seller lists. Ludlum's latest novel is *The Scorpio Illusion* (1993).

Robert Ludlum lives with his wife in Naples, Florida.

◈ *Critical Extracts*

WILLIAM B. HILL　　　What makes this book ⟨*The Scarlatti Inheritance*⟩ fascinating is the rapidity of its narration and the scope of the story. It involves high finance, cleverly concealed defalcation, cold-blooded killers, the financing of the Nazi party, mysterious death on shipboard—what would you? Would scope such as this invite the danger of improbability? It would, it does, the improbabilities occur; but if they reduce the novel almost to the plane of thriller, with more suspension of disbelief than the ordinary novel exacts, they still leave us with a narrative that is fast and intense. ⟨. . .⟩

There is brutality of a remarkably ruthless sort here, and the end offers as justice a cold-blooded murder by the hero. It is, however, a gripping tale, with the love of Canfield for his wife, Ulster's widow and the young boy's mother, as one of the dominant themes.

William B. Hill, [Review of *The Scarlatti Inheritance*], *Best Sellers*, 1 June 1971, p. 122

UNSIGNED ⟨*The Rhinemann Exchange* is⟩ an espionage thriller set in the desperate last year of the Hitler war. The situation that ignites the action (nearly five hundred sanguineous pages of it) is preposterous but intellectually undemanding. Germany has perfected a gyroscope airplane-guidance system but lacks the industrial diamonds needed to complete its terrible rocket missile; the United States has access to tons of industrial diamonds but its aerophysicists can't get the kinks out of its top-priority gyroscope. So a corrupt military-industrial cabal on both sides agrees to a secret, treasonous exchange, and Rhinemann, a German Jew (an "expatriot," in the author's vocabulary) living in Buenos Aires, is selected to handle the transfer. The United States, being no fool, sends a top agent, Captain Spaulding (Groucho Marx may be amused to learn), to Buenos Aires to look after its interests but (as is classically customary in spy stories) refrains from telling him the whole truth. Mr. Ludlum reads like a Hearst feature writer of the twenties—staccato sentences, one-sentence paragraphs—and he expresses himself with some abandon: "Kendall was an authoritative rodent who was not awkward in the tunnels of negotiated filth." The result, nevertheless, is reasonably entertaining.

Unsigned, [Review of *The Rhinemann Exchange*], *New Yorker*, 14 October 1974, pp. 202–3

BARBARA PHILLIPS Since 1970, with the regularity of swallows returning to Capistrano, Robert Ludlum has produced a novel of international intrigue mingling romance and violence. *The Rhinemann Exchange* (1974) was recently shown on network TV screens. Last year's *The Gemini Contenders* was on the best-seller list for 17 weeks. The latest entry, *The Chancellor Manuscript*, is a dual main selection of the Literary Guild.

While there is nothing literary about *The Chancellor Manuscript*, the story idea is certainly inventive. J. Edgar Hoover does not die naturally in his sleep, but is assassinated. Why? To keep him from revealing the contents of his secret files which, according to this novel, contain enough damaging information to ruin the lives of every man, woman and child in the nation. ⟨. . .⟩

There is no doubt that the book is entertaining. The characters are stock, the style melodramatic, the hero's durability preposterous. But the plotting is skillful, and the narrative races along with the speed of the expensive cars that Ludlum incorporates so lovingly into the plot. The novel also contains details about the secret workings of intelligence agencies that seem frighteningly accurate, as though Ludlum had his very own "Deep Throat." ⟨. . .⟩

It is fashionable to maintain that internal conspiracies and international intrigues are the commonplace events which investigative reporters and fiction writers say they are, so no wonder we're all confused as to whether art or life is the real thing. Anything can happen and probably does in a world where daily headlines scream about Korean bribery of U.S. congressmen, CIA payments to King Hussein, or corporate bribery of high foreign officials. But if Mr. Ludlum's novel has any basis in fact, even the most respected among us had better review his past indiscretions.

Barbara Phillips, "*Chancellor Manuscript:* New Ludlum Thriller," *Christian Science Monitor*, 31 March 1977, p. 31

PETER ANDREWS   *The Bourne Identity* represents Mr. Ludlum at his most breakneck. In the first two paragraphs of his preface, he manages to snuff out three espionage agents and unleash a secret international terrorist killer to prey on the flanks of the Free World. On the opening page of his narrative he has a trawler smashing itself to pieces in an ocean storm while a man, pursued by an armed assassin, rushes out on deck. The man takes three slugs in the back, one in the head, and plunges into a roiling ocean— now we're talking about plot development. Three pages later he is picked up by some fishermen, and two pages after that, his life is saved by an alcoholic remittance man who is probably a doctor, but you can't be sure. Is this the sought-after terrorist? We may never know. The bullet that creased his skull also gave him total amnesia. The doctor, however, notices that the man's face has been entirely rebuilt by plastic surgery. He is a creature without a name, without a memory, without even a face of his own. But wait! There is a tiny piece of microfilm embedded in his flesh. On it is the number of a secret bank account in Zurich. . . . And most important, in case you think I have given anything away, there are still some 500 pages left to go. Mr. Ludlum has barely addressed himself to the task at hand. Does anyone really want to bail out now?

Some of Mr. Ludlum's previous novels were so convoluted they should have been packed with bags of bread crumbs to help readers keep track of the plot lines. But *The Bourne Identity* is a Ludlum story at its most severely plotted, and for me its most effective.

Peter Andrews, "Momentum Is Everything," *New York Times Book Review*, 30 March 1980, p. 7

ROBIN W. WINKS   Ludlum does make for compelling reading, if one is not paying close attention. *The Matarese Circle* is no less silly than the earlier Ludlums but it is better written. To be sure, the little annoying slips are still there: the hero thinks to escape "to Melanesia, the Fijis, . . . any of a dozen Sunda islands" (if you don't spot the problem here forget it), and the exact nature of the terror that awaits is remarkably vague: the Matarese council, a body of incredibly well-placed descendants of a Sardinian bent on revenge and world-dominance, "sends in the experts, and provides covert financing. Fanatics do not labor over the source of funds, only their availability." We never really learn more about how one of Ludlum's international conspiracies works, since someone can be counted upon to hurl a bomb at our hero before anyone can get down to details. *The Bourne Identity*, the current best-seller (equally long: Ludlums generally run to a dependable 500-plus pages), requires the reader to believe that a top-flight killer has so lost his memory that he cannot recall whether he works for Us or Them, and none of the many attempts to kill him by both sides helps much. He is succored by a Canadian whom he first kidnaps from a conference in Geneva; despite rough treatment, she naturally falls in love with the mysterious Bourne. Yet Ludlum seems not to have bothered to swat up on Canada, since Europe is his setting, and so he has the lovely Marie St. Jacques appealing to Versailles and other French symbols long abandoned by any French Canadian. He gets the functions of the Treasury Board in Ottawa wrong, and he insists, redundantly, that our heroine is a *French*-Canadienne.

Robin W. Winks, "Mysteries," *New Republic*, 25 November 1981, pp. 38–39

BRUCE E. BRANDT   ⟨. . .⟩ we find ⟨in Robert Ludlum⟩ an author who has increasingly turned to conspiracy on a grand scale. Thus, in *The Chancellor Manuscript*, a cabal of five men is revealed to have directed every major action of the United States since the depression. They have made mistakes, such as an industrial relationship with Germany that backfired into a world war, but most of their actions, such as the assassination of J. Edgar Hoover, are clearly good, and they are essentially benevolent rulers. Unfortunately, one of them is a traitor, and a vital portion of Hoover's secret files are seized by members of an even more mysterious, evil and deadly conspiracy—the black militants. These all speak Swahili, a suggestion of alien influence corresponding to the real-life insistence of right-wing conspiracy theorists that only outside agitation could dupe our contented minorities into unwise and unwarranted action. The power of conspiracy is global in *The Holcroft Covenant*. Here Ludlum begins with the premise that a group of Nazi children were smuggled out of Germany at the end of the war and raised in foster homes all over the world. As adults, these children have all risen to prominence, apparently because they really are genetically superior to the rest of us, and they succeed in taking over the world from the inside. At the end, Ludlum's hero devotes himself to a lifetime of assassinating these new leaders, but the final message seems to be that though we can defeat the Nazi on the battlefield, we are not vigilant enough to keep him out of office or off the supreme court.

This ominous vision that grants the protagonist a personal and largely moral victory in a world where evil is otherwise triumphant is amplified in *The Matarese Circle*. Ludlum's portrayal of the Circle's first meeting, which culminates in the murder of all the witnesses and its baptism in the blood of its founder, is spectacular, but the core of the vision is archetypally pure: this small band of men is committed to the destruction of the world order, and its Corsican origin, intended to recall Napoleon's efforts to conquer the world, renders it sufficiently alien to account for such opposition to society. They are responsible, we learn, for virtually every political death since Sarajevo, a list including Trotsky, Stalin, Beria, the Kennedys, King and Franklin Roosevelt. Initially they were hired assassins, but now they kill simply to increase world chaos, for such chaos enhances their opportunities to seize power. To the same end, they finance such groups as the PLO, the Red Brigades, the Weathermen, the Minutemen, and the Ku Klux Klan, and they have heightened the distrust between the United States and the Soviet Union. They have infiltrated everywhere, and Ludlum shows a Matarese meeting that includes high U.S. and Soviet officials. Their real coup is that one of them, a liberal Massachusetts senator, is about to be elected president. The supposed scion of an old New England family, the real Appleton, we learn, died years before and his place was taken by the son of the leader of the Matarese, a use of the changeling motif that again insists that evil is alien and that things are not what they seem. The final horror is revealed by the leader of the Matarese only at the very end:

> "Governments as we have known them are no longer viable entities. They must be replaced."
>
> "By whom? With what?"
>
> The old man softened his voice; it became hollow, hypnotic. "By a new breed of philosopher-kings, if you like. Men who understand the world as it has truly emerged, who measure its potential in terms of resources, technology and productivity, who care not one whit about the color of a man's skin, or the heritage of his ancestors, or what idols he may pray to. Who care only about his full productive potentials as a human being. And his contribution to the marketplace."
>
> "My God," said Bray. "You're talking about the conglomerates."

Yes, the ultimate enemy is the man in the gray flannel suit. Ludlum's surprise is in a sense no surprise. Historically, money interests and organizations whose allegiances are perceived as transcending national boundaries have often proved suspect. Failure to discriminate on the basis of race, ancestry or religion is perhaps a new twist on the image of corporate evil, but for Scofield this signifies the increasing depersonalization of life under the conglomerates: "In your world there *are* no identities! We're numbers and symbols on computers! Circles and squares." The novel has not prepared us for such a concern on Scofield's part; his major humanitarian aspect, his weariness of killing people, seems more a case of "professional burnout" than conscience. Nonetheless, this fear is the logical extension of Ludlum's premise, for as we have seen, the value of believing in a conspiracy is not only that it imposes a pattern upon events, but that it affirms, despite the opposing claims of Masons or Catholics or Mormons or whomever, that we know what we are about and where our values lie. The vision of conspiracy is an antidote to alienation, and to the extent that conglomerates are representative of the increasing dehumanization and impersonality of the industrial world, they will increasingly be seen as conspiracies.

Bruce E. Brandt, "Reflections of 'Paranoid Style' in the Current Suspense Novel," *Clues* 3, No. 1 (Spring–Summer 1982): 64–65

ALAN FURST   Yes, our old buddies the Fascist Generals are at it again ⟨in *The Aquitaine Progression*⟩, up to their beastly plots in the umpteenth novel of the decade. Always the same guys, with the white truffles and the black Mercedeses, hanging out in their chateaus in the South of France with muscle-bound servants (all named Jacques) and their wiggy sex lives. I guess with old guys it just takes tickling. But say this for them: They are superwealthy, as always, and they *are* cultured and speak in only the most sophisticated tones. And as for the dark, hushed corridors of secret power, these guys are where it's at. ⟨. . .⟩

The Aquitaine Progression is, like Ludlum's nine previous novels, a comic book for adults, written with all the subtlety of a man cutting down a tree with a car. The experience of the book is generally akin to reading somebody's completed crossword puzzle: you know what's coming next, and there it is. Same principle as the Chinese water torture. ⟨. . .⟩

Writers of the Ludlum school of espionage ⟨. . .⟩ attempt to overwhelm with volume: they may not be able to do a good sentence, but will at least give you a lot of them. This concept invades plotting and all other aspects of the novel. Unable to create one deliciously appropriate corpse? Then strew a few hundred around for the reader to trip over. The books themselves seem to grow longer and longer—in part a function of the $17.95 cover price—keeping half the chain saws in Oregon busy day and night. ⟨. . .⟩

I read an espionage novel earlier this year where a scientist and a spy have a brain transplant so that the spy can do the scientific dirty work. As I read, a persistent little voice in my head kept whispering, *I don't believe this, this is bullshit.* Nobody's screaming for Shakespeare, just a light cruise with plenty of good scenery.

The genre freak—lamp just right, radio turned down—sets out for a juicy evening with certain nonnegotiable demands. Authenticity of dialogue (George Higgins's stop-and-start diction is riveting because it's palpably real), an urgent sense of locale (Jerry Westerby's trip through Southeast Asia in le Carré's *The Honourable Schoolboy* may be the best it has ever been done), and a plot that somehow imitates the red-light/green-light passage of actual human time. In other words, a lot of reality in the fantasy.

The good productive genre writers—Ross Thomas, Elmore Leonard, Robert Parker, Nicholas Freeling, my beloved George MacDonald Fraser, to name a few—can generally be counted on for a book a year. But I read more than ten books a year, and I just can't be bothered with any more Fascist Generals.

And if I can't find a good book to keep me company in this life, maybe they already *have* taken over the world and we just didn't notice.

Alan Furst, "Thrilled to Death," *Esquire* 101, No. 4 (April 1984): 211–12

THOMAS R. EDWARDS   ⟨. . .⟩ what is it that all we recumbent, reasonably well-to-do fellows *want* from what might as well be called a ludlum? First the thing needs defining. A *ludlum*: a long, turgidly written, frantically overplotted novel, the literary equivalent of seriously wielding a plumber's helper. Its subject is conspiracy, the secret scheming of our collective enemies, foreign and domestic, and the equally secret and almost equally frightening counter-scheming of our supposed friends and protectors, the CIA or the NSC or the even more sinister "Consular Operations" branch of the State Department, which I fervently hope is Ludlum's invention. To put it more grandly, the subject is the dreadful subsumption of private selfhood and its moral sense into a morally indeterminate public life. Ludlum's heroes are respectable, successful men—lawyers, scholars, businessmen—who are entrapped and used by hidden power; some of the entrappers are on our side, some not, and the hero's task is to get them sorted out. But in an authorial move almost de rigueur in such fiction, the difference between good and bad is kept maddeningly obscure, and the hero's fate is simply to survive and find some private happiness outside the labyrinths of power which sometimes seem to enclose us all. ⟨. . .⟩

Ludlum is careful to write just as badly as he can. His characters are given to remarks like "There's a rotten growth in our collective armor," and I treasure the moment when one of them, a relatively sane psychiatrist, mutters "Don't ask me where these people find their metaphors." But his conventional shoot-'em-up action prose has its own kind of interest:

> The assassin threw himself over the row of flowers, clutching the warm barrel of Bourne's machine gun, wrenching it downward, leveling and firing his own gun at Jason. The bullet grazed Bourne's forehead, and in fury, Jason yanked back the trigger of the repeating weapon. Bullets thundered into the ground, the vibrations within their small, deadly arena earth-shattering. He grabbed the Englishman's gun, twisting it counter-clockwise. The assassin's mutilated right arm was no match for the man from Medusa. The gun exploded as Bourne wrenched it free. The

imposter fell back on the grass, his eyes glazed, within them the
knowledge that he had lost.

It would be hard for writing to make action seem less realistic than this—
in such a situation, for example, who would have this preternatural awareness
of what particular bullets were doing? But if the details are clumsy (did the
gun "explode" or just fire?), the passage makes dim if inadvertent contact
with a great tradition of violence in literature. One combatant, Webb, is
called "Bourne," "Jason," and "the man from Medusa," while the other is
"the assassin," "the Englishman," and "the imposter"; a firearm can be a
"machine gun," a "repeating weapon," or just a "gun." If this is the elegant
variation that identifies so much bad prose, still some of it sounds oddly
like the variable formulaic epithets of Homeric and other oral epics, those
metrical conveniences which also suggest that great men and gods and
natural forces need more than one name if their magnificence is to be
properly known. (The names "Jason" and "Medusa" help too.) And while
I doubt that those bullets "thundered" into the ground ("thudded"?) and
that very much of the earth was shattered by their "earth-shattering" impact,
still the enlargement of small human violence into huge natural violence
is normal and necessary in heroic writing. Neither Ludlum nor the reader
needs to be conscious of such effects for them to *work* as similar ones do
in the *Iliad* or *Beowulf*.

Thomas R. Edwards, "The Dark Side" (1986), *Over Here: Criticizing America 1968–
1989* (New Brunswick, NJ: Rutgers University Press, 1991), pp. 194, 196–98

DAVID WILTSE   Reading Robert Ludlum's latest thriller 〈*The
Bourne Supremacy*〉 is a bit like watching a blacksmith forge a very long
chain. The making of the first few links is interesting enough as an exercise
in brute manipulation. What is lacking in finesse and artistry is made up
for by lots of noise and energy. But after watching the smith link together
a foot or so of chain, one perceives a certain sameness to the effort. The
chief suspense is in how long the man will keep at it. 〈. . .〉

Webb/Bourne, 〈. . .〉 although he doesn't realize it for most of the book,
is out for nothing less than the preservation of civilization as we know it.
Although a largish burden for one man, this is not necessarily a terrible
idea for a story. James Bond has saved us all more than once from similar
fates. But then Bond has always had charm, intelligence, taste, imagination,

humor and massive sex appeal on his side. Webb/Bourne, alas, has none of these assets.

Robert Ludlum has given his hero, and his readers, very little to work with in lifting this behemoth of a book off the ground. Vivid characters would help, or interesting dialogue. Mr. Ludlum is having none of that, however. A chain is strong, but not very subtle.

> David Wiltse, "Chopping Down a Forest of Bad Guys," *New York Times Book Review*, 9 March 1986, p. 12

BOB WOODWARD   Some years back Ludlum said in an interview, "I don't spend a great deal of time on things that don't move the story." It was a good practice, which he executed skillfully, creating stories that had the feel of one coherent, breathless chase. *The Icarus Agenda* instead lurches along, weaving a hyperbolic patchwork, picking up and discarding two fundamentals along the way—characters and subplots. ⟨. . .⟩

There is endless, banal dialogue as if Ludlum had to jack up the word count and pad it to 677 pages to give a big-book appearance. The characters have little depth and display little of the psychological or technical sophistication a reader might reasonably expect from his other novels. There is not enough realism. For example, the heroes speak on the domestic and international telephone all the time, conducting the most sensitive conversations knowing they are up against those possessing the latest eavesdropping technology.

The portrait of Washington and its institutions is off, a minor matter if the story held up or Ludlum had created a plausible and interesting alternative Washington. Instead he attempts to take the Washington that exists and graft onto it some simplicities and remove the infighting and intrigue which make Washington forever interesting. ⟨. . .⟩

⟨. . .⟩ Ludlum has a tendency to repeat, making sure nothing gets lost on the inattentive or careless reader, say on the airplane or in front of the TV. *Italics*, CAPITAL LETTERS and exclamation points! assist throughout. But enough. A fine escapist has flown too close to the sun and nearly crashed.

> Bob Woodward, "The Ludlum Diversion," *Washington Post Book World*, 21 February 1988, pp. 1, 13

OTTO PENZLER   Robert Ludlum has become an eagerly collected author because of sheer immense popularity. His type of action-espionage thriller has influenced so many subsequent writers that the term "Ludlum-esque" has become an accepted shorthand definition of the sort of novel that he singlehandedly made so incredibly popular.

Typically (though certainly not exclusively), two figures of heroically grand proportions are at the focal point of a battle between Good (generally someone from the United States) and Evil (generally someone from a Communist country). Each has colleagues, bosses, whole departments, but no one on either side is competent to deal with the titans. Ultimately, the battle of wits and martial skills decides the fate of the world.

Disbelief has to be suspended (often a nearly hopeless endeavor) and few readers are able to follow the numerous convolutions of the plot, but Ludlum has acquired a readership of millions that simply *must* turn one more page to discover what happens next. While the very notion of realism is alien to the entire Ludlum opera, the goals of escapism are virtually defined by it.

> Otto Penzler, "Collecting Mystery Fiction: Robert Ludlum," *Armchair Detective* 22, No. 4 (Fall 1989): 382

JOE QUEENAN   Several years ago, one of my neighbors threatened to lend me a Robert Ludlum novel. I can't remember the title—*The Heuf-schneugel Algorithm*, *The Polyphemus Conundrum*, *The Lebensraum Substra-tum*—but the threat was sufficiently serious that I left town for the summer. Fortunately, by the time I got back, my neighbor had died from some rare, macrobiotically induced disease. I took this as a sign from God, as, I'm sure, did he.

Alas, there are no dead neighbors to rescue me from *The Bourne Ultima-tum*, Mr. Ludlum's latest offering, which already is flying high on the best-seller lists. The book, the final installation in a trilogy that began with *The Bourne Supremacy* and *The Bourne Identity*, describes the final showdown between the vicious but likable American superkiller, Jason Bourne, and his thoroughly unacceptable nemesis, the Jackal. As is often the case with rectangular objects in this genre, the book is littered with mangled append-ages, splattered brain tissue, elderly men on dog leashes getting their heads sucked into furnaces, and innocent children led to the slaughter. Neverthe-less, I didn't like it. ⟨. . .⟩

Readers who have no previous experience with Mr. Ludlum needn't worry: *The Bourne Ultimatum* is loaded with recapitulations, so you won't have to go back and not be able to read the two previously unreadable books in the unreadable trilogy in order to not be able to read this one. Suffice it to say that the Jackal and the assorted Bournes are sufficiently mad at each other, that no one is safe in this sizzling novel of international intrigue that races back and forth from the moist, misty mornings of Monser-rat to the plangent pomp of Paris, to the creepy crepuscules of Crabcake Corners.

Joe Queenan, "Bourne in America!," *Wall Street Journal*, 22 March 1990, p. A12

JAMES POLK   In this latest thriller ⟨*The Scorpio Illusion*⟩ from the prolific Robert Ludlum, the beautiful, anarchistic Basque terrorist Amaya Bajaratt ("Death to all authority!" is her mantra) modestly sets out to eliminate the leaders of the United States, Britain, France and Israel. The only person able to stop her and thus save civilization as we know it is Tyrell Nathaniel Hawthorne 3d, a disillusioned former United States Naval Intelligence officer, now going to seed in the Caribbean. The two adversaries circle warily, each desperate to eliminate the other, neither able to strike the fatal blow. As the circles narrow toward Washington and the White House—Bajaratt will assassinate the President, triggering killings in Europe and the Middle East—the members of an impressive supporting cast battle for a variety of causes, only a few of which the principals understand. Cabinet secretaries, spy masters, generals, senators, a retired Supreme Court justice, a Mafia don and a mysterious *éminence grise* all head toward an incendiary denouement in the Oval Office, though few are apt to live that long. Books like *The Scorpio Illusion* seem more assembled than written—a little sex here, a lot of violence there, a scattering of irony throughout and more sudden plot twists than seem entirely reasonable. Their goal is a breakneck sort of readability, which Mr. Ludlum certainly achieves—once again.

James Polk, [Review of *The Scorpio Illusion*], *New York Times Book Review*, 20 June 1993, p. 16

◈ *Bibliography*

The Scarlatti Inheritance. 1971.

The Osterman Weekend. 1972.

The Matlock Paper. 1973.

Trevayne. 1973.

The Cry of the Halidon. 1974.

The Rhinemann Exchange. 1974.

The Road to Gandolfo. 1975.

The Gemini Contenders. 1976.

The Chancellor Manuscript. 1977.

The Holcroft Covenant. 1978.

The Matarese Circle. 1979.

The Bourne Identity. 1980.

The Parsifal Mosaic. 1982.

The Aquitaine Progression. 1984.

The Bourne Supremacy. 1986.

The Icarus Agenda. 1988.

The Bourne Ultimatum. 1990.

The Road to Omaha. 1992.

The Scorpio Illusion. 1993.

Robert B. Parker
b. 1932

ROBERT BROWN PARKER was born on September 17, 1932, in Springfield, Massachusetts, the son of Carroll Snow and Mary Pauline (Murphy) Parker. He received a B.A. from Colby College in 1954 and, after two years spent in Korea with the U.S. Army (1954–56), gained his M.A. from Boston University in 1957. He married Joan Hall in 1956; they have two sons.

Parker spent the next five years working as a technical writer for the Raytheon Company in Andover, Massachusetts (1957–59), an advertising writer for the Prudential Company in Boston (1959–62), and cochairman of his own advertising agency, the Parker-Farman Company (1960–62). At this point he decided to enter the academic community, teaching English successively at Boston University (1962–64), Massachusetts State College at Lowell (1964–66), Massachusetts State College at Bridgewater (1966–68), and Northeastern University (1968–79). In 1970 he received a Ph.D. from Boston University. Although Parker became a professor at his wife's suggestion to have more time for writing, he eventually soured on university life, believing that academicians were out of touch with reality.

Although his first two books were collaborative handbooks to literature, Parker quickly decided to turn to crime fiction, which he had read voluminously in youth. His Ph.D. dissertation had been a study of Dashiell Hammett and Raymond Chandler (subsequently published as *The Private Eye in Hammett and Chandler*, 1984), so he naturally turned to these writers for inspiration. *The Godwulf Manuscript* (1973), on which he worked for more than two years, introduced his tough private investigator, Spenser (he has no first name), a name derived from Edmund Spenser, just as Chandler's Philip Marlowe was derived from Sir Philip Sidney and Christopher Marlowe. Parker began producing Spenser novels in quick succession, including *God Save the Child* (1974), *Mortal Stakes* (1975), *Promised Land* (1976; winner of the Edgar Allan Poe Award from the Mystery Writers of America), and *The Judas Goat* (1978); their success allowed him to give up teaching and become a full-time writer.

144

In 1975 Parker's wife Joan discovered that she had breast cancer; the family's three-year ordeal, which ended in a mastectomy, is poignantly recorded in *Three Weeks in Spring* (1978). Thereafter Parker continued writing Spenser novels with regularity; some of his more notable books of the 1980s were *A Savage Place* (1981), *Early Autumn* (1981), *The Widening Gyre* (1983), *A Catskill Eagle* (1985), and *Playmates* (1989). Parker has confessed that he was initially influenced as much by Westerns as by hard-boiled detective stories in the creation of Spenser, since Parker believes that the Western is one of the last remaining genres of literature to address issues of honor and violence. Unlike the solitary detectives of Hammett, Chandler, and Ross Macdonald, Spenser has developed a relationship with Susan Silverman, which has been elaborated in several novels. The popularity of Spenser and of Parker's novels in general were augmented by the popular television series, "Spenser: For Hire," starring Robert Urich. Although Parker was a consultant for the series, he had no control over its content.

Parker has written two novels not featuring Spenser, *Wilderness* (1979) and *Love and Glory* (1983). In addition, he collaborated with John R. Marsh on a successful handbook, *Sports Illustrated Training with Weights* (1974; revised edition 1990). A slim volume of Parker's literary essays has been issued as *Parker on Writing* (1985).

In recent years Parker has renewed his interest in Raymond Chandler by writing a novel, *Poodle Springs* (1989), based upon an unfinished story by Chandler, and by writing *Perchance to Dream* (1991), a sequel to *The Big Sleep*. His most recent novel is *All Our Yesterdays* (1994). Robert B. Parker lives with his family in Cambridge, Massachusetts.

◈ *Critical Extracts*

MARTHA DUFFY   It seems that this thriller writer is not trying to put anything over on anybody. Two years ago, he announced on the jacket of his first book, *The Godwulf Manuscript*, that he had written his doctoral dissertation on Dashiell Hammett and Raymond Chandler. Both of Robert Parker's novels, about a private eye known simply as Spenser, are filled with echoes of the masters. But Parker is really not a pirate. Instead, he resembles film makers like Jean-Luc Godard, who pay homage to great directors of the past with little vignettes so blatantly similar in style that no *aficionado* could miss or fail to savor them. ⟨. . .⟩

On the evidence of *The Godwulf Manuscript* and *God Save the Child*, this could well be a long-running series. Parker's writing is clear, his plots believable and uncluttered. In Spenser he has a malleable and therefore durable hero. But despite his dust-jacket confession, Parker is holding something back; he would be no mystery writer if he did not. His real debt is not to Chandler or Hammett but to Ross Macdonald. Both Parker's plots deal with lost, unhappy young people estranged from their parents' split-level goals, but with no values of their own to turn to. Their searchings invariably bring them into the underworld of drugs and extortion that is right below their classroom windows. This, of course, has become Macdonald's sole theme.

Yet Parker is a cooler, less driven writer. Although his new book is flawed by a repetitive section devoted to a truly odious middle-aged couple, it shows a better plot and a looser, more interesting Spenser. With his knowledge of the drug trade, Parker must surely know that he is a pusher too—to mystery addicts—and take his long-term responsibilities seriously.

Martha Duffy, "Boston Op," Time, 10 February 1975, pp. 76, K10

DAVID GEHERIN   Nothing shows Parker's skill at integrating character, scene, and theme better than his description ⟨in *God Save the Child*⟩ of the Bartletts' cocktail party. Spenser has been asked to keep an eye on Marge after she receives a death threat. Feeling as out of place as a "weed at a flower show," he nonetheless agrees to attend the party in case he is needed. The first jarring note comes when the reader realizes that the party is merrily going on in almost the exact spot where Earl Maguire was murdered only hours earlier, a fact which bothers Spenser but apparently no one else. Two other incidents produce the same uneasy feeling. During the party, Spenser receives a call from the Massachusetts State Police confirming that Maguire died of a broken back. The party continues. Later he hears a recording of Billie Holiday singing her classic "God Bless the Child," a song about a deprived child which can be taken as an appropriate comment on Kevin Bartlett's predicament (and which gives the novel its title). No one but Spenser pays any attention to the song or its significance. The party continues.

This contrast between the frivolous and the tragic, and Marge's attempt to promote the former by ignoring the latter, parallels another contrast in the novel, that between respectability and corruption. The Bartletts' cocktail party is the gathering spot for many of Smithfield's finest citizens—doctors, businessmen, high school coaches, etc. We learn how deeply involved many of these same people are in crime, either as operators or as customers. Parker's point is that these respectable citizens display as little concern for the existence of corruption in their midst as they do for Kevin's disappearance or Maguire's murder.

What unifies the separate themes of the novel—the family tragedy, the corruption within the community, the sense of lost values—is Parker's emphasis on relationships: the flawed—between Kevin and his parents; the failed—between Marge and Roger Bartlett; the unethical—between Croft and his patients; the corrupt—between Croft, Trask, and Harroway; the irresponsible—between Trask and the community of Smithfield. Set against this extensive catalogue of failures, however, are some positive and productive relationships: for example, the developing relationship between Susan and Spenser; or the professional relationship between Spenser and Lieutenant Healy; or the latent homosexual relationship between Kevin and Harroway which, despite its tragic effects, is at least based on love, a commodity in short supply in the novel.

David Geherin, "Robert B. Parker," *Sons of Sam Spade: The Private-Eye Novel in the 70s* (New York: Frederick Ungar Publishing Co., 1980), pp. 38–39

CARL HOFFMAN   With *Mortal Stakes*, Parker has turned a corner, embraced wholeheartedly an idea touched on by his essay "Marxism and the Mystery." In it, the author emphasizes that hardboiled heroes like Sam Spade, Philip Marlowe, and, by implication, Spenser too, belong to the chivalric tradition, the tradition of the man of honor in a world without it. Looking back over the first three books, it seems obvious that in *Godwulf* and *God Save*, Parker was writing his way slowly up to this theme, perhaps discovering it little by little, and in *Mortal Stakes* bringing it into explicit focus. From this perspective, the negative judgment on Spenser's code at the close of the book assumes greater importance, because the recurring problem with chivalric heroes from Robin Hood to John Wayne has been their goodness, their unfailing strength and purity, which sets them so far

apart from the rest of the human race that they become unbelievable.
Hammett and Chandler both fought hard against this tendency in their
characters, Hammett by leavening Spade with a healthy dose of simple
greed, Chandler by making Marlowe a hard-drinking cynic who attains
financial success only by marrying money. Parker may be doing something
similar at the end of *Mortal Stakes*. But ⟨. . .⟩ there is a curiously insincere
feel to that final chapter, as if the author is just going through the motions
of pointing out the detective's faults, as if he only half-believes the words
he's putting in the mouths of Spenser and Susan Silverman. The suspicion
lingers that this last chapter is a *pro forma* exercise which frees Parker to
indulge his fascination with the code hero in the next two books—indeed,
to let this fascination run wild, because, in the second phase of the Spenser
series, what we get is not so much a code hero as an all-conquering fantasy
figure.

Carl Hoffman, "Spenser: The Illusion of Knighthood," *Armchair Detective* 16, No. 2
(Spring 1983): 136

W. RUSSEL GRAY   The "literary" overtones in Parker's characterization of Spenser (his name, reading tastes, poetic allusions) are not
necessarily evidence that Parker is trying to upscale himself into the
Hammett-Chandler-Macdonald league. Of that, the future will judge. It
may be fairer to Parker's intention to regard these touches as a tapping of
the heightened cultural consciousness of those who follow today's popular
arts. After all, given the fact that *Playboy* is the highest paying short fiction
market in America, it may well be that a number of readers, degreed and
un-degreed, appreciate more than centerfolds.

Parker's "pulpulist" hero exemplifies the growing belief that formal education has been somewhat oversold. Without a Ph.D. or even a B.A. he is
an impressively literate person with a social conscience. In most of the first
eleven outings Spenser has seemed as committed to healing injured family
relationships as to vanquishing or at least neutralizing the underworld's
agents of evil. He is the larger than life hero of a detective romance series
in a popular culture that has elevated "stars" to superstars. Thus Spenser
attends to the problem of evil in society like a SuperMarlowe and reacts
with the sensitivity of a SuperArcher to the distress of circumstantial victims
of family living. Such a hero excels at detecting the cankered nexus of

respectability between the underworld and family: the English professor into drug distribution, the small town police chief and doctor involved in a procuring service, a beloved tell-it-like-it-is sportscaster and blackmailer, an arson-connected insurance broker, a conglomerate chairman who condones labor racketeering and extortion, a state guidance counseling official into juvenile pornography, a congressperson in the pocket of the mob, and a reverend who is tied to drug dealing.

Parker's hero is one with whom many of his day can vicariously connect (there is fan mail in all eight languages in which the series has appeared). Spenser is admirably strong and courageous, a witty and literate exemplar of today's enlightened social consciousness, a person secure enough not to be a loner though individuality in thought and action is the source of his strength. The gyre has widened considerably since *Godwulf* in 1973.

W. Russel Gray, "Reflections in a Private Eye: Robert B. Parker's Spenser," *Clues* 5, No. 1 (Spring–Summer 1984): 11–12

DONALD J. GREINER   Rejecting Chandler's concept of the pristine hero, Parker makes Spenser more erotically inclined and thus more human. Spenser does not cheat with his partner's wife or bed down with the gangster's girl. He attracts women as easily as he is attracted to them, but his affairs are not James Bond fantasies. Brenda Loring, for instance, is so stunningly beautiful that she literally turns heads as she walks by, but she is for what Spenser calls "fun and wisecracks." Sex with Brenda is not promiscuity, but neither is it commitment. Susan Silverman is different. Heroine of many Spenser novels, Susan is a pro, a woman who unlike Brenda can talk about "hard things." In *Mortal Stakes*, however, the true fair lady worthy of rescue is soiled herself: Linda Rabb, wife of a baseball star, and former whore. Where Hammett sends Brigid to prison for murder and promiscuity, and where Chandler damns his alluring lady by combining Carmen Sternwood's posing for pornographic photographs with her drug addiction and murder rap, Parker makes his skin-flick actress a heroine. This difference reflects a change in America's social mores, a change that probably Hammett and surely Chandler would not have approved of, yet the larger point is not Linda's disgusting past but her status as a professional, as one who recognizes the weaknesses of the jock ethic, who acts like a pro in the clutch to clear up her husband's mess, and who accepts the consequences of her public exposure. Spenser does not have to sleep with Linda Rabb. All he need do is admire her.

These allusions to and alterations of Hammett and Chandler are superficial beside the heart of *Mortal Stakes*: Spenser's gradual disillusionment with the very thing that sustains Spade and Marlowe—his code. In lighter moments, his sense of self-irony is much greater than that of his forerunners, for he can make fun of his "rules": "I applied one of Spenser's rules: When in doubt, cook something and eat it. I took off my shirt, opened another can of beer, and studied the refrigerator." But such moments are rare in the grim world of *Mortal Stakes*. The more Spenser gets sucked into the grimy entanglement of prostitution, blackmail, and murder, the more he notices his own stink. Code or no code, those who play with dirt get dirty. Parker's Spenser is mired in a post-Watergate, post-Nixon, post-Vietnam United States where accepted ideals of moral persuasion and right behavior are not as clear cut as in Hammett's, Chandler's and even Macdonald's day. The result is the victorious detective as self-doubter, the winner who is no longer sure if he has played by the rules. Shooting two blackmailers from virtual ambush, Spenser vomits and thinks, "They were both dead. That's the thing about a shotgun. At close range you don't have to go around checking pulses after." And when Susan asks if he murdered them by setting them up, all he can answer is, "No, not exactly. Or . . . I don't know. Maybe."

His equivocation is as honest as it is crucial. One cannot imagine Spade in ⟨*The Maltese*⟩ *Falcon* or Marlowe in *The Big Sleep* seriously doubting his motives and methods. But Spenser must question because the shotgun blast has blown a hole in not only the bad guys but also his definition of the jock ethic, one of the cornerstones of his personal system. How can he play by the rules if he lures the opposition to a slaughter where he himself pulls the trigger? His primary problem is not the mystery itself but how to define his values. Brenda, for example, sees the jock ethic as "winning isn't everything, it's the only thing," but Spenser dismisses her quip as the jock ethic promoted by people who know little about athletes. The real thing, he insists, is more complicated.

Donald J. Greiner, "Robert B. Parker and the Jock of the Mean Streets," *Critique* 26, No. 1 (Fall 1984): 40–41

ROBERT B. PARKER and ANNE PONDER   What I write
more nearly resembles a Western than it does other detective novels. I am

certainly more like A. B. Guthrie than like Agatha Christie. I subscribe to much that Robert Warshaw said in *The Westerner*. ⟨. . .⟩

Warshaw said that the Western is the last art form that gives serious consideration to questions of honor and violence. The crucial point in the Western is not when the Westerner will draw his gun but when he won't. The point in a classic Western like *Shane* or *High Noon* is that the gun gets drawn when appropriate, rather than randomly. Where Western movies began to descend and lose their grip was when filmmakers didn't understand that or chose to demythify it, like Peckinpah's *The Wild Bunch* demythified *Shane* by substituting nostalgia and camaraderie of men in groups. The violence in the Spenser novels shares the view of the classic Western. The fact that Spenser will kill somebody is much less significant than the fact that he won't or that he does so in a controlled, almost civilized fashion. *Shane* is, in many ways, about how a hero won't kill until he must, and when he must, he does. It is not random. It is done with reason. I don't know of any other art form at the moment than the kind of books I write which considers violence as controllable, necessary, and subject to a code of behavior. The bad guys in my books will do anything, but Spenser is what Warshaw calls "the last gentleman."

Like the Westerner, the significant conflict for Spenser comes ". . . when his moral code, without ceasing to be compelling, is seen also to be imperfect. The Westerner at his best exhibits a moral ambiguity which darkens his image and saves him from absurdity; this ambiguity arises from the fact that, whatever his justifications, he is a killer of men." The same Spenser who couldn't or wouldn't shoot Harry Cotton in *Early Autumn* gets sick after he kills Leo the pimp in *Catskill Eagle*, but he shoots Jerry Costigan without hesitation. These novels are about how a man without extraordinary prestige or wealth behaves honorably. Such a character is, by definition, heroic. I do refer to some mythic patterns. For example, Spenser is a man without parents. In *Catskill Eagle* he reveals the circumstances of his birth and childhood and he fits the pattern in which the hero emerges spontaneously rather than from a traditional lineage.

Since the mythology of the Western is inhospitable to complex, interesting female characters, Spenser's world clearly exceeds the Western formula because it is inhabited by women like Susan Silverman, Linda Rabb, Rachel Wallace, Brenda Loring, and Cindy Sloan. They understand the themes important to Spenser—honor and integrity and autonomy—and one of the reasons these women are interesting is that they understand him so well.

The reader also perceives Spenser as better than he might otherwise be perceived because these good women do understand him and they explain this understanding to him.

Robert B. Parker and Anne Ponder, "What I Know about Writing Spenser Novels," *Colloquium on Crime: Eleven Renowned Mystery Writers Discuss Their Work*, ed. Robin W. Winks (New York: Charles Scribner's Sons, 1986), pp. 198–200

THEODORE WEESNER   In *Pale Kings and Princes*, the plot is not overly intricate and the chase is clear and compelling. Slipping into fictional rural Wheaton to investigate the inexplicable murder of a Worcester reporter, Spenser finds himself stonewalled at every turn, by barmaid and barber and, not least of all, by the local police. Home to a settlement of transplanted Colombians, the small Massachusetts town is believed to serve as the cocaine clearinghouse for the entire Northeast. In Spenser's way, however, are not so much intricacies of plot as murky obstacles and road-blocks, which he readily sidesteps on his way to a showdown with the town's baddest boss. Only near the end does Spenser call in reserves of mind and muscle, in the forms of Susan and Hawk, and together they go zap, bang, zip and put things right again. Whew.

Along the way, there are intimations of plausibility. They occur in the author's capturing the frosty New England air, in the smell of sauces and in the sense of humor that pervades the book. They occur in a wonderfully engaging overnight tailing of a truck north into Maine, past Portland, to the waterfront of Penobscot Bay, in an urge the reader has to blow into his chilled hands while watching a deal go down, in touches and moments as alive as steaming coffee and a cigarette at daybreak in one's own previous lifetime.

Theodore Weesner, "Cocaine Inc.," *New York Times Book Review*, 31 May 1987, p. 26

R. W. B. LEWIS   To get right down to it: Robert B. Parker's *Playmates* is the best Spenser mystery novel in many a year and as diverting and well wrought as any of the 17 novels in the series. ⟨. . .⟩

The dilemma that confronts Spenser in this affair puts ⟨his⟩ intelligence to a severe test. The racial aspect is an especially intricate mix, with black characters and white characters—players and mates on either side of the law—refusing to fall into stereotypical reactions. It can be said without giving too much away that at every turn the racial drama rings true to our current social reality.

Robert B. Parker established such an elevated standard with his first four novels, through *Promised Land* in 1976, that it would have been virtually impossible to keep it up. The level was impressively high, though, through five or six more titles, by which time it was clear that we were witnessing one of the great series in the history of the American detective story. But then, in the opinion of some, a decline set in. *A Catskill Eagle* in 1985 was an overlong chase-and-rescue story with a double-digit body count and Susan Silverman as the temporarily willful damsel in distress. Almost unthinkingly for Mr. Parker and Spenser, last year's *Crimson Joy* barely escaped the banal. The striking recovery of power in *Playmates* is all the more a matter for wonder and rejoicing.

> R. W. B. Lewis, "Spenser on the Rebound," *New York Times Book Review*, 23 April 1989, p. 13

LLOYD ROSE   There's something crazily oedipal about the very idea of Robert B. Parker's being hired to complete Raymond Chandler's unfinished "The Poodle Springs Story." Parker is probably the most Chandler-influenced of modern mystery writers. Like Chandler's private eye Philip Marlowe, Parker's wisecracking, poetry-quoting, jaw-busting Spenser (no first name) is a man out of place in the ugly moral territory through which he moves, the one uncorruptible man in a fallen world. Spenser's world is chilly, Puritan-bound Boston. Marlowe's was Los Angeles, and Chandler made it a carnival of sin, a neon-defaced landscape where the fresh ocean breeze was likely to pick up and waft along the odor of an undiscovered corpse. ⟨. . .⟩

The fragment of "The Poodle Springs Story" that Chandler left at his death, which makes up the first four chapters of *Poodle Springs*, isn't very good. He had made the mistake of marrying Marlowe off—and to an heiress no less. Chandler's notion was that Marlowe and his rich wife would spat continuously: "Marlowe . . . will hate the house she has rented for the season in Palm Springs. . . . He will detest the bunch of freeloaders who are . . . party guests. . . . She on her side will never understand why he insists on sticking to a dangerous and poorly paid profession." The bit of this bad idea that Chandler worked out was excruciatingly arch; the level of wit can be gauged by his alias of Poodle Springs for Palm Springs. Fortunately, he got very little of the story going, and Parker, stepping in at the top of Chapter Five, can take things exactly where he wants. ⟨. . .⟩

⟨. . .⟩ it's with Marlowe that Parker shows his real strength. Chandler's great artistic flaw was his sentimentalizing of his detective. Parker isn't, even here, the writer Chandler was, but he's not a sentimentalist, and he darkens and deepens Marlowe. In a bar, pumping an aging alcoholic redhead for information, Marlowe notes:

> Drunks are fragile creatures. They need to be carried like a very full glass; tip either way and they spill all over. I knew about drunks.
>   She needed another cigarette. I took one out of her pack on the bar and lit it and handed it to her. Maybe I wouldn't have made a good manservant. Maybe I would have made a good gigolo. Maybe I didn't want to think about that. Maybe that hit too close to home.

Their interview ends with Marlowe dancing with her, turning her gently even after the jukebox has run out, the pathos and sweetness of the scene undercut by his self-loathing and sense of betrayal. Chandler never really tarnished his knight; he always left Marlowe safe on the moral high ground. Parker's view of his hero is riskier: not risky enough for dangerous ambivalence, for greatness, but enough to make this book more than just a classy imitation of a master. *Poodle Springs* is a novel in its own right—Chandler's vision carried further than he carried it, and not betrayed but realized.

Lloyd Rose, "A Literary Hybrid," *Atlantic Monthly* 264, No. 1 (October 1989): 113–15

MARTIN AMIS   If Raymond Chandler had written like Robert B. Parker, he wouldn't have been Raymond Chandler. He would have been Robert B. Parker, a rather less exalted presence. The posthumous pseudo-sequel never amounts to more than a nostalgic curiosity, and it is no great surprise that *Perchance to Dream* isn't much good. The great surprise (for this reviewer) is that *The Big Sleep* isn't that good either; it seems to have aged dramatically since I last looked at it. Still, *The Big Sleep* has its qualities, and they include originality and a tremendous title—two departments in which *Perchance to Dream* is conspicuously shaky. ⟨. . .⟩

One might expect Mr. Parker to make up some ground on the plot, because Chandler is far too glazed and existential for efficient genre storytelling. *The Big Sleep*'s premise (the dying General, the two wild daughters, the vanished son-in-law) is elegant, but the murder-trail stuff is repetitive, implausible and hard to follow. Every few pages, it seems, there's a knock on the door and another new gun barrel for the reader to peer into. Mr. Parker starts strongly, and for a while *Perchance to Dream* trundles along with more uncomplicated thrust than Chandler ever cared to generate. Marlowe is furnished with an impregnable adversary and long odds against. But the denouement is a chaos of tawdry short cuts. The impregnable villain confesses instantly, and his main sidekick disappears "in the scuffle," paving the way, perhaps, for *Ay, There's the Rub*, the pseudo-pseudo-sequel of a thriller writer yet unborn.

Most seriously, the character of Marlowe collapses. Raymond Chandler created a figure who hovered somewhere between cult and myth: he is both hot and cool, both virile and sterile. He pays a price for his freedom from venality; he is untouchable in all senses; he cannot be corrupted, not by women, not by money, not by America. ⟨. . .⟩ Finding the rich nympho in his bed ("You're cute"), *Sleep*'s Marlowe tells her to leave before he throws her out "by force. Just the way you are, naked." When she goes, having called him that filthy name, Marlowe airs the room, drinks his drink and stares down at the imprint of her "small corrupt body" on the sheets. "I put my empty glass down," the chapter ends, "and tore the bed to pieces savagely."

Mr. Parker's Marlowe, more modernly, would have given her a soft drink and a long talk about her substance problem. He has no turbulent soul, no inner complication to keep in check. Mr. Parker neither understands nor respects Marlowe's inhibitions; he fritters them away, unconsciously questing for some contemporary ideal of gruff likability. By the end of the book, Marlowe has become an affable goon. This guy grins and preens and jollies things along. This guy *talks too much*.

Martin Amis, "Sin Has Come a Long Way Since 1939," *New York Times Book Review*, 27 January 1991, p. 9

MAUREEN CORRIGAN   It's not that *Double Deuce*, Parker's 18th Spenser novel, is out-and-out lousy; it's just that last year's *Pastime* was vigorous, smart and funny—a lot like vintage Parker—and so it revived high expectations for the series. And, in fact, *Double Deuce* invites close comparison with *Pastime* because it's another story about a young man's coming of age. Only this time, Hawk, instead of Spenser, plays the role of Bachelor Father. ⟨. . .⟩

I think Parker wrote *Double Deuce* with the worthy intention of trying to "de-otherize" Hawk by pairing him with a wonderful woman and by centering the story in a world where Spenser is perceived as a white outsider. But, by the end of the novel, Hawk has become even more of a cipher. His relationship with Jackie shatters when she learns, as the rest of us always suspected, that he's incapable of loving anyone . . . except, maybe, Spenser. (In a heart-to-heart chat, Spenser explains to Jackie that the only way Hawk can be himself "is to go inside, to be inaccessible." Don't try to understand; it's a male thing.) And, though Hawk presides at the violent climax, it's Spenser who really solves the murder of Devona Jefferson and her daughter.

The plot of *Double Deuce* is a rehash of old themes, and the dialogue's middlin' flat, but, Spenser fans will make it a bestseller anyway—we always do. Reading the new Spenser novel is a way of staying connected to characters we like, sort of like attending a séance to commune with the departed, even though they're only pale shades of their former selves.

Maureen Corrigan, "Hawk Takes Center Stage," Washington Post Book World, 24 May 1992, p. 6

▣ Bibliography

The Personal Response to Literature (with others). 1971.

Order and Diversity: The Craft of Prose (editor; with Peter L. Sandberg). 1973.

The Godwulf Manuscript. 1973.

God Save the Child. 1974.

Sports Illustrated Training with Weights. 1974, 1990 (with John R. Marsh).

Mortal Stakes. 1975.

Promised Land. 1976.

The Judas Goat. 1978.

Three Weeks in Spring (with Joan H. Parker). 1978.

Wilderness. 1979.

Looking for Rachel Wallace. 1980.

Mature Advertising: A Handbook of Effectiveness in Print. 1980.

A Savage Place. 1981.

Early Autumn. 1981.

Ceremony. 1982.

Surrogate. 1982.

The Widening Gyre. 1983.

A Spenserian Sonnet. 1983.

Love and Glory. 1983.

The Private Eye in Hammett and Chandler. 1984.

Valediction. 1984.

A Catskill Eagle. 1985.

Parker on Writing. 1985.

Taming a Sea-Horse. 1986.

Pale Kings and Princes. 1987.

Crimson Joy. 1988.

Playmates. 1989.

Poodle Springs (with Raymond Chandler). 1989.

The Early Spenser ⟨*The Godwulf Manuscript*, God Save the Child, Mortal Stakes⟩. 1989.

Stardust. 1990.

A Year at the Races (with Joan H. Parker). 1990.

Pastime. 1991.

Perchance to Dream: Robert B. Parker's Sequel to Raymond Chandler's The Big Sleep. 1991.

Double Deuce. 1992.

Paper Doll. 1993.

Spenser's Boston. 1994.

Walking Shadow. 1994.

All Our Yesterdays. 1994.

Mickey Spillane
b. 1918

FRANK MORRISON SPILLANE was born on March 9, 1918, to John Joseph Spillane, a bartender, and Catherine Anne Spillane. He was raised in Elizabeth, New Jersey, and attended Kansas State College. During World War II he flew fighter missions and taught air force cadets, eventually rising to the rank of captain.

Spillane had begun writing before the war for the "slick" magazines and, under pseudonyms, for the pulps. It was through his reading of the hardboiled magazines *Black Mask* and *Dime Detective* that he fell under the spell of Carroll John Daly, creator of the first hard-boiled detective, Race Williams. Spillane's fascination with the exaggerated, uncompromising characters of Williams and other crime fighters led him to contribute to comic books featuring Captain Marvell, Captain America, and other superhero renderings of the American justice system.

Spillane married Mary Ann Pearce in 1945. In need of money to buy some land in 1946, he was staked to a $1,000 advance by E. P. Dutton to write his first novel. *I, the Jury*, which he completed in three weeks, introduced Mike Hammer, a no-nonsense private eye with an overdeveloped sense of personal justice that bordered on the pathological. Although the novel was a routine tale of betrayal and murder, it was distinguished by Spillane's refusal to acknowledge the limits that hitherto had kept hardboiled fiction within the boundaries of good taste. Critics and social commentators were offended by the book's lurid sexuality and Hammer's unrestrained brutality toward men and women alike. Readers bought copies by the millions. The book has never gone out of print and was adapted for film twice, in 1953 and 1981.

Although Spillane considered Hammer a mouthpiece for his own conservative antiestablishment beliefs, he made no pretense about the commercialism of his writing. Hammer reappeared as the hero of five more best-selling novels published between 1950 and 1952 and spawned many imitators in the burgeoning paperback original market, where his exploits set the tone

158

for a curbside view of America at variance with the complacency of the times. Several of these novels were filmed, and Hammer was the subject of two television series and a comic strip.

Following his conversion to the Jehovah's Witness faith in 1952, Spillane gave up writing crime novels and retired to his home in Myrtle Beach, South Carolina, producing the occasional short story or film script, gaining recognition as a television personality, and raising his four children. He returned as a novelist in 1961, and Mike Hammer reappeared the following year in *The Girl Hunters*, which was filmed in 1963 from Spillane's script, with himself playing the lead role. In 1964 his novel *Day of the Guns* introduced Tiger Mann, an intelligence agent cut from the same cloth as Mike Hammer, whose adventures in international espionage were the subject of four novels. Spillane alternated between Hammer, Mann, and nonseries characters over another ten novels until 1973, when he again retired as a novelist.

On a bet from his publisher, Spillane in 1979 wrote *The Day the Sea Rolled Back*, a critically praised mystery novel for children and the first in a projected six-book series. Perhaps as a result of the successful television series "Mike Hammer," starring Stacey Keach, Spillane brought Mike Hammer out of retirement in *The Killing Man* in 1989. Spillane married a third time in 1983 and divides his time between homes in Manhattan and Myrtle Beach. He remains one of the best-selling writers of all time, with seven of his books among the top fifteen fiction best-sellers of the past fifty years.

Critical Extracts

ANTHONY BOUCHER   Private eye Mike Hammer ⟨in *I, the Jury*⟩ swears revenge for the murder of his best friend and tracks the killer, through some of the season's strongest scenes of sex and sadism, to private execution. Able, if painfully derivative, writing and plotting, in so vicious a glorification of force, cruelty and extra-legal methods that the novel might be made required reading in a Gestapo training school.

Anthony Boucher, "Murder, They Say," *San Francisco Chronicle*, 3 August 1947, p. 19

MALCOLM COWLEY   I am not used to having Jack the Ripper presented as a model for emulation and I confess that Mike Hammer frightens me. It has been argued that the stories have no relation to American life, that they put together the ingredients of the Western novel, the pursuit thriller, the comic strip and the animated film cartoon into a cockeyed fairy story that has no more social significance than the fun house at Coney Island. The publishers, I suppose, would like to accept this explanation: what fun! ⟨. . .⟩

What frightens me about these fairy tales is that they are entirely too close to one side of American life in 1952. We have been reading about more and more crimes of violence, especially those directed against women. Police statistics show that, while old-fashioned burglaries are decreasing, rapes, mutilations and violent robberies are growing in number from year to year. I wouldn't say that Mike Hammer had anything to do with police statistics, and the fact may be that reading these stories is a means of channeling off the dangerous impulses into daydreams. On the other hand, Mike Hammer helps to show—like the comic books and some of the animated cartoons—that the sadism is there, in the midst of our elaborate and internally peaceful culture. A few weeks ago I read about a sailor in Brooklyn who was arrested for robbing women in lonely streets. He snatched their handbags, then knocked them down, kicked them in the abdomen—like Mike Hammer—and left them gasping and vomiting on the sidewalk to wait for the ambulance. Maybe he wasn't a reader of the Mike Hammer stories, but he was part of the same moral configuration.

Malcolm Cowley, "Sex Murder Incorporated," *New Republic*, 11 February 1952, p. 18

CHARLES J. ROLO   Spillane's books have been described by Mr. Max Lerner as "really prolonged literary lynchings, strip-teases, and rapes," which pander to "our sick cravings." There is, I'm sure, a good deal of truth in this, but I don't think that the supercharge of sex and sadism is the decisive factor behind Spillane's unique popularity—those ingredients are being used by plenty of other whodunit writers without anything like the same box-office results. While the Spillane books may be bliss to the peeping tom and a delight to respectable folk who like their fictional murder laced with rough stuff, the Hammer stories also answer an altogether different, primitively moralistic set of cravings. I suspect this is the crucial underlying factor in their phenomenal appeal.

During the past two decades, monstrous evils—total war, political purges, the systematic sadism of the Gestapo—have become part of our everyday consciousness. And lately, Americans have been made more sharply aware that, here in the United States, there flourish crime networks organized on the lines of big business and well-barbered racketeers who have found answers even to the income tax. The signs are that more and more people feel personally steamed up about all this, and, at the same time, have a frustrated feeling that the individual can't do much about it. Perhaps the acutest frustration of our time is this sense that the individual has been reduced to impotence in a world where the principle of large-scale organization has spread so far into human affairs, legitimate and nefarious.

This moral indignation and this frustration in the face of large-scale evil (and neither can properly be called "sick") are reproduced more intensely in the Hammer books than in any other murder mysteries. Hammer, unlike most fictional detectives, is personally touched by the initial murder, much as we, nowadays, are touched by aggression wherever it occurs; and he is enraged (as we are angered) that smooth deadly criminals should go unpunished and even prosper mightily. Now begins the compensatory daydream in which the Superman fights our fight against the forces of evil. Hammer is not just any superman—he has The Call. Hammer is Jehovah's messenger; he is the avenging hand of the Jehovah of *Proverbs*, who ordains that "destruction shall be to the workers of iniquity." When Hammer, in the apocalyptic dénouements, pumps a bullet into the killer, he kills a part of himself—love or respect. His mission is to be the Flaming Sword.

In Spillane's books we see, as through a magnifying glass, the drama inherent in the formula of the detective story. Every murder mystery poses symbolically (in the form of the initial murder) the problem of Evil—and resolves it; every detective story therefore meets a deep metaphysical need. Some reflect more sharply than others the needs of a particular time and a particular place.

Charles J. Rolo, "Simenon and Spillane: The Metaphysics of Murder for the Millions" (1952), *Mass Culture: The Popular Arts in America*, ed. Bernard Rosenberg and David Manning White (New York: Basic Books, 1957), pp. 169–70

CHRISTOPHER LA FARGE   One can say that the readers of murder stories don't necessarily demand good English or even good writing, but simply what is usually described as "thrill-packed action." One can say that of the 24,000,000 persons who have bought or read Mr. Spillane's books many readers must be young and uncritical, and also that many must have got a vicarious satisfaction from the sexual passages reduced to such simple and unvarying animalism, either because their own lives provide no such satisfactions or because they'd like to think of themselves as having such physical prowess. One can say that in a tense world, full of hysterical shrillness, many, ⟨. . .⟩ isolated within the overlarge groupings of an industrial civilization, must derive from such writing a sort of satisfaction because the Bad get their come-uppance without the need for the delays of lawful justice. If that were all it would not be very important. But it isn't all.

There is left the popularity of a Hero who, with such a character as has been described, mocks at and denies the efficacy of all law and decency, flouts all laws, statutory, ethical, and moral, delights in assault and murder that is brutally executed, sets his personal judgment always above that of all other men but in particular above that of those to whom government delegates law enforcement (which he thereby constantly derogates), and makes the words *soft* and *honourable* synonymous. This is the sort of philosophy, *mutatis mutandis*, that has permitted to Senator McCarthy his periods of extreme popularity throughout the nation: one man will, beyond the normal processes, unhampered by the normal and accepted restraints, bring the Bad to his own form of justice. Mike Hammer's Communists and members of the Mafia are, of course, all Very Bad. They are also described as soft, homosexual, stupid, gullible, childish, or easily tricked; but at the same time as the Most Dangerous Thing in the United States. *Any* means which will, with Hammer, lead to their extirpation and in particular their death by his hands are Good. With Senator McCarthy, any means that will expose Communists, including the derogation of all Public Servants, the telling of lies, the irreparable damaging of the innocent, the sensational and the unfounded charge, is justified so long as he thinks it is the right thing to do. Each, then, reflects the other, though McCarthyism kills but careers where Hammerism (perhaps in the end more mercifully) kills life itself.

> Christopher La Farge, "Mickey Spillane and His Bloody Hammer," *Saturday Review*, 6 November 1954, p. 58

PHILIP WYLIE   In most cases Spillane uses a kind of sandwich technique. First there is a killing, then a chapter in which Hammer beats someone up, then a sex chapter, and so on for about five cycles. Inevitably there are a dozen or so chillingly antisocial speeches. These attack the law, the police, and the jury system, and espouse the philosophy that it's good news when a self-appointed vigilante like the detective-hero kills a criminal rather than let him stand trial. Always Spillane has the chief culprit killed either by Hammer or through Hammer's vengeance. Notice the titles—*I, the Jury*, *My Gun Is Quick*, *Vengeance Is Mine*. Never under any circumstance is the culprit punished by due process of law.

It is more than a little amazing that the public, manifesting what sociological disturbance I can only guess, should respond so eagerly to this particular brand of escape reading. Vulgarity is only one aspect of the matter. The far deeper crime extolled in these accounts is a dangerous and all too familiar pattern of twisted ethics. For Spillane's Mike Hammer does more than merely sin. He justifies his lust, violence, and abnormalities by setting himself above evil and the law, by making himself sole arbiter of what's right for society (and incidentally good for Mike Hammer), without regard to established law or the dignity of the individual. And he uses this dangerous demagoguery as a license for brutality, bestiality, and the most sordid kind of animal behavior.

In other words, the books appeal by direct action to every low, brutal, cruel, sadistic, lawless impulse that humanity has been trying to master for thousands of years in the effort to maintain civilization. If Spillane's millions of readers suddenly began acting like Spillane's detective, Mike Hammer, the Soviets could take us over without dropping a bomb—because the U.S.A. would be in chaos.

Philip Wylie, "The Crime of Mickey Spillane," *Good Housekeeping* 130, No. 2 (February 1955): 207

JOHN G. CAWELTI   Violence as orgasm is a main theme of Spillane's novels. ⟨. . .⟩ Spillane makes the relationship between sexual teasing and violent catharsis a part of the basic texture of his stories. In his hands, the hard-boiled structural formula of increasing involvement in a web of corruption becomes an alternating pattern of sexual provocation and orgies of shooting or beating that seem to function psychologically as a partial release of the emotional tension built up by the unconsummated sexual teasing. This structural pattern reaches its climax in the nightmarish final scenes of Spillane's novels. ⟨. . .⟩

⟨. . .⟩ Mike Hammer's orgiastic sadism is acceptable and cathartic for a mass audience because it is initiated by sentimental feelings, such as Mike's deep sorrow for a murdered friend, and justified by the unpunished evil that his investigations uncover. Weighed against the individual and social evils he confronts, Mike's brutality is made to seem a necessary and even indispensable course of action. In an urban world dominated by gangsters, Communist agents, and socialite dope pushers, the only person who can bring the elites of evil to their reckoning is Spillane's lone wolf of destruction. Spillane's social paranoia with its hysterical fears of urban sophistication, foreigners, and minority groups therefore serves an important function in justifying his hero's brutality. Similarly, Spillane's sentimentality and didacticism are given greater intensity through their eventuation in violence.

> John G. Cawelti, "Hammett, Chandler, and Spillane" (1969), *Adventure, Mystery, and Romance: Formula Stories as Art and Popular Culture* (Chicago: University of Chicago Press, 1976), pp. 186, 188–89

KAY WEIBEL   It is no coincidence that the villains of Spillane's novels almost inevitably prove to be women. In his article "The Spillane Phenomenon," John Cawelti talks about the rhythm in Spillane's novels, stating that it reaches its final climax in "violence as orgasm." Since Mike is at war in the novels, a torturous rape would provide the natural climax. In that manner the sexual and violent tensions created by the action in the novels would be resolved simultaneously. Mike Hammer is not allowed this indulgence, however, since he is a believer in female purity and a righteous avenger serving the cause of justice, and atrocities, even in war, are always committed only by the enemy. Denied rape, Mike takes the next best alternative—pumping bullets from the gun that symbolizes his masculinity into the nude body of the villain.

The Spillane novels, then, attempt to resolve for men the two-way image of male/female roles provided by the popular media. On the one hand, men were being told to settle down and be the stable provider for the decade's heroine, Mother. The success of the supersex movie queens and of *Playboy* and its imitators, however, indicated that men had another and contradictory image of themselves as adventure-seeking bachelors. Mike Hammer's solution was simple: take the best of both worlds. Have handy an attractive mother/wife for emergencies and general support, but pursue the adventurous life, including violence and loose women, as well. The unworkability of this formula is revealed metaphorically, however, in the violent death of all the promiscuous women in the novels. Since the real wife/mother would not allow the intrusion of violence and other women in the life of her stable provider, the enjoyment of these adventures must be limited—to the span of time it takes to read a Mickey Spillane novel.

Kay Weibel, "Mickey Spillane as a Fifties Phenomenon," *Dimensions in Detective Fiction*, ed. Larry N. Landrum, Pat Browne, and Ray B. Browne (Bowling Green, OH: Bowling Green University Popular Press, 1976), p. 122

MICHAEL BARSON   I: How come everybody gets knocked off in your books?

S: Well, I like the hero to win. I don't care if he's a bad guy. I never changed my conception of what the hero should be. He's as bad as the crooks themselves. He's just as mean and nasty as he has to be. But this keeps him in a certain character—you can't lose sight of him. He doesn't get washed out with everybody else.

I: You like a happy ending.

S: Oh, man, a happy ending is a success story. A good, happy, satisfying ending is the best thing in the world—satisfying, it doesn't have to be happy. In *I, the Jury*, he kills the girl he loves, but it's satisfying because she's such a beast of a character. The whole characterization of Mike was that he set out to do something—to yourself be true, see. He was going to kill her even if he loved her—he looks behind him, sees the gun she's going to blow his brains out with while she's kissing him. But she figures, He's never seen me naked—this one thing will divert him long enough. That's why she said, "How could you?" To her, as a scientist, it was an impossible thing to have happened. And his answer totally explains his character: "It was easy." That's the character I wanted to get across. See, I never intended to write a sequel to that book. That ended it right there. But, gee whiz, I had to write another . . . and another, and another . . .

I: If you've read a few Spillane books you can tell that the woman who's described as being so pure and lovely is actually—

S: Let me tell you a funny story. People say to me, "You're the guy that's always shooting women in the belly." And I say, "Mike only shot a woman in the belly once. Know why? Because he missed."

I: Let's face it—the women don't come off too well in your books.

S: You can always kill them off. If you're going to kill them off, kill a pretty one, they're better.

I: But in four of your first six Mike Hammer stories it's the woman who's the villain.

S: Well, they've got to be a man or a woman, don't they? You've only got a choice of two.

I: True.

S: *Vengeance Is Mine* was written with a purpose in mind. Because after shooting Charlotte, he could never kill a woman again. I had to get him over that thing, but it had to be a transitional stage so he could do it again if he wanted. I don't think he killed any women.

I: Mike Hammer gets really wrapped up in his killing—he gets that "kill-crazy lust."

S: Homicide and justifiable homicide are two different things. Supposing somebody kills your kid, or rapes your wife. If you've got a gun, you'll kill. That man has got to be wiped out. The only choice is very simple—bang, he's dead.

I: But Mike seems to enjoy it so much.

S: Because he's always on a personal vengeance note. He's never a paid case. Somebody is out there and deserves it. It's like hunting down a mad animal. I never put him out there to say he *likes* to kill. He *has* to kill.

Michael Barson, "Just a Writer Looking for a Buck," *Armchair Detective* 12, No. 4 (Fall 1979): 298

GEOFFREY O'BRIEN   In the world of Spillane's anarchic private eye, everything reduces to a Manichaean struggle between the essentially solitary Mike Hammer and a shadowy inexorable network of moral monsters whom it is his mission to destroy. Society and its elected representatives enter the picture only as forces seeking to deter Hammer from the fulfillment of his mission. It's all terribly ironic—the liberal do-gooders who object to Hammer's violent methods will never understand that he is protecting them from an evil that he alone can fully grasp. With the police Hammer has a love-hate relationship. He despises them when they kowtow to corrupt politicians or allow their hands to be tied by legal scruples, but acknowledges that fundamentally they fight the good fight.

Spillane's novels have a curiously dreamlike atmosphere: many things happen, but none of them seems particularly substantial; the sole reality is Hammer's consciousness, which is propelled by an apparently continuous sense of thwarted rage. This inchoate anger echoes like a litany on page after page: "Maybe it was just me, but suddenly I wanted to grab that guy in the overcoat and slam his teeth down his throat and wait to see what his two boys would do" (*One Lonely Night*); "I loved to shoot killers. I couldn't think of anything I'd rather do than shoot a killer and watch his blood trace a slimy path across the floor" (*Vengeance Is Mine*); "I hate the guts of those people. I hate them so bad it's coming out of my skin. I'm going to find out who 'they' are and why and then they've had it" (*Kiss Me, Deadly*). Psychology becomes indistinguishable from physiology: "I was just one tight knot of muscle, bunched together by a rage that wanted to rip and tear" (*My Gun Is Quick*).

There could also be drawn from Hammer's musings a compendium of familiar-sounding dicta on such topics as Communists ("So I was a sucker for fighting a war. I was a sap for liking my country. I was a jerk for not thinking them a superior breed of lice!"—*One Lonely Night*); lesbians ("She was another one of those mannish things that breed in the half-light of the so-called aesthetical world"—*Vengeance Is Mine*); and gun control ("If the D.A. wants to jug me . . . I'll throw the Constitution in his face. I think one of the first things it says is that the people are allowed to bear arms"—*Vengeance Is Mine*).

> Geoffrey O'Brien, *Hardboiled America: The Lurid Years of Paperbacks* (New York: Van Nostrand Reinhold Co., 1981), pp. 95–96

J. KENNETH VAN DOVER   Spillane may be the most daring of the supersellers; his achievement is certainly the most disturbing. There is something admirable in ⟨Erle Stanley⟩ Gardner's dogged iteration of his fables of New Deal individualism and optimism while ⟨Ian⟩ Fleming's commitment to ethical hedonism and geopolitical Manicheism is at least intelligible and, in any event, is qualified by its application in the fantastic and often parodic world of James Bond. The moral myth which provides a context for the action of Spillane heroes is neither as decent as that which guides Perry Mason nor as definite as that which governs James Bond. The very ease with which Spillane makes the transition from private eye to counterintelligence agent to hood is most disquieting, for the same voice affirms the values of each. Private revenge, national salvation, gangsterism, and vigilantism are levelled by this equation. The survival value of toughness becomes an end in itself, to be justified on an ad hoc basis by appeals *against* a particular enemy (never *for* an articulate principle)—against killers or Communists, pimps or homosexuals, blackmailers or drug dealers. Spillane's protean career is thus to some extent the result of his radical failure to establish positive values in his fiction. ⟨. . .⟩

In the fairy tales of Spillane-Hammer, the Big Bad Wolf is the narrator, and he justifies his depredations honestly by referring to the requirements of his own appetites. Hunger may be a legitimate motive for action. Certainly it will appeal to an action-starved audience. But it remains an unstable virtue. The wolf would be hard pressed to debate morality with the three little pigs. In the fiction of Gardner and Fleming, the nature of justice *is* a topic for discussion. Mason and Bond are prone to self-doubt and self-defense, and they express their qualms frequently in dialogues with their secretaries and comrades. The mission of Mike Hammer is questioned only once, in *One Lonely Night*, and there, significantly, the debate takes place entirely within the mind of Hammer himself. He is a knight for whom loneliness is a necessity. It is his very alienation from any shared community values that enables him to justify his violent actions as ends in themselves. The ultimate criticism of the ethos of Spillane's fictional world must be that it is literally undebateable.

J. Kenneth Van Dover, "Mickey Spillane," *Murder in the Millions: Erle Stanley Gardner, Mickey Spillane, Ian Fleming* (New York: Frederick Ungar Publishing Co., 1984), pp. 150–52

ROBERT SANDELS   At his back, Tiger ⟨Mann⟩ has the arrogant American intelligence establishment which he must manipulate and confound if he is to get anywhere. He mixes the chase with populist maneuverings against bureaucracy, a cliché of the hard-boiled tradition worked into every Mike Hammer novel. "Some of us still care," Tiger says from time to time, or "There are still some of us who . . ." He can't trust the CIA because it is crippled by red tape and ignorance. He must lie to police, hide evidence in felony crimes and change his gun barrel after a killing. Spillane relies so much on the Mike Hammer formula that he never allows Tiger Mann to leave the country and even rarely to leave New York City. His orders come from across the river at "Newark control." Some sense of mobility is achieved by having Tiger take cabs frequently. For exotic locales, Tiger goes to ethnic restaurants. It's as though the map of Tiger's world had been drawn by Saul Steinberg. Tiger stays in the city and waits for the international conspiracies to come to town, like visiting athletic teams.

Personal revenge, not international intrigue, dominates these stories: Tiger seeks revenge against his ex-lover Rondine who gun-shot him during the Second World War; one villain is after Tiger for shooting him in the throat and ruining a promising concert career for what is probably the only singing assassin in the genre; another wants to kill Tiger for shooting off his trigger finger and ruining a promising career as a hit-man. Politics and intrigue recede into the background like a kind of narrative Muzak. International issues are vague references, not crucial plot mechanisms. The Cold War is hardly distinguishable from sordid metropolitan crime of the hard-boiled tradition.

Spillane has constructed these novels explicitly around a particular set of political beliefs. He makes them so central to the story that the series reads like a partisan political primer. Where Fleming was content to draw his villains from Russia and the "darker races," providing them with preposterous and therefore merely amusing maniacal ambitions, Spillane tried to ground his stories in contemporary "lessons" of the Cold War. These are somber, humorless novels with nothing of the cynicism of le Carré and nothing of Bond's aloofness and occasional self-mockery. Fleming's novels actually have little to do with international politics—only with the Cold War atmosphere. Little in the way of a distinct political philosophy emerges from his work. To be sure, Bond, in his offhand and pedestrian way, subscribes to the Cold War catechism of the day in the same easy manner that he subscribes to the usual English clubman prejudices or practises brand name snobbery. Both Spillane and Fleming used the Cold War milieu as a license to commit fantasy; but, whereas Fleming's fantasies were men's magazine daydreams, Spillane used the clichés of espionage fiction to warn of true-to-life national dangers and to justify his enunciation of rightist judgments. The reader is invited to take him seriously and to react as much to his politics as to his fantasies.

Robert Sandels, " 'The Machinery of Government vs. People Who Cared': Rightism in Mickey Spillane's Tiger Mann Novels," *Clues* 7, No. 1 (Spring–Summer 1986): 101–2

GEORGE STADE   Hammer's first impulse, on meeting another man, is to slap him around. As you might expect from someone who drools, when he hugs or kisses a woman, he hurts. "I felt like reaching out and squeezing her to pieces," he says of Charlotte ⟨in *I, the Jury*⟩. And when Hammer feels like doing something, he does it: "I knew I was hurting her," he says on this occasion, as on another he says, "it was a wonder she could breathe," and on still another he says, "I squeezed her arms so hard my hands hurt." Intensity of feeling in Hammer always leads to someone else's pain. Charlotte seems to go for this sort of thing: "You love hard, too, don't you Mike?" she says admiringly.

It does not bother this cultivated and educated woman that Hammer has plebeian tastes; that he says he cannot follow the big words in her books; that when he goes through magazines, he looks only at the pictures and ignores the text; that on Sundays he throws away the news and reads only the funnies; that he needs his secretary's help to tie his tie. Nor does it bother Charlotte, in spite of her clinical experience—she's a psychoanalyst, remember—that Hammer's attitudes toward sex are full of warning signs. He is both prudish and prurient, both lustful and bashful, a firm believer in the double standard.

He is upset, for example, when Velda utters a mild obscenity, "the kind you see scratched in the sidewalk by some evil-minded guttersnipe." When Velda fusses about his intention to visit a cathouse (on business), he reassures her with the usual brag that he doesn't have to pay for it and that, in any case, as he says, "After all those pictures the army showed me of what happens to good little boys who go out with bad little girls, I'm afraid even to kiss my mother." The madam of the cathouse, by the way, "looked like somebody's mother." As he leaves, having declined a quickie offered by one of the girls, he again says "a silent thanks to Uncle Sam for showing me those posters and films."

In general, Hammer does not like forward women. He likes to do the pursuing himself. "I like to do some of the work myself," he says, "not have it handed to me on a platter." Mary Bellemy wants to peep at his beefcake, but he puts her off with an " 'I don't get undressed in front of women.' " Charlotte Manning, by then his fiancée, needs a little loving. " 'Mike,' she whispered, 'I want you,' " but he says no. " 'No, darling,' " he says; " 'it's too beautiful to spoil.' " He also tells Charlotte that once they are married, she will have to give up her job, although she is raking it in while he is not. ⟨. . .⟩

I, the Jury, then, is a manual of conduct; more specifically, it is a show-and-tell treatise on masculinity. We are shown by his conduct and told by other characters that Mike Hammer, otherwise an ordinary Joe, is extraordinary only in being all man. Never is he more polemically a man than when confronted by his moral opposites, or negative definers. These are criminals, forward women, and perverts, all of whom, by the end of the novel, have been equated.

> George Stade, "The Hard-Boiled Dick: Perverse Reflections in a Private Eye," *Perversions and Near-Perversions in Clinical Practice*, ed. Gerald I. Fogel and Wayne A. Myers (New Haven: Yale University Press, 1991), pp. 237–39

◈ *Bibliography*

I, the Jury. 1947.
My Gun Is Quick. 1950.
Vengeance Is Mine! 1950.
The Big Kill. 1951.
The Long Wait. 1951.
One Lonely Night. 1951.
Kiss Me, Deadly. 1952.
The Deep. 1961.
The Girl Hunters. 1962.
Me, Hood! 1963.
Day of the Guns. 1964.
The Flier. 1964.
Return of the Hood. 1964.
The Snake. 1964.
Bloody Sunrise. 1965.
The Death Dealers. 1965.
The By-pass Control. 1966.
The Twisted Thing. 1966.
The Body Lovers. 1967.
The Delta Factor. 1967.
Me, Hood! 1969.
The Tough Guys. 1969.
Survival . . . Zero! 1970.

The Erection Set. 1972.

The Last Cop Out. 1973.

Vintage Spillane: A New Omnibus. 1974.

The Day the Sea Rolled Back. 1979.

The Ship That Never Was. 1982.

Mike Hammer: The Comic Strip. Ed. Max Allan Collins. 1982–84. 2 vols.

Tomorrow I Die. Ed. Max Allan Collins. 1984.

Five Complete Mike Hammer Novels ⟨*I, the Jury, Vengeance Is Mine, The Big Kill, My Gun Is Quick, Kiss Me, Deadly*⟩. 1987.

The Killing Man. 1989.

The Hammer Strikes Again ⟨*One Lonely Night, The Snake, The Twisted Thing, The Body Lovers, Survival . . . Zero!*⟩. 1989.

Murder Is My Business (editor; with Max Allan Collins). 1994.

⧈ ⧈ ⧈

Andrew Vachss
b. 1942

ANDREW HENRY VACHSS was born on October 19, 1942, in New York City, the son of Bernard and Geraldine (Mattus) Vachss. After receiving his B.A. from Case Western Reserve University in 1965, Vachss undertook a variety of jobs in social work, including working as a caseworker for the Department of Social Services in New York, a deputy director of the Medfield-Norfolk Prison Project in Medfield, Massachusetts, a project director of the Department of Youth Services in Boston, and a planner and analyst for the Crime Control Coordinator's Office in Yonkers, New York. During this period he worked on his law degree, attaining the J.D. (magna cum laude) from the New England School of Law in 1975.

Vachss began a private practice in New York in 1976 but continued work in public service. Since 1975 he has been director of the New York City Juvenile Justice Planning Project. He has lectured widely on law and criminal justice at Boston University, New York University, John Jay College of Criminal Justice, and Fordham University. He has also been a relief worker assisting children in Biafra.

Vachss's first published book was a sociological study, *The Life-Style Violent Juvenile* (1979), written with Yitzhak Bakal. He had written a novel early in his career, but it was rejected by several publishers. Years later he wrote another novel, *Flood*, which was published in 1985. This novel introduces the private investigator Burke (no first name is given), who with a variety of offbeat sidekicks hunts down a child-rapist. Most of Vachss's subsequent novels revolve around Burke and his associates, take place in New York City, and deal relentlessly and uncompromisingly with the issues that Vachss has faced as a social worker and lawyer: the abuse of children, juveniles as criminals, and the brutality of urban life. Although his novels have sometimes been criticized for excessive violence, Vachss has been praised for unflinchingly facing some of the ugliest and most intractable problems of modern society.

Vachss has produced novels regularly since the mid-1980s, including *Strega* (1987; winner of the Grand Prix de Littérature Policière), *Blue Belle* (1988), *Hard Candy* (1989), *Blossom* (1990), *Sacrifice (1991)*, *Shella* (1993), and *Down in the Zero* (1994). He has written a variety of short stories published in magazines and anthologies; they have recently been collected in *Born Bad* (1994). Recently Vachss has experimented in multimedia publications combining comic art and text: *A Flash of White* (1993) and *Drive By* (1993).

Andrew Vachss is married to Alice Vachss, chief of the Special Victims Bureau for the district attorney's office in the borough of Queens; she has recently written an account of her work, *Sex Crimes: Ten Years on the Front Lines Prosecuting Rapists and Confronting Their Collaborators* (1993). Vachss continues to practice law and to write in New York.

◈ *Critical Extracts*

HELEN DUDAR   Andrew H. Vachss, a New York lawyer awesomely knowledgeable about the seamier sides of city life, wrote his first novel some years ago with the hope of showing the world "how you produce a genuine card-carrying sociopath." The manuscript is yellowing in his files, in a bedding of rejection notes he recites with deadpan relish: " 'This book made me throw up,' and 'I think it should be suppressed,' and 'If he ever writes a book human beings can read, send it to me.' " ⟨. . .⟩

Nobody of any importance in this book ⟨*Flood*⟩ has more than one name. Flood is a small, fierce woman with a killer karate chop who hires a detective to hunt down the rapist-killer of her best friend's child. Burke, self-described "great scam artist," is the unlicensed private eye who conducts the search. A living lesson in justifiable paranoia, he assumes most coin phones are tapped, never travels to any point in a straight line and maintains an office elaborately wired against intruders and guarded by a giant Neapolitan mastiff named Pansy. The cast of wonderfully bizarre characters enlisted to help Burke and Flood includes Michelle, a transvestite prostitute; the Mole, an electronics genius who lives under a junkyard and is available for complex illicit jobs, and Max the Silent, a deaf-mute Tibetan powerhouse who can bend brass knuckles. ⟨. . .⟩

Mr. Vachss, who is wiry, intense and chronically wry, not unlike a character out of a Vachss novel, views the possibilities with restrained enthusiasm. "A lot of things," he says, "have already exceeded my wildest fantasies. It's sold at least 500 copies to my certain knowledge."

Helen Dudar, "An Attorney Turns to Fiction," *Wall Street Journal,* 16 September 1985, p. 22

NICK KIMBERLEY   Andrew H. Vachss is an American lawyer specialising in juvenile delinquency and child abuse. That should lend authority to his first novel, *Flood,* about a man nicknamed Cobra who specialises in sodomising children. Sadly, Vachss allows his righteous anger to run away with him. The world he describes is a humourless caricature: the city as jungle; the solitary hero routing evil with an iron discipline born of experience as a convict and mercenary. His people, like his dogs, react instinctively to stimuli: no time here for thought, talk, or rational behaviour. The novel orchestrates genuine anxieties—about violence, the break-up of the family, the lack of care, and of caring—into an unpleasant survivalism: if you want to get by out there, you'd better carry a knife and a few grenades. Burke, the hero, has built a world which no outsider can penetrate. You end up thinking he's the one who's deranged, not the Cobra.

Paranoid visions of urban decay are a staple of modern crime fiction: Vachss' utterly nasty novel offers no hope for social being; in this psychotic world, it's kill or be killed.

Nick Kimberley, "Cobraphilia," *New Statesman,* 15 August 1986, p. 31

RON TATAR   This ⟨*Flood*⟩ is a first novel that mixes hardboiled conventions with elements of spy-novel gadgetry. The combination results in an entertaining romp. ⟨. . .⟩

Burke's attitudes toward people are best summed up in his description of an informant named Michelle. "Her gender may be a mystery, but in my world, it's not who you are, it's how you stand up."

Mama Wong provides food and information. Max the Silent helps with the rough stuff. Max cannot hear or speak, but he is the deadliest man in town.

These are just some of the supporting characters who make *Flood* a perfect example of an '80s pulp. I mean that in the best possible way. Secret clans, electronic wizardry, street cynicism, nasty bad guys, Eastern mysticism, and an obvious love for life's unique individuals make this a book that is fun to read.

Ron Tatar, "Private Eye," *Armchair Detective* 20, No. 1 (Winter 1987): 85–86

DAVID MORELL   For the past year, I've surveyed every novel in this category ⟨the mystery story⟩ that publishers felt fit to submit, and if Andrew Vachss' *Strega* had been sent to me, I'd have put it far, far at the top of my list.

It's wonderful. The words do leap off the page. The plot is fresh. The principal character is original. The style is as clean as a haiku.

"It started with a kid."

So *Strega* starts. One paragraph. Six syllables. Like the 440 cubic inch engine in the car the hero drives, the book thrusts into motion. A woman's child has been threatened. A raspy voice on the phone tells the mother he'll leave the child alone if the mother goes jogging in Forest Park, without any underwear, while he watches. I raged. I wanted a hero to crush the maggot and help the mother and her child.

I did get a hero, but so different, so unorthodox I felt startled. His name is Burke. No first name. To put it another way, he has many first names, but you don't know which is authentic. He's an orphan. A child of the state. An ex-convict. An outlaw. His irreverent first-person voice is delightful. ⟨. . .⟩

Strega. As Burke explains, the Italian word means "a witch-bitch you could lust after or run from. You could be in the middle of a desert and her shadow would make you cold. And I had taken her money." Strega is the woman whose child was threatened, the mother who had to run through the park. After Burke crushes her victimizer, she asks Burke to help her confront an even more obscene victimizer. During a day-care activity, the 8-year-old son of Strega's best friend was sexually violated. A photograph was taken. If the photograph can be found and torn up in front of the child's eyes, he might be able to cancel his nightmarish memory.

Burke's quest is the substance of the plot. But as he searches, he comes to realize that Strega conceals a dark secret. Sultry, steamy, and dangerous, an emotional vampire, she reveals her shocking motivation at the close of the book.

Andre Vachss' earlier novel about Burke was *Flood*. I'm on my way to buy it. This author's a contender. Keep an eye out. Watch for him.

David Morell, "The Heart of Evil," *Washington Post Book World*, 12 April 1987, p. 6

BILL BRASHLER   A sleuth who lives not just on society's edge, but on its underbelly. An Amazon of a heroine whose thoughts never assume the proportions of her body. A city full of mercenaries, psychopaths and deviates. An unsmiling author with an open collar and an eye patch.

Such is *Blue Belle*, the third episode in the sullen existence of Burke, the outlaw private eye created by Andrew Vachss. It is a book so ferocious, with characters so venal and action so breakneck, that you dare not get in the way. ⟨. . .⟩

⟨. . .⟩ Vachss knows the turf and writes with a sneering bravado. In Burke's world guys have "cement mixer eyes," and "everybody's lying but you and me." Burke prowls the city with a seething, angry, almost psychotic voice appropriate to the devils he deals with.

Bill Brashler, "Burke's Law: A Vivid Quest for Vengeance," *Chicago Tribune Books*, 4 September 1988, p. 5

SARAH SCHULMAN   Burke's third adventure ⟨*Blue Belle*⟩ takes place in contemporary downtown Manhattan; his assignment is to track down an elusive van driver who is shooting teen-age prostitutes in rapid succession. Employed by a pimp, Burke often plays both cop and robber but has his own version of moral clarity. While he is not above spying, gambling and money-laundering, he has a special hatred for child molesters and those who kill for fun.

Burke's stripper girlfriend, Belle, is herself a child of incest and looks to him for emotional healing. As a character, Belle has special problems. She says things like "I love you. I pay attention when you talk. I learn things. You want to mistreat me? I'll still love you."

Burke's other pals have more to offer. There is a Chinese money-launderer, assorted Latin prison buddies, who owe him a variety of favors, a transsexual named Michelle and a short black man named Prophet who says things like "Cutting up slime ain't no crime." In other words, Burke is a liberal. He's slightly sexist, slightly macho and slightly boring.

Sarah Schulman, "Bigots and Bashers," *New York Times Book Review,* 9 October 1988, p. 41

RICHARD GEHR   ⟨*Blue Belle*⟩ opens with Burke earning a bundle at the expense of some Wall Street creeps while whining about lower Manhattan's new gentry, "who get preorgasmic when you whisper 'investment banking.' " He lives like a paranoid war criminal in a heavily fortified bunker along with a vicious yet lovable Neapolitan mastiff named Pansy—not all that different from the newcomers he despises. A loner among loners, he has a father complex on account of his institutional upbringing; Vachss reads savviest in scenes involving supercynical Burke with the police, attorneys, and family agencies.

This stems from Vachss's impeccable credentials as a lawyer in the fields of juvenile justice and child abuse (he still lectures and trains on the subject). His indignation at pedophiles, pimps, and pornographers is righteous as hell and has grown over the course of the books. Now Burke's personal torments seem secondary to the children's crusade he has undertaken ("I was going to be a scam artist. But I kept running into kids. And they keep pulling me into what I didn't want to be"). What's good for the world is bad for Vachss's fans; Burke's scams are much more intriguing than his social services. In *Blue Belle*, the "kids" are menaced by the Ghost Van, which appears out of nowhere to torment New York's underage girl hookers, who are either offed on the spot or sped to a Times Square porn palace to star in snuff films. ⟨. . .⟩

Yet the city's inherent freakiness appears to have rubbed off on Vachss/ Burke. Belle, the novel's lust interest, is a strapping 29-year-old blond stripper endowed with inordinate t&a; she appears much younger, however, speaks in a "little-girl" voice, and is herself an incest child. The surly kiddie defender wastes no time falling for this big baby, whose predilections run toward spanking and buggery ("If I try to sit on your face again, you going to give me another smack?"). But since all good things must end for Burke, the former swamp sister falls in the line of duty. Vachss might consider giving Burke a rest, too. The line between virtue and vice is always problematic, and with Burke's secret proclivities uncovered, he should probably be kept off the streets for a while.

Richard Gehr, "Righteous Brother," *Village Voice*, 29 November 1988, p. 66

RHODA KOENIG   A lone warrior outside the worlds of "citizens" and "monsters," Burke owes much to Raymond Chandler and Robert B. Parker, with such appurtenances as an all-wise exotic mother figure and an all-powerful deaf-mute sidekick. But the New York he inhabits is not borrowed from anybody and shimmers on the page as gaudily and scarily as it does on the street, with its "teenage robot-mutant millionaires" dealing crack, its ever-present hustlers, and its thriving trade in children's flesh. It is the last that inflames Burke—his creator is an attorney specializing in child-abuse cases ⟨. . .⟩—and leads him to sting the "freaks" in a number of ingenious scams ("Let them write the Better Business Bureau") and a few cases of (to Burke) justifiable homicide.

⟨In *Hard Candy*⟩ Burke's teenage girlfriend from his old, bad neighborhood, where "foreplay was for people with money," asks him to bring back her own teenage daughter, in the hands of the leader of some undefined cult. But the mother is a hooker with some unspoken motives, and another player in the game is Wesley, the superkiller who doesn't hesitate to behead the daughter of a Mafia don when his bill isn't paid. Vachss's tough, tense prose takes us expertly through this unsavory story, whose level of cynicism may be gauged by Burke's response to an implausible remark: "Yeah. And Donny Manes stabbed *himself* to death."

Hard Candy will tell you many things about crime I hope you don't already know, which are interesting, if dismaying, to learn. Some may object to the author's casting an extralegal avenger in the leading role, but Burke is anything but heroic. Like the childen he arrives too late to save, he is crippled forever by the abyss he has gazed into, and his automatic chivalry is the motor reflex of the emotionally dead.

Rhoda Koenig, "Publish or Perestroika," *New York*, 5 June 1989, p. 57

CAROL ANSHAW   Burke's main missing part seems to be a sense of personal ironic detachment. He takes himself more seriously than even your average ultra-macho private eye. Although no one seems to be after him, Burke lives in a maximum-security apartment presided over by a killer attack-dog. Though he doesn't seem to get an undue number of calls, he has all his messages elaborately screened through the phone at Mama Wong's Chinese restaurant.

Basically a loner, he nonetheless clears a little space on the ground where he stands, so women can worship there. His basic attitude toward the female gender puts him somewhere in the company of Andrew Dice Clay. Burke's idea of a witty personals ad is: "Woman wanted. Disease-free. Self-lubricating. Short attention span."

Blossom is Burke's fifth appearance between covers. This time he leaves his Manhattan turf behind him and heads for Merrillville, Ind., where an old jail-cell buddy has family troubles. His young cousin has been charged with a grim stack of serial killings—shootings of necking couples in parked cars. Burke quickly (operating on tough-guy instinct) decides the kid didn't do it. Who really did is sure to be some filthy sicko scum because these are the bad guys in society, as Vachss constructs it. ⟨. . .⟩

Vachss draws his villains as right-wing paramilitary nutcases, making his story a perfect circle of violence and loathing. The good guys want to get rid of the filth and scum whose intent it is to get rid of the filth and scum. In a world like this the only difference in belief systems is one's definition of filth and one's choice of clean-up method.

That Vachss' books are popular scares me a little. I don't like thinking I'm the only reader made morally queasy inside his airless, closed loop.

> Carol Anshaw, "Doing Evil unto Evil," *Chicago Tribune Books*, 8 July 1990, pp. 3, 11

MARILYN STASIO   "I'm a criminal," boasts Burke, the ex-con hero of Andrew Vachss's *Blossom*. "I'm a *contrabandista*. An outlaw." In his fifth crusade against the pimps, child molesters, porn merchants and assorted sociopaths who make him see red, the unlicensed New York investigator also reveals himself to be a chest-thumping egomaniac whose he-man exploits have fallen into predictable patterns of vicious crime and savage retribution.

Answering a former cellmate's plea to clear a teen-age relative of a murder charge, Burke takes his vigilante code of justice to a mill town in Indiana.

Here he assembles a band of taciturn men and plucky women to help him track down (with intent to kill) the "piquerist" who is getting his sick kicks from sniper-shooting women.

"Burke knows freaks like nobody else," notes one admirer. That he does, and with a thoroughness that is also evident in his understanding of guns and country blues. Such sagacity does not extend, however, to human beings, who are simplistically categorized as "freaks" or "family" by Burke and overdrawn to comic-book scale by Mr. Vachss.

Marilyn Stasio, [Review of *Blossom*], *New York Times Book Review*, 15 July 1990, p. 26

JAN HOFFMAN   Vachss's passionate rage on behalf of abused children (*Blossom* is dedicated to a boy who didn't make it to his fourth birthday) surges through these otherwise conventional genre novels, making them distinctively harrowing, ugly, upending. Each novel contains several scenes illuminating aspects of child abuse, from a pedophile attempting to explain his lust (*Strega*) to therapists chipping at the wall built up by a child (*Hard Candy*). In *Blossom*, Burke, who travels to Indiana to help an old cellmate, extracts a terrible confession from his pal's teen-aged nephew about how he's been seduced for a "special love" by a preacher. And the young killer Burke stalks this time was tortured by his parents and became so psychologically twisted that the local proto-Nazis rejected him. Now he gets his sexual jolts from shooting at couples spooning in parked cars.

Blossom has much the same strengths and weaknesses as its predecessors. The novel is pus-mean and shockingly original with respect to vices of choice. While the degree of putrefaction will hit neophyte readers harder than veteran fans, *Blossom* is still stuffed with enough pedophile kidnappers, teen prostitutes, stacks of sadistic pornography, and prison-yard tales to give Sam Spade a happy attack of the creeps. Moreover, the authority with which Vachss writes about such underworlds is rather unnerving.

Jan Hoffman, "Maniac," *Village Voice*, 16 October 1990, p. 74

CHARLES CHAMPLIN   Andrew Vachss is just about the toughest of contemporary crime novelists, a New York lawyer specializing in juvenile-justice cases, who exposes his knowledge of the world's darkest side, and his rage at it, in novels that are not so much narratives as fragments of a mosaic of evil. ⟨. . .⟩ *Sacrifice* is Vachss' sixth tale of the horrors wrought upon children. This time his ex-con protagonist Burke is trying to help a child so badly abused that he has taken temporary refuge in a second, murderous personality who, or which, has murdered a baby but has no memory of it.

Burke has a circle of helpers that somewhat resembles the gangs who used to abet Doc Savage and the Shadow, including a deaf and speechless Chinese of enormous speed and stealth, a chap called The Prof who speaks in rap, a woman who runs a Chinese restaurant and hates all customers except Burke and his pals, assorted Jamaicans and others. He is haunted by all the friends, including many women, he has lost violently in earlier books.

The combination of pulpish devices and empurpled rhetoric occasionally comes close to defeating Vachss' intentions. "This isn't a city. It's a halfway house without a roof. Stressed to critical mass. . . . Fear rules. Politicans promise the people an army of blue-coated street-sweepers for a jungle no chemical could defoliate. . . . The walls of some buildings still tremble with the molecular memory of baby-bashing violence and incestuous terror."

Yet despite the stressful writing, Vachss waves a powerful light across a city landscape that few writers go near, and none portray so convincingly. It is unpleasant, but it is also mesmerizing in its intensity.

> Charles Champlin, [Review of *Sacrifice*], *Los Angeles Times Book Review*, 9 June 1991, p. 13

GARY DRETZKA   After a one-book detour into the hinterland, Vachss returns to familiar territory in *Sacrifice*. His no-nonsense P.I., Burke, is reunited with his dedicated band of superheroes—Max the Silent, the Mole, the Prof, Mama, Pansy the dog—in their continuing pursuit of human "predators," especially those who prey on children.

If you've already bought into Vachss' series, *Sacrifice* will bring a welcome return to the seamy New York streets that served so well in *Strega* and *Blue Belle*.

Here he and his cohorts work against the clock—indeed, a ticking emotional time bomb—to find the crack-ravaged murderer of an infant and simultaneously try to save a young boy from the various personalities devouring him from inside. This involves tracking down the boy's sadistic parents and dealing with their horrible cult in a way that should unnerve any dues-paying ACLU member.

In the meantime, Burke tries to fend off the grasping hands of the city's jaded police and social agents. He also enlists some interesting practitioners of voodoo in his battle with twisted followers of witchcraft and satanism.

Sacrifice, as spare and tense as anything Vachss has written, again teaches us more than we care to know about sex offenders, child abusers and others of the truly evil among us. We also are drawn deeper into the darkness of Burke's being:

"There's others like me. Children of the Secret. Raised by so many different humans. Those who ignore us, those who tortured us. No place to run, so survival becomes all. For us, a religion. Nourished on lies so that we alone know the truth. An army of us. You can't see us, but we find each other. Like a special breed of damaged dog, responding only to the silent whistle."

Vachss' books are as bleak and disturbing as the crimes he describes, yet such virtues as friendship, kindness and loyalty are rewarded and good generally triumphs over evil. This Marvel Comics approach to crime-fighting will be off-putting to many, but those who have stayed with Burke through his five previous adventures know how difficult it is to break the habit.

Gary Dretzka, "Crime for Summertime," *Chicago Tribune Books*, 16 June 1991, p. 7

JEFF YANG   Burke, the antihero of Vachss' previous books, is a PI/ conman with a radically nontraditional "family." In *Shella*, the first non-Burke book, Vachss strips away this veneer of quasi-domesticity, leaving his hardcase protagonist without friends, without a home, without even a name. "John Smith" or "Ghost," as he's variously called, is a noir archetype as bare as unfinished furniture. The plot, too, has been sanded down into a taut monofilament—Ghost is looking for a ghost from his past, a woman who calls herself Shella:

> Some social worker in one of the shelters told her she had to
> come out of her shell. So they could help. A shell, that's what she
> needed. So she turned it around, made it her name. She told me
> it was all she had that was really there.

Ghost is a zen monster, a killer who works with his hands and without a second thought. Shella, his virgin/whore/dominatrix love, is a figment through most of the book, spun out of flashbacks that reveal nothing but the shell that makes her name. As people inconveniently get in the way of Ghost's search, the book moves relentlessly toward its conclusion, one corpse at a time.

Despite its linear focus—or maybe because of it—*Shella* isn't as riveting as Vachss's Burke stories. He was always able to wring edginess from his portrayal of a society hovering beneath the radar—a world of back alleys and shuttered rooms, with its own code of honor, its own food chain. Ghost is too deadly to fraternize with; even in the underworld, he's an alien. Interaction with other characters is minimal, and most of the book is told from Ghost's point of view. What dialogue there is serves primarily to emphasize his status as a killing spirit among the living: "Hey, come on, Monroe. This guy don't look tough to me," says one lowlife to another. "Cancer don't *look* tough either," replies his fellow thug. "You're out of your league." He is. Ghost kills him. ⟨. . .⟩

⟨. . .⟩ perhaps Vachss has steeped too much in his own mania, believes too much in his own myths. The prose in *Shella* is boiled to the bone; the characters are so knife-hard that they've become pure caricature. It's not surprising that the climax, the meeting between ghost and shell, rings hollow. Even the book's final twist, involving a killer more insidious than the baby-rapers and assassins of the Burke novels, comes off as a tawdry attempt to bring contemporary issues into an increasingly dated noir milieu. Flush with Hollywood money for the rights to his earlier works, Vachss might do well to remember how easily *hard* can become *brittle*.

Jeff Yang, [Review of *Shella*], *Voice Literary Supplement* No. 115 (May 1993): 7–8

GEORGE STADE   ⟨. . .⟩ the plot ⟨of *Shella*⟩ is preposterous, the characters based on rumor, paranoia and light literature, the dialogue unlike anything anyone has ever said, anywhere. In this respect *Shella* is like Mr. Vachss's other novels, whose hero and narrator is Burke, another psychopath with whom his creator is in love. In *Shella* there is the same self-pity and self-congratulation as in the Burke novels, even the butterfly symbolism and sentimentality about dogs.

When it comes to style, however, *Shella* is an improvement over its predecessors. Burke tells his stories in a style that is both laconic and garrulous: the sentences are short or fragmentary, but there are pages of them given over to fulminations against urban depravity and sexual predation, especially of children. Ghost, on the other hand, is laconic and affectless; in *Shella*, the righteous indignation is expressed through particulars, rather than by tone or outright assertion.

Ghost's character and Shella's gradually revealed savagery, as it turns out, are explained (and excused) by backgrounds of childhood neglect and abuse. These are serious matters, but as Mr. Vachss uses them they feel like moral blackmail, pretexts for murder and fantasies of revenge. It is no use, of course, knocking the other guy's fantasy fiction: the genre's fiction is to allow in the imagination what we deny ourselves in the flesh, and it is just as likely to siphon off dangerous emotions as to encourage them. If you are boiling over with vengeful fury upon which you cannot act, Mr. Vachss may be the man for you—now that Mickey Spillane is out of style.

> George Stade, "Looking for Her in All the Wrong Places," *New York Times Book Review*, 23 May 1993, p. 14

EDWARD BRYANT   Although the title's typoed right on Mark Nelson's fine composite front cover, that's about the last misstep for *Drive By*, the new Andrew Vachss chapbook from Crossroads Press. Dark fantasy maybe for white folks in the suburbs, this is all too accurate reality for inner cities. The story—in dramatic terms, it's more of a vignette—is the bleak portrait of a black kid getting caught up in a cycle of urban violence. On a more technical side, *Drive By*'s a good object lesson in comics storytelling. After Neal Barrett's introduction, the reader should sequentially read Vachss' prose version, Joe R. Lansdale's story treatment, and then the comics realization by Lansdale and artist Gary Gianni. Think of this as a crisp, effective Rosetta Stone for anyone interested in graphic adaptations.

> Edward Bryant, [Review of *Drive By*], *Locus* 32, No. 2 (February 1994): 61–62

◈ *Bibliography*

The Life-Style Violent Juvenile: The Secure Treatment Approach (with Yitzhak Bakal). 1979.

Flood. 1985.

Strega. 1987.

Blue Belle. 1988.

Hard Candy. 1989.

Blossom. 1990.

Sacrifice. 1991.

Shella. 1993.

A Flash of White (with others). 1993.

Another Chance to Get It Right: A Children's Book for Adults. 1993.

Drive By (with others). 1993.

Born Bad. 1994.

Down in the Zero. 1994.